THE DRIVE FOR POWER

THE DRIVE FOR POWER

Arnold A. Hutschnecker, M.D.

M Evans

Lanham • New York • Boulder • Toronto • Plymouth, UK

M. Evans
An imprint of The Rowman & Littlefield Publishing Group, Inc.
4501 Forbes Boulevard, Suite 200, Lanham, Maryland 20706
http://www.rlpgtrade.com

10 Thornbury Road, Plymouth PL6 7PP, United Kingdom

Distributed by National Book Network

British Library Cataloguing in Publication Information Available

Library of Congress Cataloging-in-Publication Data Available

ISBN 13: 978-1-59077-322-2 (pbk: alk. paper)

♾™ The paper used in this publication meets the minimum requirements of American National Standard for Information Sciences—Permanence of Paper for Printed Library Materials, ANSI/NISO Z39.48-1992.

Printed in the United States of America

The unleashed power of the atom has changed everything, except our thinking; Thus we are drifting towards a catastrophe beyond comparison. We shall require a substantially new manner of thinking if mankind is to survive.

—Albert Einstein

Acknowledgments

The completion of this book, my fourth, has left me with two dominant feelings—one of gladness that the mountain looming ahead of me has finally been scaled, and the other of gratitude towards all who have contributed to the completion of this book.

The feeling of gladness is not a sense of pure joy, but more one of satisfaction that a job that had to be done has been completed.

"Why do you do it," my friends asked, "if you find writing so toilsome?" And I answer, "Not doing it is worse—" Aside from a natural drive to succeed, there is, I believe, deep within men of responsibility, a need to leave this world just a fraction less wicked than when they entered it.

My gratitude is mixed with feelings of humble acknowledgment that go back to all my teachers, even the poor ones: the crisp, all male Ph.D.'s I had in high school, and later on my medical professors—some famous, others stern-faced scientists, and still others warmhearted, concerned physicians. Their words remained imprinted on my mind, as did the earthy words of wisdom of my father and the gentle wit of my somewhat dreamy mother.

I am deeply grateful to my patients, who have enriched my life and taught me the greatest lesson of all: how to learn understanding and be a physician, and how to cope with the many-faceted adversities of life.

I owe gratitude to a dedicated group of men, friends and fellows of the American Association of Psychoanalytic Physicians, all psychiatrists and psychoanalysts. Dr. George Train, a scholar, a thinker, and a humanitarian, made valuable suggestions, as did his brother, Dr. John Train, and Drs. Maria Fleischl and Ed Pinney, Jr., all M.D.'s and psychoanalysts. Also, I wish to thank Harrison Salisbury for his very perceptive understanding of my psychopolitical ideas.

As to the book itself, I was fortunate enough to benefit from the experience of a good friend, herself a successful writer, Lucy Freeman, whose enthusiasm for some of my new ideas was most encouraging. Jeanne Bernkopf deserves credit for her part as a most capable, sharp-pencilled editor, as does Pamela Veley for her kind and talented assistance. Special thanks go to my secretary, Evelyn Gruen, for her many overtime hours typing the manuscript.

A.A.H.

Contents

Preface

"Experience is fallacious and judgment difficult." So said Hippocrates, and his words have served throughout this book to remind me to avoid any temptation to present patent solutions or oversimplified interpretations of the complex and dynamic drive for power that exists in all people—from the President of a country to a politician, a struggling actress, or an ambitious salesman. As the need to win gains momentum it takes control of our actions, determining our man-woman relationship, our life style, even our very survival in an uncertain and ever more complex growing world.

The aim of this book is to demonstrate the competitive drive for immediate or distant goals by the introduction of a new field that I hope offers new ways of thinking: I call it psychopolitics, which is an application of psychodynamic principles to political life, with the emphasis on political leaders. And I have attempted to show how we, the people, can learn to elect healthier political leaders, mature men and women who will live up to their commitment rather than use power as a vehicle for their own ambitions.

The signs of power play go back to infancy. The drive for power encompasses the force that motivates the dreams and actions of a child as he grows into adulthood which in turn determines how he will use this enormous source of energy: for good or evil, for creation or destruction, for peace or war. Because both creation and destruction are lodged deep within the human mind, it is there that the understanding of self-fulfillment and love for peace must be built. All of us all over the world, rich or poor, wise or ignorant, have the right to self-determination, the right to unfold whatever potential we possess without fear of harrassment or exploitation.

On a collective level, a healthy drive for power will help build a new world without violence or the threat of war. To accomplish this goal requires the teaching of healthy human values along with the three R's. Self-awareness and inner security will enable people not only to build their own more meaningful lives, but also to elect mentally and physically healthy leaders whose sense of reality will unite all humans in a cooperative effort for a better and more peaceful world. As a physician, I consider it part of the wider task of preventive medicine to work for a world in which every individual can find a place without fear or a threat to anyone's basic need for security.

Arnold A. Hutschnecker

THE DRIVE FOR POWER

I

A Doctor's Dilemma

IT WAS Saturday, November fifth, 1960, a peaceful evening at my country home in Sherman, Connecticut. It was also three days before the presidential election between Richard M. Nixon and John F. Kennedy.

My wife and I were watching an old movie on television when, shortly after nine-thirty, the telephone rang.

To my "Hello," a masculine voice responded, "This is the Associated Press." He gave me a name, one I had not heard of.

Then he said, "Doctor Hutschnecker, did you by any chance hear the announcement that on Monday there will be a statement about the health and fitness for office of the two presidential candidates?"

"Yes," I said. "I heard it on the radio this afternoon."

The voice continued, "We have been informed that you are Vice-President Nixon's doctor, and we would like a statement from you about his health."

He couldn't be serious. There had been no secrecy about the Vice-President's visits to me. His limousines and Secret Service men had been clearly in evidence in front of my door. At the time I was engaged in the practice of internal medicine, and Mr. Nixon came simply for occasional checkups and to discuss how to deal with the stresses of his office, including the many official dinners he had to attend—in short, how to stay fit. There was no evidence of any illness.

3

But did the reporter expect me to give a statement about the Vice-President's health? I answered him, "You can't be serious."

I added, "In the entire United States there isn't one physician who would give a shred of information about a patient. Much less to a stranger over the phone who might be anybody."

"You can call the Associated Press and verify that I am a reporter there," he said.

"That won't be necessary," I replied, "because there will be no statement."

I could have said simply, "No comment," but that could imply that I was hiding some secret information about the Vice-President's health. If I had said he was in good physical condition, my statement might lead other reporters to besiege me with questions as to when Mr. Nixon had come to see me and the reason for his visits. But the main reason for my uncommunicative answer was my strict belief in a physician's foremost obligation to guard and protect, under any circumstances, a patient's right to absolute confidentiality, a point debated during my appearance before the House Judiciary Committee to testify in the case of Gerald Ford before his confirmation as Vice-President of the United States. Even a positive statement about Mr. Nixon's health would in my mind constitute an infringement of that confidentiality.

I did make clear to the Associated Press reporter that Mr. Nixon had discontinued his medical visits several years before, when gossip columns stated that he was seeing a Park Avenue psychiatrist. The reason for these rumors was that, in 1951, I wrote one of the first popular books on psychosomatic medicine and thereby made people think I was a psychoanalytically oriented psychiatrist. I was still an internist, but I had long been interested in the emotional conditions—the misery, the tension, the unhappiness—that lay beneath the clinical symptoms of the people I had treated. And I had long been troubled by the question as to what it was in the depths of a human mind that drove one patient to recover, another to die of the same disease.

At any rate, Mr. Nixon and I had yielded to the urging of his political advisers that he not see me any more professionally, and yet it had been a good, that is, trusting doctor-patient relationship. How strange, I thought, that a man in public life would be allowed, even encouraged, to visit a heart specialist, say, but would be criticized for trying to understand the emotional undercurrent of his unconscious drives, fears, and conflicts, or possible neurotic hangups. Was there something wrong with trying to learn how to cope with the realities of life more effectively, how to protect positive-controlled aggressive forces from the pollution of overambitious negative or even self-defeating inner compulsive drives?

The beginning of psychosomatic thinking had been part of my medical training at the Charitée, the medical hospital of the School of Medicine of the University of Berlin, for it was there I first learned of the ability of the human psyche to twist or deny a situation. The psychic, often unconscious interplay between a signal and its response can, and often does, lead to disastrous decisions that in turn have the capacity to destroy outright the creativity and accomplishments even of a man of superior intellect.

I have always been intrigued by self-made men, especially by the political leaders I had chanced to meet or observe. Some were like meteors that have a quick brilliant rise, then burn out. A man's enormous creativity can be overshadowed by his unconscious yet powerful wish to die. The wish is not always seen in one final act of dying but rather in a number of self-destructive decisions before the end. Some men possess such a heroic self-image that they would rather die with their boots on than be judged weak by themselves or by posterity.

When Watergate began to dominate the American political scene, I resisted the pressure from newspaper and television correspondents to comment on some of the events, but I did state that *reasoning power alone* would not provide a satisfactory explanation of all the bizarre actions of those young and not-so-young men in responsible positions. The plotting and scheming could not be explained simply as insatiable hunger for power or doggish loyalty to a leader. No conscious level of intellect could explain fully their motivation. There was something in the character structure of these men that was neurotic and pressing enough to produce criminal thinking and abnormal behavior, possibly in the hope that their cleverness would be noticed by their leader, that they would bathe in the glory of recognition.

In dealing with the Associated Press reporter that November night in 1960, I was aware of how easily a careless remark could be misinterpreted. After he made a few more attempts to gain some information from me, including for whom I would vote in the coming presidential election, the reporter finally said somewhat sadly, "I am worse off now than before I called you."

I pondered how this particular problem would be resolved long after I hung up.

The anticipated statement on the health issue of both candidates did not take place on Monday, and it did not become an election issue. After Election Day, considering the narrow margin by which President Kennedy won (0.2%), I could not help but wonder how the election might have turned out had President Kennedy been obliged to give a statement of his back ailment, later described as Addison's disease, had I given Mr. Nixon a clean bill of health.

Eight years later, when Mr. Nixon became the country's thirty-seventh President, the long-forgotten incident was revived.

Newsweek magazine, in its November 25, 1968, issue, wrote about Richard Milhous Nixon and myself that "the doctor-patient relationship probably would never have got out of

Hutschnecker's consulting room had columnist Drew Pearson not followed up a tip and nosed into the matter during the 1968 campaign."

On November 14, 1968, a Thursday, a story had flashed on the United Press International wires, datelined Washington, D.C. I think it is important to get the facts on the record, because so much has been distorted and misrepresented since. The story in its entirety appears in the Appendix.

The story started:

> Columnist Drew Pearson, who has been involved in disputes involving several Presidents, has raised the question of why Richard M. Nixon, now President-elect, consulted a New York physician several years ago.
>
> Pearson related to an audience at the National Press Club Wednesday that he was told the visit concerned "psychiatric problems" and occurred at some time in the 1953-61 period that Nixon was Vice-President.
>
> The physician is Dr. Arnold A. Hutschnecker, currently a psychiatrist with offices at 829 Park Ave. in New York. Dr. Hutschnecker told UPI that when he was treating Nixon two or three times a year from 1950 to 1955 it was "for strictly medical problems."

Drew Pearson said he had telephoned me twice at my office five days before the 1968 election. On the first call, he said, I admitted treating Mr. Nixon when he was Vice-President, but when he called back that afternoon I told him that Mr. Nixon consulted me about strictly medical problems, not for psychotherapy.

Mr. Pearson said he decided to write nothing about it at the time, but now he told the National Press Club:

> Now subsequently Dr. Hutschnecker has told others and confirmed the fact that in the interim between my call at 9:30 in the morning and 4 P.M. he got a call from the

Nixon office and that he had changed his story to me. And he did confirm to others that he had treated or advised Nixon over psychiatric problems. And he had expressed some worry privately that Nixon had problems—or did have a problem—of not standing up under great pressure.

I denied the Pearson allegations as soon as they appeared; I made clear to the press that I had never made any such statement, had never received any such call from Nixon headquarters. And I learned subsequently that Mr. Pearson's source of supposed information was a very sick former patient of mine, a paranoiac schizophrenic who was out to get President Nixon because he hated the President with the same passion he hated his own father.

And I began to wonder how a believing public can be protected against a reporter who would use as his source of information an unemployed psychotic at war with the world.

For me to remain silent would have meant to agree with the allegation that President Nixon lacked mental stability. Yet to speak up against outright lies was to come close to violating the obligations of confidentiality.

So I decided that the best way to close the incident would be to write an article for a national magazine, an article that would deal with the basic anxiety people have about the emotional stability of any political leader, about the confusion in the minds of people, or perhaps an exploitation of that anxiety by an opposing camp. I could make clear the falsifications and simply set the record straight.

The thought of clarifying a still lingering confusion about President Nixon's health and the relationship between the president and me was not confined entirely to myself. A reporter called asking for an interview in depth for the Sunday magazine section of the *New York Times*. We set a date. I was surprised when the reporter arrived. I did not expect a lady as glamorous as Gloria Steinem who arrived in a mini, as was the style in 1968. She was brilliant and utterly charming, and we talked for three and a half hours about many things but little concerning President Nixon and the relationship I had with him.

Miss Steinem's article never appeared, but the editors of *Look* magazine asked me to write the story myself, which I did: its title was "The Mental Health of Political Leaders." It was published on July 4, 1969. This article inspired several psychologists to follow up my ideas. Bruce Mazlish, professor of history at the Massachusetts Institute of Technology, stated in his book *In Search of Nixon:*

"As the physician who presumably treated Nixon, he [Dr. Hutschnecker] had a unique opportunity to understand him—as a person, if not as a President. At the very least, then, Nixon's doctor preceded us in the purely psychological side of our study. . . . Dr. Hutschnecker, however, is very discreet about his 'treatment' of Nixon, and no clear picture of the relationship emerges." He suggested my records be opened fifty years from now, in order not to violate professional confidence.

Ever since Drew Pearson's two columns about me, I have not been able to shake an impression. "There goes the President's shrink," I occasionally hear people say at a theater or some other public place, indicating their belief that the relationship between President Nixon and me has not really ended.

There was even a play on Broadway in 1972 titled *An Evening with Richard Nixon and . . .*," written by Gore Vidal. The play was a biting satire on the President and such former political leaders as George Washington, Franklin D. Roosevelt, and Thomas E. Dewey. The actor George Hall played Dr. Hutschnecker, listed on the program after Barry Goldwater and Hubert Humphrey and just preceding Spiro Agnew. One scene showed the President on a couch in my office, holding a silly discussion as I treated him medically by bandaging one leg over his trousers. The aim was to ridicule the President but even more to make him appear unstable, ready to "break down" at almost any new crisis. It also meant to cast doubt that I had really discontinued my professional relationship with the President. It seemed to imply that I was covering up an emotional instability and it seemed to say that a man who may have gone to a psychotherapist must be considered incompetent for leadership, certainly for the presidency of the United States.

Thus the dilemma of a doctor who treats a national leader. To tell or not tell is not the question. He cannot tell.

II

A Politician's Unforgivable Sin

EVERY SINGLE human, in whatever socioeconomic position, has within him or her a drive for power, a force that can help unfold the potentials inherent in a personality. This force can lead to fulfillment or failure, happiness or misery, depending on the individual's set of values; and those values in turn determine the sum and sequence of his near or distant goals. Because of this, every individual has also the power to contribute to the advance of civilization—or to its destruction. For it is the direction of the power drive that leads one man to create—and another to kill.

If unharnessed, uncontrolled, the drive for power may cause one man to run amok, destroy all that stands in his way, and may cause another to overextend himself until he breaks down from exhaustion.

If turned against the self, the power drive may paralyze a person's natural will to live, rendering him powerless, weak, self-condemned to live a parasitic existence.

Man's drive for power needs cultivation and balancing if he is to use his enormous source of energy to his best advantage: meaningfully and creatively.

I think of it often in the terms a scientist once explained atomic energy to me. A friend of mine, João Muniz, the Brazilian amabassador to the United Nations, worked diligently and with enthusiasm, as was his nature, on the idea of creating a United Nations agency for the use of atomic energy for peaceful purposes. When, in October 1956, he finally succeeded in bringing about a conference of the member nations that approved the idea of an International Atomic Energy Agency, he invited me to a reception in New York because he thought I would enjoy meeting some of the atomic scientists. I asked two of the nuclear physicists sitting at our table, "Can you explain in simple terms how we obtain atomic energy? All I know is that after an atomic explosion there is an enormous mushroom cloud that rises to the sky, spreading death and destruction. How do you harness this incredible, violent, deadly power?"

One of the atomic scientists laughed, took a piece of paper out of his pocket and drew a sketch to explain how the enormous burst of energy is led, if I remember correctly, into giant reactors and converted into electric power.

I often use this example to show how a man who is driven by a near-explosive power drive must learn to convert this dangerous force into even-flowing, controlled energy, if he is to build his life and attain his goals, rather than destroy himself and others. The need to balance the power drive lies in every healthy human being, be he shopkeeper, secretary, farmer, poet, stockbroker, housewife, financier—or exalted political leader. There is a constant battle in each of us between the forces of excitation and inhibition. It is the balance of power that enables every one of us to cope with the resistance, fears, rejections, crises, and threats to our everyday existence. As a hard-driving talented designer, who is a patient, often quotes me over and over as saying, we have a cupful of energy every day and what matters is how we spend it. Do we build like a mason, brick on brick, or do we dissipate our energy, or do we fail to use the contents of the cup at all?

One successful businessman came to me because he thought he was heading straight for a breakdown. He felt he was losing control of his temper; he had threatened to hurt his wife physically and became frightened. "I seem to be operating at an unbearably high pitch," he said. "I feel if there is one more bit of pressure, I won't be able to stand it; I'll blow my top."

I asked, "What do you mean by blowing your top?"

He said quietly, "Go mad—crazy. Lose control of my senses. Not know what I might do."

"Has that ever happened?" I asked.

"No," he said. "I never quite felt the way I do now. Before, I could manage somehow, but now I feel driven. I have never worked this hard before." He seemed to be near panic as he spoke about his life. "I figure there are only so many years left for me. I must accumulate all the money I can, which isn't easy these days, what with inflation, taxes, my responsibilities and the economic slump. If I don't hurry, I may end up with nothing, comes my old age. And my wife doesn't understand that I do this for her, because I may go before she does. She keeps nagging me and warns me to slow up, and I get mad. I actually feel I could kill her because I think she is selfish and stupid."

I could not tell him at a first meeting when I was just gathering facts about him that it was not so much the hard work that caused his hypertension but the rage, anger, self-pity, and the constant fear of failure that kept driving him on. If he did not gain perspective or review his values so he could gain control of his superdrive, I thought, there would be no old age for him to worry about or to enjoy. Would he accept therapy, at such a point, in order to know himself? Or would he want some "instant" pill, one quick "magical" word of reassurance? He decided to come back. "I just have to," he said, which indicated he wanted to do something about his disturbed condition.

The fear of going crazy, or of having what many people call a nervous breakdown, does not necessarily signify a psychotic personality or a breakdown. But while the fear can be only an imagined anticipation of impending disaster, it can nevertheless, if unrelieved, cause a breakdown or in Pavlov's words, a state of "protective inhibition." Such a state is an automatic, unconscious, temporary withdrawal from everyday demands in order to protect the brain cells from permanent damage. Nature brings on a sleepy state so that the brain cells can recover. A breakdown may force a person into a respite from conflict, afford him the rest he would not otherwise give his body or his nerves. When a person withdraws because of physical illness, he is protecting himself from dangerous states of exhaustion and encouraging healing processes in his body. Even a common cold can be protective, producing an excuse for avoiding some taxing unpleasantness or preventing more serious damage to the body, either physically or mentally.

While anyone under prolonged stress can suffer a nervous breakdown, the danger is greater for people who have high ambitions and who are exposed professionally to heavier pressures, especially, of course, political leaders.

It was after World War I that I decided to become a physician in order to help repair some of the damage done to the bodies of young men. But as time went on, I could not reconcile myself to the fact that some leaders—political fanatics or bored and depressed men, gamblers, who thrive on excitement—could cause thousands of torn bodies which individual physicians are then called upon to mend. It's insane, I have thought so often, it's medieval thinking. The doctor's job, I therefore reasoned, must go beyond skillfully putting back together the fragments of human flesh shattered in the battles of war.

The more I experienced the political upheavals in Europe, uprisings, street battles, and, eventually, the gathering clouds of World War II, the more I was determined to devote myself to the study and possibly prevention of war. To this I have given all the time my practice has left me, all my thoughts, my energies, my hope and work, including this book.

The incredible incompetence and mental instability of many leaders, the sacrifice by men in power of millions of human lives has impelled me to dare to undertake an examination of the phenomenon of war, though I know that one man alone cannot succeed in bringing under control the last of the ancient plagues still unconquered by man.

We live with a kind of limping logic. If a man who kills another man is judged temporarily insane, how do we judge a political leader who orders his peoples to engage in mass murder? Are we dealing with human rights or the rights of a lynching party? The difference seems to be that under the guise of "national honor" a leader can arouse the support of a nation in the goal of mass murder while the single attacker is considered a common murderer hated by all. But the purity of logic has begun to win acceptance, or we would not have had, for the first time in history, a judgment at Nuremberg. Today, a leader who advocates war must be sure to keep a position of power lest he be tried as a war criminal.

Any average man or woman who feels emotionally upset can go to a psychoanalyst, but a leader who might be under the greatest stress imaginable, such as the President of the United States, is denied the seeking of such help. Is this rational thinking for the last third of the twentieth century?

Why should a political leader who is in a position to decide the issues of war and peace not be allowed the benefits offered by psychotherapy—the science and art of the human mind. Why must our leaders play the role of supermen, hold the image of the ship captain who never sleeps?

Paradoxically and unfortunately, in our United States we are quick to condemn leaders if they dare to seek better mental health even though the building or strengthening of emotional and mental health in a leader would safeguard our, the people's, state of security, our state of well-being, perhaps even our very survival. After all, once a nation elects mentally unstable men to positions of power, the emotionally healthy, hard-working, concerned, responsible members of that nation will have little chance to determine their destiny. Decisions affecting our economy or our foreign policy are made by the men in power with the aid of their advisers who all too often are eloquent theoreticians with little wisdom of life. These advisers, frequently propelled by their own ambitious drives, work with statistics and computers in sterile rooms, removed from human interaction; they almost never do the fighting and the dying. The experts, older men who "know best" what is good for the country, send the young to die. I have often thought of the unconscious motivation of filicide, the killing of the son by the father, the opposite of Freud's Oedipus complex.

Many leaders have been propelled since childhood to overcome a painful or enormous sense of insignificance or an unconscious fear of death. Driven by their compulsion to make a mark in history, to live on at the expense of almost everything, including their own self-esteem or happiness, they are undeterred by the blood spilled for their own glory. Pessimists, including Freud, question the existence of any real progress in man's civilization, and many cynics call the idea of permanent peace naive, unrealistic, a fool's dream. But I believe in progress because I feel the basic goodness in man outweighs all evil and that in spite of all resistance, ultimate peace will prevail.

This nation, so progressive in most other matters, has a seemingly abysmal fear of mental illness. It is a problem rooted in ignorance. Even the term mental illness has not fully lost its association with a person obsessed by the devil, the hopelessly insane.

Fortunately, the term "insanity" has become obsolete in

modern psychiatry though it is still being used as a "vague, legal term for the psychotic state." According to the glossary of the American Psychiatric Association a psychotic state connotes:

a) mental incompetence
b) inability to distinguish "right from wrong" and/or
c) a condition that interferes with the individual's ability to care for himself or which constitutes a danger to himself or to others.

When I was a student at the University of Berlin, the professor of psychiatry told a story his own professor had told to illustrate the general attitude towards the mentally ill. As head of the Royal Prussian Psychiatric Hospital, my professor's professor had the job of inspecting the Royal Insane Asylum, tucked away in the country. He described how he would drive to the asylum in a horsedrawn carriage, wearing his top hat, for his monthly visits. He would find all the inmates lined up in military fashion awaiting him. He would address the inmates collectively with the question, "Are you all still nuts?" Whether or not there was a reply, he would then make the same entry in his book, month after month, year after year: "Condition unchanged." Then he would return, top hat in place, to the city.

At that time it was believed that the psychotic, or the more severely disturbed mental patients, would remain more or less in a chronic state of diminished control of their impulses, or loss of contact with reality. Such people were locked up to protect society or themselves, and any thought of recovery, or even of erroneous diagnosis, was dismissed.

Now physicians differentiate between neurotic and psychotic disorders. The first is an emotional maladaption due to unresolved unconscious conflicts, a condition that yields to psychoanalytic or other forms of psychotherapeutic treatment. Psychotic disorders, considered by many physicians to be genetic, yielded first to treatment by electric shock, then insulin and other therapies; today a vast armament of psychopharmacological drugs has enabled many people to leave mental hospitals in a short time.

Years ago a corny joke circulated among doctors concerning the difference between the two types of mental illness. "The neurotic," it went, "builds castles in the sky. The psychotic lives in them." To which a cynic added, "And the psychiatrist collects the rent."

Through antidepressant or mood-elevating drugs, some patients become able to receive psychotherapy and thereby not only become competent and productive but able to build within themselves self-esteem, security, healthy value judgment and a capacity to enjoy their existence. Psychotherapy has reclaimed many wasted lives, has helped many to build outstanding careers and to find satisfaction and happiness.

In the spring of 1972 the question of a man's mental illness became a campaign issue, for that was when Senator George McGovern chose as his running mate Thomas F. Eagleton, a promising young senator. Suddenly the rumor spread that Senator Eagleton had been in mental hospitals, and the senator himself disclosed he had had three hospitalizations, including electroshock treatments, for psychiatric reasons.

The controversy raged. If the Democrats won, could the country afford to have a mentally disturbed man in the second highest position, or, to use a common phrase, "one heartbeat from the Presidency with his finger on the atomic trigger"? Senator McGovern was stupefied and poorly advised. He proclaimed at first that he was backing Senator Eagleton a thousand percent. But he yielded to public pressure, and chose a new running mate.

My respected friend Harrison Salisbury, the first editor of the Op-Ed page of *The New York Times*, asked me—it was more of a gentle urging—to give a professional opinion on the

Eagleton case in the form of an editorial. Because it was so close to the national elections—about two weeks before—it was with great reluctance that I decided to tackle the issue. (*See* Appendix.) Mental instability is a term as disturbing as it is confusing and mysterious. The question had to be raised: What is mental health and what is mental illness? Are we talking about psychotic behavior that cripples a man's rational thinking and distorts his view of the world of reality; or are we talking about neurotic symptoms that may interfere in various degrees with his functioning in a world of reality, without basically distorting that world? And the, there was the even more frightening question: What is insanity—where is the dividing line between sanity and madness?

In the column headlined "The Lessons of Eagleton," which appeared on October 30, 1972 (election day was November 7) I said that evidently the fear was that under the pressures of his high office an unstable leader could break down and possibly make unsound or destructive decisions.

"Generally speaking," I wrote, "it takes insight and enormous courage for a person to decide to go through a process of self-examination as in psychotherapy, when he must come to grips with the person he really is and his place in a world of reality. Consequently, to consult a psychiatrist is not necessarily a sign of mental instability and may often speak more for than against a political leader.*

It almost seems as though in political life ghosts once called upon the scene never leave it, or rather, that old fears never die. Almost a rerun of the same charge that faced President Nixon—the charge of having been treated by me—came when

---

*Other units of the news media interviewed me on TV. When I asked one of the newscasters why they always came to me, he answered, "We go to others also, but we come to you first because you are the authority on political leaders," a statement that made me wonder how such "authority" is determined.

President Gerald Ford, then minority leader of the House of Representatives, was nominated by President Nixon to be Vice-President, after the resignation of Spiro Agnew. There were rumors, followed by denials, that Mr. Ford had been a patient of mine.

Mr. Ford told the Senate Rules Committee, which conducted hearings on his nomination on November 1, 1973, that this charge was a "lie," that the only time he saw me was when he spent fifteen minutes in my office and, he added, "I think he [Dr. Hutschnecker] lectured me about leadership." He said he was "disgustingly sane," that "under no circumstances have I ever been treated by any person in the medical profession for psychiatry."

"If one thing was made perfectly clear in this first slow, polite day of Senate committee hearings on the nomination of Representative Gerald R. Ford to be Vice-President, it is that consulting a psychiatrist or psychotherapist is still an unforgivable sin for an American politician." Thus wrote Linda Charlton in *The New York Times* reporting on the opening day's hearing.

Six days later I appeared in Washington, invited there to be sworn in as a witness in the Gerald Ford case, to answer questions on two points of concern: Ford's mental stability and his credibility. I was confronted with questions at a hearing of the Committee on Rules and Administration of the United States Senate, indeed a dignified body of men, on November 7, 1973. The problem had arisen because Robert N. Winter-Berger, a former lobbyist, had charged in his book, *The Washington Payoff,* that Congressman Gerald Ford had been my patient for about one year, after the pressures of his position as House minority leader began to make him "irritable, nervous and depressed." If true, this statement could have jeopardized Mr. Ford's appointment.

Because of Watergate and the resignation of Vice-President Agnew, Congress was determined to use extreme caution and engage in careful scrutiny before confirming the new nominee for the vice-presidency.

The chairman of the Senate Rules Committee, Senator Howard W. Cannon of Nevada, asked me almost at once, "Are you acquainted with a man by the name of Robert N. Winter-Berger?"

"Yes, I am," I replied.

"And when and where did you first meet Mr. Winter-Berger, if you recall?"

"I met him first at a dinner party, and it must have been in 1966, because my wife was still alive then, and she talked with him. He became interested in what she told him about a [my] trip to the Soviet Union and to the Pavlov Institute," I explained.

"And what was your relationship after that with Mr. Winter-Berger?" asked Senator Cannon.

I said that the ex-lobbyist had shown a strong interest in talking to me about the process of conditioning as Pavlov used it, and had asked whether it was applicable to political life or political leaders. I told him that is what the Russians are doing all the time. A few days after the dinner, he had telephoned and asked to see me. I gave him some time after hours with regular patients.

Senator Cannon asked, "Was Mr. Winter-Berger ever a patient of yours or is he now a patient of yours?"

"Never," I replied.

Then the senator asked, "Have you had occasion to meet Congressman Gerald R. Ford, the minority leader of the House of Representatives?"

"Yes, I have," I replied.

"And when and where did that occur?"

I testified that there had been a telephone call making an appointment for Mr. Ford. I thought perhaps Winter-Berger had urged him to see me. But as I told Senator Cannon, Mr. Ford "did not come as a patient." The time was November

1966, I recalled.

I also told the Senate that Mr. Ford and I had a general discussion about the problems of political leaders and the control of aggression. We discussed no personal problems of Mr. Ford's.

"Did you give him any advice concerning medical or physical or mental problems?" asked Senator Cannon.

"No," I said. "The only thing I said was that we better stay out of any war in Southeast Asia. I thought that would not be a very good thing . . . but that is not medical."

"Did you bill him—did you submit any bill to him for services?" asked the senator.

"Never. No," I said.

I said I saw Mr. Ford a second time when I visited friends in Washington. He had suggested that if I ever came to Washington, I should call him, and so I did. He invited me to his office. We again discussed the war in Southeast Asia. "Well," I said, "if we would get out of Southeast Asia, that would be in the best interest of the country, and the other way it would just support Communism. I thought that was not the way to fight it."

The senator then asked me, "Did Mr. Winter-Berger ever indicate to you that he had suggested that Congressman Ford visit you?"

I said that Winter-Berger had vaguely mentioned a connection with Mr. Ford, that "he would be involved with Mr. Ford."

"Did he say in what way he was involved with Mr. Ford?"

"Yes. I asked him, 'What do you do?' and he told me he was a lobbyist. And I said, 'What kind of profession is that?' And so he explained it. And I kidded him and said, 'You call that a profession?' "

"What was his explanation?"

"That he represented companies and is paid for it. I asked him, 'Why do you do it?' He said, 'I make more money that way.' And I said, 'Than what?' And he said, 'Than being a lawyer.'"

Senator Cannon then quoted from Winter-Berger's book, saying "At one point in this book, he states, and I quote, 'At one point, Jerry Ford told me that the pressures of being minority leader were beginning to make him irritable, nervous, and depressed. I told him about Hutschie, that is, Dr. Hutschnecker, and about Nixon, suggesting that he ask Nixon if Hutschie were doing him any good. This was how Ford became a Hutschie patient for at least a year.'"

Then the senator asked me, "What is your response to that statement?"

I said, "There are actually two questions there. As to the discussion between Winter-Berger and Mr. Ford, I cannot comment. I do not know what took place. But as to the whole thing, this is sheer imagination or fantasy. Untrue. Mr. Ford never complained about feelings of nervousness or fatigue or exhaustion, or anything of that sort, and never called, ever— except for the first time when I saw him."

"So you have only seen him on those two occasions so far?" asked the senator.

"Yes. One time at my office and the second time in Washington."

"And your answer, then, is that he was never a patient of yours, and the relationship of patient-doctor never did exist between you?"

"It was never discussed. No," I said.

Then the senator brought up the original controversial question, saying, "As you know, Mr. Winter-Berger also alleged that you had treated President Nixon. And without getting into any details of the patient-doctor relationship, can you tell us whether or not President Nixon has been a patient of yours?"

I replied that President Nixon came to me "strictly in my capacity as an internist."

Senator Mark O. Hatfield, in his questioning, pursued this point further. He asked, "You never had an occasion to help

Mr. Nixon as a patient in the field of psychiatric medicine?"

"No," I replied.

Senator Hatfield then quoted from Winter-Berger's book: "That night Hutschie told us that his greatest difficulty with Nixon as a patient was teaching the man not to try to think on his feet. Nixon, said Hutschie, is the sort of man who should rehearse even a casual conversation." Senator Hatfield then asked, "Now, that would imply psychiatric counseling, rather than internal medicine, would it not?"

"Correct, if it were true," I said. "But it happens not to be true. It is total invention, from beginning to the point he tries to make."

"It is a total untruth?" said Senator Hatfield.

"Totally. Absolutely," I said.

Senator Hatfield quoted another passage from the book, which said, "Hutschie later told me that in May 1970, after the violent national reaction to Nixon's announcement of the invasion of Cambodia, Nixon went to his Florida home for the weekend, and Hutschie was there, making an emergency house call, trying to piece together Nixon's shattered ego."

I said, "Absolutely untrue. I did not see Mr. Winter-Berger in 1970. The whole story is total invention."

"So that at no time did you visit Mr. Nixon in Florida for the purpose of psychiatric counseling?"

"No."

"Or any other place for psychiatric counseling?"

"No. I have never been to San Clemente or to Florida," meaning, of course, the winter White House.

Senator Marlow W. Cook of Kentucky wanted to know, "What do you think of him [Winter-Berger] . . . What [is] your insight in relation to your profession . . . ?"

I said, "He was basically an angry man . . . very thin veneer of polite behavior . . . I asked him, 'What do you want to get out of life?' And he said, 'I want money.' He wanted power."

Toward the end of the session, when we were again discussing Winter-Berger's personality, Senator Cannon asked, "Doctor, is it possible that a person having some of the traits that you describe here could or would state something, allege something, to be the truth, and perhaps even believe that it were the truth in his own mind?"

I said, "There are people who are mentally disturbed, and they really do not know the truth. We see situations all the time—if you take an automobile accident, two people will describe the same incident, swearing what they saw is the truth, but the way each one sees it may be distorted.

"I cannot say how sick Mr. Winter-Berger is. But from the way his book was presented, this was a deliberate attempt to hurt other people. I thought about it. I could not help but think of Schopenhauer, who described why people write books. He said there are two types of writers: those who write out of conviction and those who write for money. But I think there is a third reason, and that is vindictiveness—to get even with someone. This book is a direct, vicious attack with the intention to hurt people.

"In my own case, I have done him no harm. I saw him several times, I was friendly. I answered some questions he wanted answered. And I don't know why he went into what you call 'hitting someone under the belly,' in a way which is the most harmful to a professional man—to say that you 'leak' information, that you drop names of your patients, that you have no conscious scruples about what is confidential material—just spilling it out as though I had said all those things."

Senator Claiborne Pell from Rhode Island, a man with a seemingly delightful sense of humor, then asked why I did not sue Winter-Berger for libel. I replied, "I talked with my lawyers after I considered it. I felt if I had sued him, it would have only promoted the book. And that is what I did not want to do. And I had a feeling that is what he speculated I would do." I did not mention that in all my life I never sued anybody—not because I am timid, but because court actions absorb one's mind destructively. I wanted to avoid publicity, but also I did not want to bring President Nixon's name into this matter.

By way of a summary, I told the senators that Winter-Berger "may have wanted to push Ford into something Ford did not want to do. And the book is really aimed at destroying Ford. This is just my feeling. And he mentioned me incidentally, as a tie-in with Nixon, to give it just a little more color."

The senators, including the chairman, thanked me for appearing. Senator Cannon said, "Doctor, we thank you very much for taking the time to be here with us and helping the committee out in its work."

Thirteen days later, on November 20, 1973, I set off again for Washington, this time to appear before the Judiciary Committee of the House of Representatives. As I walked in I was amused to see some members reading the column I had written for *The New York Times* Op-Ed page, titled, "The Stigma of Seeing a Psychiatrist." (*See* Appendix.)

While I found the majority of the congressmen, especially the chairman, Congressman Peter Rodino, very courteous, a few pressed me hard to "share" my impression of Senator Ford with them, in spite of my frequent denials that he had ever been a patient of mine. The testimony took up 100 pages of record.

Congressman Robert W. Kastenmeier of Wisconsin asked, "Granted that your two interviews with Mr. Ford were not in depth, they have been somewhat superficial, could you nonetheless share with this committee your analysis of the psychological makeup of Mr. Ford?"

I replied, "No. I think that would be a very unfair attempt on my part. The reason I make statements in regard to Mr. Winter-Berger was that he engaged in a direct attack on me and my statements were a sort of defense. But as far as Mr. Ford is concerned, I have some personal impressions, but it would be most unfair to state them . . ." Under some pressure I added: "He struck me as an open, honest personality, but that is as far as I would go."

Mr. Kastenmeier said he understood I was "producing a book . . . which may shed some light on political personalities you have known and we may look forward to seeing Mr. Ford, Mr. Nixon, and others in that book, is that correct?"

"Possibly," I answered.

And when Congressman Don Edwards from California also asked me about the book I replied, "I am interested more in the structure of what makes a political leader. If I use examples, it is only to make points. But the book does not deal primarily with the personalities and then draw a theory. I start with a theory and then use some examples."

There was again discussion about Winter-Berger, and Congressman Kastenmeier again entered the interrogation and said, "It is ironical if not paradoxical that the witness is able to give us so much insight into Mr. Winter-Berger but the person we are really interested in, Mr. Ford, considering that the witness is really, I would say, expert in connection with the analysis of political leaders, this is one of his obviously profound interests, that he cannot share with us somewhat better insight, if you will, analysis, of Mr. Ford."

I explained again that I had spoken in my own defense when it came to Winter-Berger but that I could not reveal confidential matter when it came to President Nixon or Congressman Ford.

Congressman Jerome R. Waldie of California asked what Mr. Ford said during the meeting. "What did he tell you he was there for? He stays only fifteen minutes, he is anxious when he arrives, what did he say to you when he got there in that fifteen minutes?"

"I didn't say he was anxious," I said.

"Well, you said he betrayed anxieties."

"I did not use the term anxious."

"That makes it a very weird fifteen minutes unless he was there for some ascertainable purpose," said Congressman

Waldie. "What purpose did he come to New York to see you for?"

"That I cannot answer because that is something that transpired between Mr. Winter-Berger and Mr. Ford," I replied. "What Mr. Winter-Berger told Mr. Ford as to why he should see me, or what possible use I could be to the one or the other, is an assumption on my part. But I cannot assume why Mr. Ford decided to come."

"I don't want you to assume. I want you to tell us what Mr. Ford told you the reason he came," said Congressman Waldie.

"I am sorry. I am not holding back, but I don't recall."

"Well, did Mr. Ford not tell you any reason he was there?"

"After he told me he was not coming as a patient—naturally I asked—he said something to the effect—that he just wanted to meet me."

"And did he say why he just wanted to meet you?"

"No. He said that Mr. Winter-Berger impressed upon him that it might be of some value or interest for him to meet me."

"Did you ask him what sort of value or interest he thought might be obtained?"

"No. I was not involved in any analysis. We just chatted."

"Did you draw any assumption of what value he might obtain from meeting you?"

"No, I can't say this."

"Let me ask you this. Were you perplexed by his visit?"

"No, I was not."

"Did it seem to you a usual thing to happen in your office, to have a nationally known politician wander in and say, 'I am not a patient, but this fellow Winter-Berger,' a fellow you don't like and distrust, 'says I ought to meet you because we might have some value that each might get from the other'?"

"He just didn't 'walk in.' I knew Mr. Winter-Berger had announced that he might come, and eventually there was the phone call."

There followed long discussion as to the actual date when I

had last seen Winter-Berger. Then, to conclude the session, Congressman Wayne W. Owens asked, "Dr. Hutschnecker, if I were to come to your office and say I am a political figure and I feel the need for your professional service, but it must be completely confidential, would you accept me as a patient? The fact of my visit to you must be completely confidential."

I said, "I answer with reservation, because I don't take every patient."

"I understand."

"I have a discussion first."

"Assuming that I qualify financially and otherwise?" said Congressman Owens. "You would take me and promise me confidentiality?"

"Absolutely."

"And my name would not appear, therefore, on your books. Would you take me under a—in effect, if I were to tell you my political career could be in danger if the fact of my visit—"

"Right. I may use another name or I may have some other indication. I don't think I ever put, for instance, Mr. Nixon's name in the book. I kept his record apart from the other records."

"Did you handle him under a false name, an assumed name?"

"No, but I just crossed off the time and so I know it, and kept his record locked up someplace else."

"So a political person could come to you and be treated by you and his name never appear on any of your records?"

"That is right. That is correct."

"If you were asked whether in fact that person had ever been a patient of yours, would you keep that fact confidential? If you were asked under oath?"

"I would have to say that I cannot reveal it."

"So if you were asked under oath you would not reveal it?"

"I would not. I could not."

"Would you refuse to answer the question, or would you answer in the negative?"

"If I saw a situation, let's say, a national emergency, then we have a very tricky, difficult situation. But as a general procedure, I would not reveal the name."

"You are aware of the penalties for perjury?"

"Yes."

"If you give an incorrect answer under oath?"

"Yes, I know that."

"And your knowledge of those penalties notwithstanding, you would not reveal under oath that you have treated such a patient to whom you had given such a promise?"

"I would ask the chairman to consider this, to try to understand that if I take someone on and give him the reassurance that I will not reveal his name, I will not do it," I said.

"Then how should we be assured, as this committee today, that you have not treated Gerald Ford?"

"All I can tell you, and I say it under oath, is that I never treated him."

"But you have already said that had you treated him and given him a promise of confidentiality—"

"I would have said I refuse to answer, had I treated him."

At times it seemed to me that some of the congressmen were driven more by their own need to win than by an objective interest in obtaining the facts. Eventually, Mr. Rodino, the chairman, obviously to cut short further questioning, said: "I am satisfied this witness spoke the truth." And later he added, "Thank you for your great patience."

On the plane home, I thought once again that in our attitude toward psychoanalytic help we are still living in the dark ages, and yet we can land men on the moon and engage in a conversation by telephone with the astronauts, or have a photograph flashed from Mercury, 20 million miles away.

Before my appearances as a witness in Washington, an FBI agent had visited me to get the facts on Mr. Ford. We had an interesting discussion as to what kinds of people would visit an office such as mine. Some would come, I explained, because they were in a quandary about themselves and how to cope with life. Others wanted to learn why they were standing in their own way to success, or had ended up by failing. Or why their marriage was about to break up. Perhaps a student would come because he could not cope with the demands of school or could not concentrate, or was afraid to become a dropout. Some wanted to find their way back to school. Then there were those who had thought that wealth and social standing would make them happy, and who now suffered from depressions and suicidal ideations because their values had let them down.

The agent shook his head in wonder when I told him that in my office marriages had been saved, not just mended temporarily, careers had been built or rebuilt, and people had reconstructed their lives rather than allowing them to remain in broken pieces. Not all marriages could be saved, I added, for some were so destructive that husband and wife were better off separating.

The FBI man was startled to learn about an area of life of which he had practically no awareness. He seemed to be realizing, all at once, that life cannot be understood in terms of a simple, rigid rule of right or wrong, or the Hollywood formula of the good guy and the bad guy.

I told him that the majority of my patients were *not* mentally sick people, but people of superior intellect who had the courage to come to my office to try to find out who they were, and who wanted to overcome destructive or depressive conditioning. I think I used the term "hangups." They were people who work hard, and with disarming honesty, to become inwardly free and concerned about other human beings, rather than making believe that all that mattered was to go full speed ahead while hiding their inner selves carefully behind a mask of conventionality.

The FBI agent, a well-educated and alert man, expressed his amazement, saying, "And I thought only mentally sick people go to a psychiatrist. By golly, I have learned more in this hour here than in all my life." He took one of my books with him. After he left I wondered whether he ever would consider seeing an analyst should he find himself in a state of conflict or acute confusion. Or, would he, conditioned as he seemed to be, continue to look at therapy from the standpoint of his career as an unforgivable sin?

III

The Mental Health of Political Leaders

I F W E are to protect ourselves against political leaders who in acting out their inner drive for power plunge a nation or half the world into risky ventures or bloody "little wars," we must try to understand these leaders as human beings.

We must try to gain awareness of their personality, their character structure and the way they use their innate super-drive. As people, are they cynical-negative or are they be-nevolent-positive? Do they say a glass is half-full or half-empty? Do they have an unconscious fear of death and a resultant need to display their power to be reassured of being alive? Do they have the solemn sense of a mission? Do they see themselves as liberators, as St. Georges who will slay all the evil dragons? Do they feel compelled to change the world in their image in order to achieve immortality?

Once we elect a leader, mentally stable or unstable, Congress

33

notwithstanding, we the people hand over our destiny, our future, to all the complexities that make up his personality.

I for one do not share the somewhat cynical political axiom that nations deserve the leaders they elect. There exist conditions such as worldwide periods of hope or hopelessness that affect the mood of the voters and their search for a strong protective leader. There may be distrust and fear and a consequent desire to bolt the doors and seek safety in isolationism.

Man's inspiring hope of "One World" has been swallowed up by a heavy fog of pessimism and seems to be lost, replaced by corrupt and selfish partisanship, by people who would like to return to the womb, or retreat to a fortress existence and pull up their drawbridges. Though it is too late in history for that because we have become too interdependent, we, nevertheless have seen, since World War II, a regressive trend, a disintegration of larger countries into a score of independent splinter states. The emergence of new national entities, especially in Africa and Asia, fostered by fanatical clansmen and achieved mostly by the use of force and of violence, resembles the process of mass regression into smaller tribal societies with embroiling sibling rivalries. The new states stress their individuality by emphasizing what divides rather than what unites the family of man, underscoring segregation, racial superiority, political dogmatism or religious bigotry, thereby disrupting the building of a family of man with a healthy pursuit of common human goals.

Today the battle cry is not for peace but for war in the name of liberation and freedom, and violence is being advocated as an essential element for attaining "justice" through power in many corners of the world, including our own. In Northern Ireland people of the same blood kill one another in the name of the same God; in the Middle East fanatical leaders stir up holy wars.

Psychoanalysts know that all the noble reasons given for the use of violence are basically rationalizations. For whatever the legitimate reasons, if men in positions of power were of good will, most of the differences could be resolved peacefully. But there is a remarkable absence of good will because of man's compulsive need to fight, to live up to some chauvinistic slogan of national honor. Actually, a call to arms would have little appeal if there was not a tendency to violence in the deeper nature of man. It may well be, as Freud, quoted by Ernest Jones, put it, that "the very emphasis of the Commandment 'Thou shalt not kill' makes it certain that we are descendents of generations of murderers, whose love for murder was in their blood as it is perhaps in ours."

Many historians, as well as political, military and other leaders, are actually blatant in their condemnation of peace. They equate peace with passivity, with weakness, with atrophy and decay. Baron von der Goltz, a German Field Marshal, said: "The warlike spirit must not be allowed to die out among people, neither must the love for peace get the upper hand." And another Field Marshal showed his complete disregard for the value of human life and his distortion of values when he said, "War is part of God's world order. In it are developed the noblest virtues of man: courage and abnegation, dutifulness and self-sacrifice . . . without war the world would sink into materialism." If any of our military officers think the same, they do not say so. One U.S. captain answered my questions about the army in a quick statement: "The U.S. Army is the greatest peace organization in the world." Well learned, I thought.

President Truman fired General MacArthur not only because the general disobeyed his commander-in-chief, but because President Truman had doubts about the general's proposal for a huge American military presence in the Near East and his intent to invade China. He said of MacArthur, "I have given it a lot of thought, and I have finally concluded—that there were times when he wasn't right in his head." Merle Miller in his book *Plain Speaking* quotes President Truman as saying, "I fired him because he would not respect the authority of the President, I did not fire him because he was a dumb son-of-a-bitch, even though he was (though that's not against the law for generals, if it were, half to three-quarters of the generals of the world would be in jail)." People want their heroes to remain unblemished and they become upset at any diminishing of their demigods, but clinically (as his own doctor told me) MacArthur was not a stable personality.

What is it in leaders that makes them pursue violence instead of peace? First let us ask: What are the dynamics of leadership? What is it that creates that iron will, that undeviating superdrive that makes a man go through obstacles, deprivation, humiliation and defeats, and yet enables him to retain an unshakable belief in himself and a single-mindedness of purpose and will?

That which distinguishes a leader from other people, especially when confronted with obstacles, is his almost fanatical quality, an obstinate, undaunting determination to go ahead, to live and toil for the sole purpose of reaching that ultimate position of power.

To understand this phenomenon of drive, we must understand the origin of human aggression. We find valuable clues for such understanding in the painstaking studies Ivan Petrovitch Pavlov, Russian physiologist and Nobel Prize winner, discoverer of the conditioned reflex, conducted first on dogs, then on people, which led to his classification of four types of behavior.

By exposing dogs to planned stress, Pavlov found four distinctly different kinds of reaction: the strong-excitatory, the lively, the calm imperturbable and the weak-inhibitory.

Humans react to stress in a similar way. In more familiar psychological terminology, we would call the first type the hostile-aggressive. It is this group that provides the vast majority of leaders in all areas of life—political, industrial, business, professional and sports, as well as in the arts and sciences—

actually in all areas of competitive activities, including the man-woman relationship, marriage.

In the political arena, de Gaulle may serve as a prime example of this type, for his quarrelsome stirring up of troubles in the name of the glory of France. His arrogance and demands led Churchill to remark that of all the crosses he had to bear, the cross of Lorraine was the heaviest.

Type two, the aggressive-adjusted personality, has the widest threshold of tolerance and is capable of applying critical judgment and control under stress. Though people of this type are the most ideal leaders, few leaders are found in this group. A great leader like President Lincoln could, in the course of his harsh struggle with the adversities of life, slowly mature and outgrow his hostile-aggressive behavior and eventually become the man who saved the union and wrote the Gettysburg Address. And yet we may ask, would a better-adjusted President have handled the secession of the Confederate States differently at the outset? That we can never know, but we do know that several authorities have come to the conclusion that Lincoln was a very emotionally troubled man. Elwell Crissey, who after thirteen years of research wrote the book *Lincoln's Lost Speech*, sent me a chapter of a new book he is writing, a chapter called "Mr. Lincoln on the Psychiatrist's Couch." In it Mr. Crissey refers to the late Senator Albert J. Beveridge of Indiana, whom he considers "the most indefatigable research scholar ever to study Abraham Lincoln," as having come to the conclusion, along with his consultants, that "Lincoln's personality, character and private life were so abnormal that only a psychiatrist could hope to make sense out of their unbelievably mixed-up patterns."

And Mr. Crissey quotes the psychoanalytic evaluation of Dr. Thaddeus Kostrubala, Director of Psychiatric Inpatient Services for the Maine Medical Center, Portland, Maine, and assistant professor of psychiatry at Tufts University Medical School, that Lincoln's "life-long battering by traumatic shocks would have unsettled his mind even if Lincoln had been of phlegmatic temperament." He describes Lincoln as "habitually depressed." And yet, against all odds Lincoln succeeded in preserving the integrity of the union and in freeing the slaves.

Type three, the passive-dependent personality, is not one who seeks a fight, but instead evades confrontation. Such a man tends to compromise and rationalize, as long as he can give the semblance of saving his honor.

Lincoln had some of these characteristics, which proves only that people cannot easily be fitted into some stereotyped categories. We can only assume there is a dominating or prevailing tendency. A stable personality has a greater resiliency to mood swings.

People of this type may become good administrators, but their aggressiveness has been so sublimated or inhibited in their formative years—often finding safe expression in intellectual or other pursuits—that they tend to adhere to conventional or rigid standards. These are the dependable employees with records of long service. In political life a man like Neville Chamberlain, for instance, would repress spontaneous gut reactions, conditioned as he was to be the perfect, cool Victorian gentleman who has contempt for a fight, evades a battle and rationalizes little gains as solutions, totally unaware of the dangers in the world of grim reality.

Type four, the weak-inhibited personality, could never be a leader by his own efforts unless put there in a line of succession in a monarchist system, as with King George VI of England; King Ludwig II of Bavaria who drowned himself; Czar Nicholas II and a long line of incompetent and weak leaders. What is so often true of weak leaders also holds true for the sons of leading self-made men in business or industry. In our own country, President Harding allowed men who had supported and directed his campaign to become part of his cabinet; these men took advantage of a weak leader and bled the country financially.

Types one and four are most likely to break down under pressure. They have a tendency to overreact in the face of danger, type one with overaggression and type four with further withdrawal. James V. Forrestal, first secretary of defense, a type one with an inner personality structure of type four, according to studies by Arnold A. Rogow, a political scientist, was not considered to be mentally ill by his associates. They thought that he was suffering only from fatigue; the psychiatric care he needed came too late to prevent his suicide.

Types one and four lack an inner resiliency or strength, but they can show a measure of temporary strength in coping with a crisis. As Dr. Karl Menninger has put it, you either break the situation or the situation breaks you. After a break, a type one personality may emerge stronger and more in control of his churning aggressive drive, even able to reorganize his life. But if his mental resources are inadequate, the situation will break him and then the full force of his power drive will be directed against himself. He then inevitably seeks death, in one act of suicide or in many little self-destructive actions.

A tragic example of the love-hate struggle in man, of the idealist who is unaware of the hostility within himself (a mixture of type one and type three) is President Thomas Woodrow Wilson. He felt destined to bring peace to a war-torn world, and yet unconsciously he helped create the conditions that led to World War II. One of the few deep psychological studies of a President that exists is the recent book *Thomas Woodrow Wilson, a Psychological Study*, by Sigmund Freud and William C. Bullitt.

The authors state that one fact in Wilson's childhood "stands out with such prominence that it dwarfs all the rest," the fact "that Tommy Wilson's father was his great love-object." With most political leaders there is a classic hate for the father and a need to unseat him. This was true in Hitler's case and true of Stalin and Mussolini. Perhaps because their fathers died when the dictators were in their teens they could not release their adolescent hostilities and consequently remained frustrated. But the *image* of the father remained within, as it does with all of us, and the childhood battles continued to be waged— unfortunately on a worldwide front.

Wilson's formative years were absorbed and dominated by his father, the great figure of Wilson's childhood. In comparison, Wilson's mother was a very small figure. His father was a minister and wanted his son to become one, but this was the one thing on which Wilson defied his father: he insisted on becoming a statesman.

Never in his life, by thought, word or act, did Wilson express hostility to his "beloved" father. But, according to the authors, Wilson's repressed hatred of his father continued to seek discharge, driving him to violent and unreasonable hatreds of other men who unconsciously were father substitutes to him. The authors claim that many times in Wilson's life he "slipped . . . toward neurosis," and finally "toward the end of his career, he nearly plunged into psychosis."

They describe Wilson as

a rather pathetic little boy, a child to whom one cannot refuse sympathy. He was weak, sickly and nervous, retarded in his development, his eyesight was defective and he suffered constantly from indigestion and headaches . . . his early relationship to his father doomed him to expect of himself all his life more than his body or mind could give. The nervousness and discontent which marked his life were early established.

When Wilson "crossed the ocean to bring to war-torn Europe a just and lasting peace, he put himself in the deplorable position of the benefactor who wishes to restore the eyesight of a patient but does not know the construction of the eye and has neglected to learn the necessary methods of operation."

Because of the deep unconscious identification with his minister father, Wilson had the goal of "saving the world." But his hatred of Germany and of Russia, and his championing of the terms of the Versailles Treaty only served to sow the seeds for World War II. As Freud and Bullitt state, the German colonies were annexed by England, France and Italy, the Allies

> dismembered Austria, Hungary and Turkey, severed East Prussia from the body of Germany, disemboweled Tyrol, confiscated the German merchant marine and all the German private property upon which they could lay hands, and placed a burden of tribute upon Germany without limit of time or amount. . . .

> The German submission produced no elation in Wilson. His hatred and loathing of nearly all mankind, which must have been at bottom a hatred and loathing of himself, had reached a fantastic pitch. He was overflowing with bile. And the hatred which he had not dared to loose against either Clemenceau or Lloyd George burst against Poincaré, President of the French Republic, who on the occasion of Wilson's arrival in France had made him feel inferior by speaking better without notes than he had been able to speak with notes.

> Wilson also hated Senator Henry Cabot Lodge "with a violent hatred. He was compelled to try to defeat Lodge as he had never dared try to defeat his father."

The Senate's refusal in 1919 to ratify the Versailles Treaty was "the supreme expression of the neurosis which controlled his life." He had a mental and physical collapse. After meeting with the Senate to discuss the existence of "secret treaties in 1917," his physical condition grew worse, he suffered daily headaches and became intensely nervous. Over the objections of his physician, he decided to tour America appealing to the people to support him in his fight for the treaty—his fight against Lodge. His physician warned him that his speaking tour might result in a fatal collapse. But Wilson insisted on going. His first speech on September 4 at Columbus, Ohio, "showed that he had left fact and reality behind for the land in which facts are merely the embodiment of wishes." He forgot that his mother was an immigrant from England and his father's parents immigrants from Ulster and said, "I have been bred and am proud to have been bred, of the old revolutionary stock which set this government up." The next day in St. Louis, he described his opponents as "contemptible quitters," whose "ignorance" and "aberrations" amazed him. On September 13, he began to suffer from violent headaches which continued without interruption until his collapse on the train on September 26. He was suffering, in addition, from indigestion, neuritis and irritability. His face was gray and the left side of it and the eye twitched.

On September 25, at Pueblo, Colorado, "poor little Tommy Wilson, who had learned to talk like God by listening to his 'incomparable father' talked like God for the last time. The facts in his address were fantastically distorted: 'Not one foot of territory is demanded by the conquerors, not one single item of submission to their authority is demanded by them.' " That night on the train he collapsed. The trip was canceled by his physician. Three days later, at four o'clock in the morning, he fell on the floor of his bathroom in the White House, his left side paralyzed by thrombosis in the right side of his brain. The authors state that Wilson's superego and his conflicting desires with regard to his father, drove him to a campaign of feverish speechmaking which culminated in the bursting of a blood vessel in his left eye.

"He was driven to destruction by the old conflict he had never been able to solve, the conflict between his activity toward his father and his passivity to his father. He had never solved the major dilemma of the Oedipus complex, and in the end he was destroyed by the same 'incomparable father' who created him."

He lived four years and four months after his collapse but he was a "pathetic invalid, a querulous old man full of rage and tears, hatred and self-pity. He was so ill that he was allowed to receive only such information as his wife thought would be good for him." He remained in title President of the United States until March 4, 1921, but during the last eighteen months of his administration Mrs. Wilson was in large measure the chief executive of the United States. He refused to accept the Lodge amendments to the treaty, which was defeated at Wilson's behest. Only when Harding was elected President was the treaty ratified.

Bullitt's letter of resignation as assistant in the Department of State, attaché to the American commission to negotiate peace, is particularly moving. He wrote to Wilson:

> I was one of the millions who trusted confidently and implicitly in your leadership and believed that you would take nothing less than "permanent peace" based upon "unselfish and unbiased justice." But our Government has consented now to deliver the suffering peoples of the world to new oppressions, subjections, and dismemberments—a new century of war. And I can convince myself no longer that effective labor for "a new world order" is possible as a servant of this Government.
>
> Russia, "the acid test of good will," for me as for you, has not even been understood. Unjust decisions of the Conference in regard to Santung, the Tyrol, Thrace, Hungary, East Prussia, Danzig, the Saar Valley, and the abandonment of the principle of the freedom of the seas, make new international conflicts certain. It is my conviction that the present League of Nations will be powerless to prevent these wars, and that the United States will be involved in them by the obligations undertaken in the covenant of the league and in the special understanding with France. . . .
>
> That you personally opposed most of the unjust settlements, and that you accepted them only under great

pressure, is well known. Nevertheless, it is my conviction that if you had made your fight in the open, instead of behind closed doors, you would have carried with you the public opinion of the world, which was yours; you would have been able to resist the pressure and might have established the "new international order" based upon broad and universal principles of right and justice of which you used to speak. I am sorry that you did not fight our fight to the finish and that you had so little faith in the millions of men, like myself, in every nation who had faith in you.

The sad truth was that President Wilson had no faith in himself, he hated himself as he hated the Germans, and his hatred stemmed from the childhood hatred of a father he had never been able to defy. He had repressed that hate, and when we repress an emotion, we cannot deal rationally with it. So it erupts irrationally on innocent targets. President Wilson had a chance that few men possess to change the history of the world from its violent course, but he was unable to take that chance because of the violence within himself.

We can see in American political life in more recent years, evidences of the drive to power that has plunged us into "limited" wars, that has continued the violence by decisions made behind closed doors without letting the people "in": We have had two wars in Southeast Asia, including an invasion into neutral Cambodia. *"Ubi solitudineum facinut, pacem appelant,"* said Tacitus—they make a desert and call it peace. "Limited warfare," a so-called "sophisticated solution," is still in reality mass murder, just smaller in scope than the big wars; it is carried out under the direction of men who have not abandoned the ancient, savage policy of seeking power through violence.

World War II came as a storm of human creation which could gather force only because of the enormous incompetence and cowardice of the political leaders, especially in France, England and in Germany. A psychopath, Hitler, was allowed to run amok and the leaders in Europe trembled but closed their eyes and failed to act at a time when every child in Germany knew about the growing rearmament. People were so paranoiac about Communism that they rationalized away the acute German military danger. "We are going to use Hitler for a while to stamp out Communism," said the old, aristocratic, military clique and the steel barons in Germany, a thought that found sympathy in Western Europe, especially France, and, to some degree, in the United States. The war ran its bloody course, accompanied by a breakdown of the moral conscience of the world. Even the Vatican closed its eyes and concluded a concordat. Hitler, the mass murderer, had gained respectability. The voices of sanity and morality were ignored. People were scared and did not care as long as they thought Nazism would not affect them. People thought more about possessions and money than law, ideas and human rights.

It is easy to say that a psychotic individual, such as Hitler, should never be permitted to lead a nation. But who was there to prevent his assuming power? Who in Germany was mature enough to know that his glowing promises and the hypnotic excitement he was able to stir came from a man who was mad? And even those who knew had no power to stop him. Undoubtedly we need to find ways of preventing psychotic men from gaining political power. But if we rule out the neurotic leader, we would rule out every man. It is impossible to be "civilized" without to some degree becoming neurotic.

With potentially dangerous political leaders as with a political criminal, our problem is the same: we cannot arrest a man until he has committed a crime. If a leader has enough poise and appeal, which he must have in order to be elected, no matter how criminal his intentions, people will follow his glib tongue and silvery promises.

A leader's hostility, overt or hidden, and his blind drive to win, cause him only too often to forget his campaign promises or programs. The Johnson-Goldwater presidential race of 1964 may serve as a good example of the violence that stirs in leaders. The one candidate was open in his political philosophy, and the other deceitful, though perhaps lacking conscious awareness of his deceit. Goldwater was honest enough to state that he would not oppose the use of nuclear weapons to end the conflict in Vietnam; his was an irresponsible, but open display of violence. Johnson promised peace.

But it was not just the different policy that swung the tide and caused Johnson, the man of peace, to win in an unprecedented landslide, surpassed only by President Nixon's victory in 1972. There was also a question of health. Goldwater, it was rumored, had suffered two "nervous breakdowns" while Johnson had had a heart attack. To many people a physical illness is acceptable—Eisenhower was reelected in spite of a heart attack—but a "nervous breakdown" has the connotation of mental illness, which frightens people away from a candidate.

There was still another point of difference. While Goldwater appeared to be a rigid, militaristic ultraconservative, Johnson presented the "image" of a more flexible, reassuring father-teacher figure. He seemed to be a secure realist, motivated by inner idealism. When he spoke, he sounded like a conjuring missionary. Perhaps he believed the part he played; certainly the people believed him. Even those who tend to solve conflicts by the use of arms felt reassured by Johnson's strength and accepted the promise of his new Great Society. He was known to be ruthless in his drive. His ambition almost burned him out. It kept driving him so fast and furiously and with such blinding effect, that the story has been told that when someone asked a page boy if he had seen Senator Johnson, then the newest and youngest majority leader, the youth replied, "I haven't seen anything but a burning bush."

The faith in Johnson was so deep that his almost 180-degree turn in the field of foreign affairs, particularly Vietnam, caused many people to go on trusting him. The majority of people admired the stamina with which President Johnson had pushed through reforms and new legislation on the home front. Therefore they believed that he knew where he was going on the international front as well. But soon more and more people felt betrayed. Only a short while after he became President, Johnson gathered "hawk" personalities more closely around him, angry men, men who thought in terms of force, of power, with little reverence for human life. People who suited his violent personality, such as General Maxwell Taylor and General William Westmoreland; men who were considered to be brilliant but cold as human beings, such as Henry Cabot Lodge, Robert McNamara and a glib, aloof McGeorge Bundy. All of them fit Harry Truman's description of experts: "I know all about *experts*. I said an *expert* was a fella who was afraid to learn anything new because then he wouldn't be an expert anymore." Peace had no chance. Secretary of State Dean Rusk projected his inner anger and weakness as he passionately supported the war and the bombing and burning to force a little country into submission.

Was President Johnson, the skillful wheeler-dealer in domestic affairs, naive enough to believe the superoptimists who promised that victory was just around the corner? Or was there something deep within his personality that reacted readily to violence? It is a basic psychological experience that hostility begets hostility and enmity breeds conflict and makes the hostile-aggressive personality think in terms of violent solutions rather than peaceful settlements. And so we saw Johnson, the compassionate man, using his immense powers to send more and more young men into war to kill and to be killed. And we also saw some of the young people's passionate reaction to the violence of the war spill over into the streets of American cities, an interaction many people in government did not understand.

It is not the job of psychologists to judge a man. Their job is to consider and evaluate human behavior objectively. Many

people have difficulty understanding the contradictory behavior of the human mind: for example, that aggression and
inhibition can hide under a facade of benevolence. Or the
meaning of ambivalence, the two-sided oneness that makes a
man speak with the conviction of friendship and brotherhood
though inwardly he is moved by active antagonism. The
tragedy of Lyndon Baines Johnson was that this man of great
stature, intelligence, and enormous potential meant well
perhaps but ended up like all people who delude themselves
believing they desire the good and somehow create evil. He
was another mentally unstable American President.

I find it of interest that President Johnson, an aggressive
personality, veering near the borderline of violence, did not
break down under the stress of the presidency, probably because he could release his aggression by supporting a war, the
ultimate expression of violence, and by sending others out to
fight. When he could not release his aggression fully and when
he experienced disappointments and frustrations while reaching for the presidency, he broke down physically with a heart
attack.

General Eisenhower, as President, was an entirely different
type of leader, psychologically speaking. Surprisingly, he did
not show the typical characteristics of the hostile-aggressive
personality. President Truman called him weak and a moral
coward, yet he was assertive enough to attain the highest rank
in the United States Army and the nation's highest office. He
showed evidence of a passivity found in many military men
who grow up in a hierarchy of clearly defined rules and regulations.

One remarkable feature for a military man was President
Eisenhower's comparative absence of rigidity, and it was this
quality that probably helped him to get along with people.
Without this ability, he could hardly have managed, as a com-
mander of the Allied armies, to deal with the difficulties involving Allied chiefs of staff, the jealousies of the British generals,

and an obstinate, quarrelsome and demanding Charles de Gaulle. President Eisenhower possessed another rather unusual quality for a general: gentleness. During his terms as President he resisted with determination any pressure for war, perhaps thereby creating the inner emotional climate of frustration that can become a contributory factor in heart attacks. Certainly President Eisenhower's scrupulousness in holding to his campaign promise of peace kept the United States out of war, in spite of the relentless pressure by the military and a driving, rigid, hostile Secretary of State, John Foster Dulles, intent on "brinkmanship."

The ancient axiom that leaders are born, not made, or to use Aristotle's words, that "Men are marked out from the moment of birth to rule or be ruled," has been challenged recently by a new breed of gentlemen in gray who say, "Never mind the destiny set by the stars; we know how to promote products, even human ones; we call it image building."

And so public relation supersalesmen have expanded their field of operation from the marketing of soap and other commodities to the building of salable images of politicians, and they have dared to go as high as the making of a President. The use of refined and highly sophisticated techniques, especially in the field of television, has been initiated by this new breed of imaginative, aggressive specialists who seem little bothered by what we call conscience and who wage a fierce competitive battle with their rivals for the mind of the public.

This making of public opinion seems to include two areas: the issue and the candidate.

First the issue. Hostility and fear are the most primitive and the strongest bonds uniting a group. Therefore, people must be made aware that an "imminent danger" threatens not only the welfare of the state but their very existence. This threat may be political, socioeconomic, religious, racial, or whatever else will cause people to join together because of their fear. Senator Joseph McCarthy gained enormous power by whipping people into a paranoiac frenzy over the threat of Communism; brother began to distrust brother as the country reached a state of mass hysteria that was out of all proportion to the reality of the danger.

More realistic but also paranoiac in its overall framework has been the use of the cold war to unite the people in the fear of losing all they cherish as their national heritage, to focus their hostility on a common enemy out to destroy the American way of life. It is one thing to recognize real danger and to prepare for it properly and effectively, but another to manipulate people by exploiting their fears so that they remain in a perpetual state of hostility.

The second area, the candidate, centers on the creation of a political leader. His image has to be built up so that he catches the imagination of the people and allows them to identify with him. He must appear strong and human and secure and admirable, and yet arouse in the public the feeling that he is one of them, which means that he symbolically represents the wish in every man to elevate himself to a lofty position of power. President Kennedy gave the illusion of a knight in shining armor who would cure all our ills—from inflation to corruption to war to the threat of Communism.

The candidate is presented as a man of superior intellect who recognizes, before anyone else does, all the dangers, real or imagined; who understands the needs of the people; who has empathy; and who can arouse mass optimism and diminish mass depression, fear of the future, and the hopelessness often produced by inner discontent and maladjustment.

Under pressure people have a tendency to regress, that is, to become like the helpless children they once were, seeking the protection of a strong, trustworthy and benevolent father. Conditioned in childhood, they will follow a father, that is, a leader. If a leader can arouse the public's confidence in his ability to cope with any danger, he can also arouse the hostility of the public to the pitch of fighting it. Thus hostility and fear may create a warlike spirit as well as feelings of devotion and a willingness to follow.

Leaders, especially the heads of governments, use the power of propaganda. They always have. A French historian, André Siegfried, speaking of the United States, points out the important role public opinion plays in "inspiring, orienting and controlling" the policy of the nation: ". . . It is more spontaneous than anywhere else in the world and more easily directed by efficient propaganda techniques than in any other country . . ."

American politicians know this, and while the public is in the habit of excusing borderline ethical methods or even excesses by saying "politics is dirty," the fear of public opinion or exposure has acted as a deterrent against derogatory distortions and falsehoods by a candidate. The betrayal of the basic trust of the people was perhaps the main cause of the arousal of condemnatory reaction in the Watergate case, and its ignoble "dirty tricks" phase. As Donald Segretti, a pitiful youngish man who used his brain destructively, said, "Looking back on it, none of these activities, I believe, are ones that should be included in the American political system," a mild condemnation of the viciousness of his own dirty tricks inventions.

In other cultures, especially dictatorships, where there is no restraint on human rights or dignity, propaganda is used to brainwash a total population. "All propaganda," Hitler, a master of this art, said, "must be so popular and on such an intellectual level, that even the most stupid of those toward whom it is directed will understand it. Therefore the intellectual level of the propaganda must be lower the larger the number of people who are to be influenced by it." And Goebbels, his propaganda minister said: "It is the absolute right of the State to supervise the formation of public opinion." To instill fear, he threatened: "If the day should ever come when we [the Nazis] must go, if some day we are compelled to leave the scene of history, we will slam the door so hard that the universe will shake and mankind will stand back in stupefaction."

In the task of finding a niche for himself, it is natural that a man will test himself and try to apply a sharp yardstick to measure his potential, as well as the sum of his moral and ethical conscience, so that he can compare it with another man's. Only if he recognizes that someone is superior to himself in handling a task of enormous responsibility, and only if he possesses sane judgment, as well as controlled envy and ambition, can he accept another man as a leader.

A leader may be insecure, may suffer from inner turmoil and anxiety, but nevertheless he will have to convince an apprehensive and critical public of his ability to act without delay and with wisdom and restraint.

To be a leader a man must be aggressive. He must be stirred by a drive aggressive enough to move an inert mass of people. And he must be decisive, for otherwise he will arouse anxiety and insecurity in the psyche of the people (one of the reasons McGovern lost). He must also have self-control, for otherwise he will overreact, act out his own aggression—out of proportion to the challenge.

Political leaders should be men of great courage, for they may be called upon to meet a crisis that can affect the life of a nation or the world.

When, upon the urging of a group of nuclear scientists, Einstein wrote the fateful letter to President Roosevelt to convince him of the necessity of splitting the atom because the Germans were involved in that very project, the President had to make a decision: to develop this country's own atomic plants or to dismiss the idea of competing with the Germans. But where was he to get five billion dollars without congressional approval, in order to secure the secrecy of the work? His decision is history, and the Manhattan Project an incredible demonstration of human will.

But there is always the question as to how much of a man's decision is motivated by cool visionary sense, how much by uncontrollable drive to power, and how much by churning inner hostility. It is in the very depths of the human mind, where the struggle between love and hate is fought, that the decision is made which can lead to war or peace.

If we look at the presidential race between Kennedy and Nixon, we see how both areas, the issue and the candidate, were used. One issue was mass hostility: the enemy was Communism, feared to a point that we must, according to Nixon, go to war for the possession of two small islands off the coast of mainland China. The other was not only which man would be the better defender of our cherished freedom and our national integrity, but also which man could we trust more? And here we see that third element that has grown into fearful dimensions: the skill of the political supersalesmen and the power of television.

After the 1960 election, when I had a breakfast chat with Mr. Nixon—not a hidden professional visit, but a meeting of friends—he told me of the reports he had received about the debates. People who had heard the candidates on the radio favored Nixon because of his stand on issues, whereas those who watched television were taken by the charisma of Kennedy.

I have my own thoughts as to why Mr. Nixon lost, primarily that his advisers guided him poorly. But let us examine Mr. Nixon's own explanation of why he lost that election. In his book *Six Crises* written in 1962, he presented three points:

1. The campaign from all standpoints was too long, causing physical and emotional wear and tear on both candidates.
2. He should have saved himself for the major events, such as television appearances.
3. His belief that he had "spent too much time on substance and too little on appearance" when he was on television. He said, "I paid too much attention to what I was going to say and too little as to how I would look."

> He wrote, "Where votes are concerned, a paraphrase
> of what Mr. Khrushchev claims in an ancient Russian
> proverb could not be more controlling: 'One TV pic-
> ture is worth ten thousand words.' "

From this point of view, Kennedy had an enormous advantage. The American public had been conditioned by Hollywood and the television industry to a kind of hero worship for
an idol, and Kennedy, as we have noted, came close to fulfilling
the Hollywood image. In addition to his looks and his winning
personality, he was trained to deliver his lines and to make his
points; effectively stabbing his index finger into the air as if
actually touching a point—an attitude many people began to
copy. All of this he did superbly, except that the sharp observer
could notice the rigidity of the cornea of his eyes, which must
have come either from fear or from the medication he needed
to take for the sickness of his adrenal glands.

As the press noted, in addition to fatigue and his knee injury,
Mr. Nixon had suffered a debilitating, painful and depressing
rejection by an authoritative father figure. Former President
Eisenhower, in a seeming projection of absolute neutrality,
failed to give his substitute son any real support during the
crucial first weeks, and when he finally came out for Nixon it
was too late, and he was sharply mocked by Kennedy. The
relationship between Mr. Nixon and President Eisenhower
was in many ways reminiscent of the ancient conflict of father
and son, the elder man watching critically the performance of
his son, as if saying "show me."

President Kennedy came from a different psychological
background. A hard-driving, power-hungry, ruthlessly determined and overly aggressive father, psychologically classified
as a hostile-aggressive type, had trained his son for leadership
with almost the precision of a scientist adept in Pavlovian
methods of conditioning. Personally, I was struck by a strange
parallel between Frederick the Great of Prussia and President

Kennedy, in that both had ruthless fathers who had carefully mapped out the careers of their sons, preparing them for their destined future, one with Europe's best-trained Prussian army and money, and the other with a mass of political power and money.

A very attractive young woman, a patient of mine, told me that once when she was a dinner companion of the "Ambassador," as Joseph P. Kennedy was known, he said to her, "I wanted power. I thought money would give me power and so I made money, only to discover that it was politics, not money, that really gave a man power. So I went into politics." And that indeed created for him a position of power. He used his power to attain the satisfaction of being the United States Ambassador to the Court of St. James. Not being able to go far beyond this prestigious position, he was living out his ambition by molding his son for the highest symbol of power, the presidency of the United States.

Strangely enough, in spite of his charisma, charm and quick wit, President Kennedy did not, psychologically speaking, display the features of the truly hostile-aggressive type of leadership. With all the admirable talents and features he possessed, he impressed me as a rather tragic figure, not only because of the cruel fate that struck him down at the zenith of success, but because of his constant need to prove his masculinity and his courage. Even after he was elected President, his brother Robert, considering himself the intellect, mocked the President-elect as "all muscles, no brain."

President Kennedy did possess a leadership quality. He assembled around him young, brilliant advisers (though some like McNamara and an arrogant theoretician, McGeorge Bundy, proved to have a disastrous effect on the United States policy in Southeast Asia), and most of all he aroused the enthusiasm of the world for his new, youthful, vigorous policies.

Since President Kennedy suffered from a disease of the adrenal glands, his overcompensating display of "guts" becomes clinically more understandable, as does his almost fatalistic insistence on going to Dallas despite strong warnings and on riding in an open car. How much genuine "will to live" did Jack Kennedy have? Or how strong was his unconscious death wish, or his need to defeat death by outstanding acts of courage? Nobody really knows, often not even the person in question. The day President Kennedy was shot, every decent human being's brain stopped functioning for a moment. The day he died, something died in everyone who shared his belief in what he had set out to do. Evil had triumphed for a moment, but it did not extinguish in people the belief in the basic goodness in man, nor the hope for a happier future.

We have just passed through a crisis more complex than that which afflicted the country when Kennedy was assassinated, for then there was a smooth succession of power. Recent events severely tested this nation's faith in the integrity of the leaders at the helm. Disturbed, confused, and shocked, we nevertheless took pride in our workable judicial system. But looking back, we still scold ourselves because of our complacency and blind trust in our elected officials. Today we ask ourselves: How could we have let it happen in the first place?

As we painfully watched our government riding out a storm, we also took heart in seeing the emergence of the strength of the Constitution and the birth of new ideals, for in no other country would a people be allowed to watch openly the testing of the governmental and judicial systems.

The nation survived the death of Kennedy; we have survived Vietnam, though we are still paying the price for the costly and shameful blunders there, and now we have come through Watergate. But coming through is just the beginning. There is a two-fold lesson to be learned. The first was well expressed by Gerald Ford on March 30, 1974, when he said that "never again could the [Republican] party allow their Presidential candidate to bypass the regular party organization and set up a campaign that would make its own rules" and "dictate the terms of a national election" by "a clique of ambitious amateurs." Unfortunately, these amateurs, immoral and scheming, served their leader with such blindness and unprecedented monomania that they confused what they thought best for the man with what was best for the country. The disaster that followed was inevitable because of the basic self-destructiveness of this "clique," men who misused their position of power, hurt the people, gravely injured the office of the Presidency, and, as is the case with emotionally immature people, ended up wounding themselves.

The second lesson we can draw from the tragic chain of events is that we must reverse the general breakdown of morality, put an end to the disrespect for and rapacious mishandling of human rights by men in all areas of government, down to the pompous little official who confuses a means to an end with an end in itself. His low-scale drive for power may be evident in discourtesy and often dehumanizing treatment of the people he is ostensibly serving: he lets them wait, forces them to stand in line, even encourages them to lie. People will plead guilty, in traffic court, for example, even though they are not guilty, because they cannot afford to lose working hours and because they want to get out of a stifling atmosphere. This is corruption, nurtured by a callous bureaucracy. And it is corruption when a man "makes a deal"; turns witness for the prosecution in order to avoid conviction and a prison sentence.

Once the doors to corruption are open, there is no limit as to its destructive consequences. They may run through endless departments and, in principle, lead to a tragic spectacle such as Watergate.

In all fairness, we cannot expect a political leader (and less from a small official) to feel genuine love for his fellow man even if he kisses babies and shakes hands. But we have matured enough to demand finally to be treated as adults: with respect, with openness, and as free individuals. But if we wish the security of personal freedom and privacy, we must learn to choose our political leaders wisely, not just by their membership in a political party, but by objective value-judgment of a political leader, as explained in my chapter on psychopolitics.

A colleague of mine, a psychiatrist, intrigued by my interest in political leaders, called me to inquire how psychology could be used to help political candidates to win elections. "I plan," he said, "to set up an organization to introduce a new branch of political psychology similar to industrial psychology—would you join?"

I said, "Absolutely not." I strongly oppose the forming of an institution which aims to use the experience of a psychiatrist to help candidates' election to political office. This might lead to incompetent and corrupt individuals learning enough psychological gimmicks and salesmanship to be elected. The psychiatrist had betrayed his own thinly veiled drive for power.

We, the people, must be convinced of a future political leader's inner values, of his basic goodness, creativity, his strength of character, his ability to handle his hostility and the aggression around him with dispassion and control and his vigor in making decisions that will bring safety and peace to the nation. To help secure this type of leadership is the aim of my concept of psychopolitics.

IV

Pied Pipers in Politics

I F IT is true that since time immemorial man has fought and died for freedom, considering it the highest human value, what mystical force would cause him to surrender his freedom, sometimes without a fight, to a tyrannical leader?

Is it the strength of a leader's hypnotic persuasion or is it the leader's power to arouse a slumbering need for excitement that is capable of beclouding rational judgment and conscience. What is it in an often paranoiacally—that is, irrationally—stirred-up leader that ignites a latent force in the minds of his followers? Is it simply a conditioned reflex that makes man react automatically to a set of well-established signals?

When I think back to the early thirties (I was living in Germany at the time), or when I see a swastika, my ears still resound with the hoarse shouting and ravings of Hitler, who

59

had mesmerized his audience and forged a mass of people into one body, inducing in them such a state of ecstatic intoxication that they regressed to a primitive, unthinking level of mental functioning. He roused his people to mass hysteria, put them into a state of trance, free from conscience (superego) control, and made them feel the pride of Teutonic knights as they screamed their frenzied battle cry: "Sieg Heil, Sieg Heil!" A friend of mine, a very young physician who started by denouncing Hitler's speeches as stupid, was sucked into the reasonless spell of the frenzied mass. A civilized, friendly patient of mine in Berlin, an architect, left his brown coat with the swastika armband and cap hanging in the foyer when I visited him professionally. He too had fallen for the propaganda of One People, One Reich, One Fuehrer. Where was this man's intelligence?

Twenty years before that, when Wilhelm II shouted from his balcony, "I know of no [political] parties anymore, I know only Germans," and "I lead you towards glorious times," as he declared war in 1914, all that the masses heard were the words "glorious times." They felt a rare closeness toward one another, a rare feeling of excitement as they roared their approval. Nobody put up real opposition. The young university students eagerly volunteered and marched together to get to the front in Flanders, singing as if drunk as they stormed ahead into the deadly fire of the newly employed French machine guns. They were blinded by their sense of omnipotence and carried along by their enthusiasm; they felt stronger than the bullets that destroyed them. We students in high school could not wait to be eligible to join the war. We wrote a composition on how sweet it was to die for the fatherland, the slogan so deeply ingrained for generations in the German people that our response to it was one mass-conditioned reflex.

When, at the outbreak of World War I, Jaurès, the French socialist, warned the people against the insanity of war, he was murdered. The French, too, had been conditioned in their hate against the deadly peril of their arch enemy, *les sales prussiens.*

Nietzsche had soberly warned the world against "a herd of blond beasts of prey, a race of conquerors and masters with military organizations, with the power to organize, unscrupulously placing their fearful paws upon a population perhaps vastly superior in numbers—this herd founded the State." This herd, drunk with a sense of power, intoxicated by the belief that they were a race of supermen, became Hitler's ravaging, murdering, armored hordes and laid waste to half of Europe.

Why do men resort so readily to mass murder when dispassionate and intelligent reasoning could solve most political problems?

If World War II could not have been prevented, it could at least have been delayed had the French reacted to Hitler's march into the Rhineland, and if the leaders of the European Allies had not been so miserably weak, inadequate and shortsighted. Some unfortunate decisions of our own government in its pursuit of cold war policies during the past nearly three decades has given us a gruesome example of paradoxical intent and helped produce violence instead of security, hate instead of peace. We can understand a people's determination to fight off an aggressor, as when the United States retaliated after the Japanese attack on Pearl Harbor, or when Poland and Russia tried desperately to defend themselves against Germany's brutal and unprovoked assault. But when wars of *conquest* are launched and fought, the long-established barriers of civilized behavior are broken down and man's lust to kill is awakened.

In the summer of 1973 I went to Munich and visited a former grade school friend I had not seen in forty years. He told me that for most Germans he knew, the war had been the greatest experience of their lives. Though he himself had resisted joining the Nazi party, as had his father, he had represented the powerful German chemical industry as a lawyer. He did not say it but he seemed to share with his fellow Germans the glories and defeats of the war, both deep emotional experiences. (He had managed to get out of Berlin with one suitcase during the bombardment the night before the Russians stormed the city.) Doubtless the emotional extremes he felt—extremes such as few people experience under ordinary conditions—were heightened by the sharing.

A fifteen-year-old schoolgirl in a village near Munich told me about the driver of the school bus, a man who hardly ever talked. She said he never read a newspaper or a book, or showed interest in anything that was going on in the world, except for driving his bus. One day he said to her very suddenly, "If Hitler were to call me again, I would go to Stalingrad—with joy." This, the decisive defeat of the German Eighth Army was what he chose to return to, rather than some other victorious or less bloody battle. "If that isn't crazy thinking," said the girl, "I don't know what is." This man, like my former school friend, felt that his life was made far more exciting by the drama of war.

Most of the studies of man's urge to kill or to make war look to his primitive heritage, his savage ancestry, for an explanation. And yet few animals kill except for food or survival. What is there about man that is different?

When Cain slew Abel, he became, biblically at least, the first man to kill another. The motive was not survival, or the acquisition of land, which has been given lately as a cause of why men fight and kill each other. The reason given in Cain's case was jealousy. Not jealousy over a woman, either, but over a father's love.

Of more modern vintage, there was the case of a young man serving a term for having murdered one of his two brothers. After a few years, he was released on probation for half a day, so he could go home to see his family. During that brief period, he managed to kill his remaining brother. It is all too easy to whip men up to the passion of murder—the unconscious envy of other men who they feel possess something they do not: land, wealth, a woman, or a mother's love. My mother and father love my brother better than me, and if I can get him out of the way forever, there will be just me left and they'll have to love me best, says the mind of an infant, and sometimes that attitude is never outgrown.

Murder is in the blood of man when he loses control, when his instincts overpower a weak superego or an assertive conscience—when, as the legal term describes it, he becomes "temporarily insane." War has been called "collective insanity." Masses of men kill other masses of men in the same way one man kills another, except for the deployment of highly sophisticated weapons and macabre intellectual strategies aiming at the highest number of body counts and the philosophy that who wins is "right."

If we apply the psychodynamic tests of a person to a nation, could we not question the mental stability of the architects of the two American undeclared wars, the one in Korea, the other in Southeast Asia? Have these wars in the Orient reached their objective, if defeat of Communist aggression or of the Communist philosophy has been the goal? Can we teach people democracy and happiness by the sword? I remember saying to President Gerald Ford that our prestige will go down and the Vietcong, driven by a fanatical belief, will probably end up gaining not only the support of the people (as was the case in China) but also territory. That was in 1967. I am not glad that my prediction came true.

The outcome was in my mind inevitable because of the corrupt, tyrannical, undemocratic rule of the Thieu regime. We fought the Communists presumably to keep Communism from spreading, but failed. But suppose we had stopped Communism in Vietnam, what was to stop it from starting in Africa or South America or wherever people are socioeconomically repressed? Would our political and military crusaders not insist that we send troops there too? How long can we arrogantly play the role of God's police, telling other people how they should live? Especially if we truly believe, as I do, in the democratic principle? Give each peasant two acres of land, I have often said, and there won't be Communism; that is perhaps a naive formula, but it is cheaper than our involvements, and it is bloodless.

There are, of course, aggressors and defenders and in the future we must ask ourselves who are we going to defend— the larger part of the population or a corrupt upper class? Get rid of the deplorable conditions, and there will be no need for the so-called "liberators." In Western Europe, Marxist ideology has not been able to win the upper hand because of the fairer socioeconomic conditions and the greater degree of social justice.

The pied pipers on the one side—the political fanatics with a firm belief in their "superior" Communist ideology—and the pied pipers on the other side, out to "protect" the people from their liberators, are reminiscent of Gustavus Adolphus of Sweden who, by force of arms, brought Protestantism to Northern Germany. He was deeply convinced that Protestantism would bring the people salvation and greater happiness, even at the cost of dying.

Why do people who know they will have to do the fighting and the dying follow leaders who never put their own lives in danger? Why do older men send younger men, their sexual rivals, into battle? The older men may do so because of real conviction, but more often than not it is because of their inner hostility and craving for glory. It is for this that younger men must pay with their lives?

To understand why men follow a leader, we have to understand two principles; one, Pavlov's theory of conditioning, the other, Freud's interpretation of the functioning of the human mind.

Pavlov proved by his experiments with dogs that a new stimulus or signal can set off an old established response, and he showed how a specific response can be developed by a specific signal. He taught his dogs to salivate on signal by blowing a whistle or switching on a light each time the dog was given a piece of meat. Then the signal was given, without the meat, and the dog still salivated. A conditioned reflex had been established in the brain; the stronger the signal, the greater the salivation.

One Pavlov experiment aimed at a study of the effect of morphine. Every afternoon, at a specific time, an assistant in a white coat would give a dog a hypodermic injection of morphine. The dog would react by getting drowsy and vomiting, as many people do, since morphine is eliminated into the stomach. Then the dog would fall asleep. After the fifth time, when the assistant in the white coat appeared, the dog began to vomit and fell asleep even before he received the injection. A white coat and a needle were the signals for a specific response. The dog was conditioned.

The conditioned reflex is an arc or short circuit in the cortex (or outer layer of the brain) between the signals coming into the brain and the reactions. The brain reacts in a specific way to a signal, a word, a symbol, a smell, a sound.

To explain what happens when patients are disturbed and regress to a lower or earlier level of functioning, unable to perform well or to think clearly, I often use the following example:

Pretend you are at a railroad station out in the country. You are waiting for a train and staring at the rails. You know from the shininess of the rails that trains run along them. There are parallel rails but they are rusty, no longer in use. A switch directs the trains along the shiny rails, but occasionally it sends a train along the old rails.

When we outgrow our first conditioning, a switch directs us to act maturely and use the new rails. But if under enormous stress there is an acute regression, the switch is overloaded and the train of our thought or action returns to the original rusty rail until we recover in ten minutes or the next day, or perhaps even in a month—until we take hold of ourselves, snap out of things, as we say.

The old rusty rails, the first conditioning, is the sum of our very early experiences, long forgotten, that form the unconscious.* A presidential order, a picture of the White House, a flag, enemy, war—all these symbols are signals causing specific reactions. The unconscious may drive us to act out of motives of hate even though we want to act out of motives of love. For in the unconscious, two opposite emotions, such as love and hate, can exist side by side. We can love and hate at the same time, though we may be conscious only of the feeling of love, as Bleuler, the Swiss psychiatrist explained when he first used the term "ambivalence." The physician often hears a patient stress his will to live even as he commits act after act of self-destruction or slow suicide. We can say we want peace and yet unconsciously wish and prepare for all-out war.

It is an involuntary brain reaction—a conditioned reflex—that prompts the unreasoned feelings of men following their leaders into self-destruction as the bands play and the flags wave. Basic training sets new signals to which the brain reacts; hate is cultivated; the repetition of a signal to storm, to shoot, to run a bayonet into the belly of a sandbag is practiced over and over until the signal sticks and the brain blocks out all other feelings except perhaps fear. Men are induced into an irrational state by a long process of conditioning until their responses become automatic and they reach a level of superexcitation.

*Psychoanalytically, the unconscious pattern is, in the words of Lawrence Kubie, a mirror reflection of the conditioned reflex.

The psychological mechanism of ambivalence was vividly demonstrated by the four-year-old son of a patient of mine. Angered by his mother's refusal to give in to a demand he made, he announced, "Mother, I am going upstairs, and take father's gun, and load it, and shoot you dead." The mother's reply was rather remarkable. All she said was, "I'm sorry to learn that's the way you feel about me," and walked away. Her remark perplexed the boy and after a while broke his anger. Overcome by fear of his mother's rejection, and in a state of confusion, he ran to her, clung to her and exclaimed, "I love you! I love you!" The attitude of the mother struck me as wiser than that of many statesmen, who all too often respond to a smaller, less powerful country's expression of hostility with equal hostility, rather than trying to solve the conflict amiably.

Later in the book I will go into detail on other psychological mechanisms, including rationalization, projection, displacement, that explain how a man can turn his childhood hate on innocent targets. For now, though, we can state that on a very primitive level, as in an individual's psychotic acting out, the act of killing can provide an enormous relief from unbearable inner tension or repressed violence.

At a scientific meeting, one researcher presented five cases of murderers he had examined for the state of New York. One woman, I remember, a seemingly kind, docile housewife, had received a phone call from her mother-in-law, who made another of her frequent demands for money. The younger woman calmly took a gun she kept hidden, got into a taxi, telling herself that money would no longer matter, drove to her mother-in-law's house and shot the older woman. Then the daughter-in-law telephoned the police, reported the murder and sat down to wait for her arrest. During her psychiatric examination, the woman told of the great inner calm and satisfaction she felt at the deed of murder, an experience she obviously enjoyed so intensely that nothing else—not even the death penalty—mattered to her.

War, a savage yet legitimate mass murder, sanctions not only release of violence, but heretofore unacceptable sexual promiscuity and, in a subtle way, homosexuality, since it throws men together in intimate living conditions and deprives them of women. As David Rabe, playwright and Army veteran of Vietnam, commented on the time he spent after his discharge haunting go-go bars in Philadelphia to do research for his play *Boom-Boom Room*, "It was the only place I felt comfortable after the army. There was the same sense of primate violence and the same sense of indiscriminate behavior being acceptable that there is in the Army." One of the young American fliers who was a prisoner of war said to novelist and short-story writer Grace Paley in an interview, "Gosh, Grace, I have to admit it, I really loved bombing." The son of Mussolini once remarked how much fun it was watching people run for shelter from his machine guns; there was an excitement in war he had never experienced in everyday living.

Man is conditioned psychologically from his earliest memories to obey a father or mother as the all-powerful symbol of authority. For a child, his mother and father *are* society. When the child becomes a man, if he has not fully matured and is not able to do his own thinking, he will blindly follow the powerful image of the father of his country. Because of his ambivalence, he has not only feelings of love but also, and often more strongly, unresolved deeply repressed feelings of hatred for his father and mother and sisters and brothers. Under the banner of war these may be let loose. Danger produces enormous excitement which, to some people, the automobile racer for instance, makes life meaningful for the moment. It is a triumph over death until death finally triumphs over the man who cannot live without excitement.

But there is another kind of excitement, the quiet excitement that comes out of creating and building. It is harder for man to grasp and requires enormous perseverance and self-discipline to achieve, but it is the only kind of excitement that is consistent, satisfying and not destructive.

The immature man, who all too seldom questions the reason for his existence, has no exciting goals, is not high up on the socioeconomic ladder and is apt to lead a drab life. Usually he will repress conscious awareness of his regressive drive and be unable to mobilize and channel his aggression into creative, meaningful and enjoyable pursuits. He will live with little self-esteem, near the border of depression and more often than not feeling bored, lifeless and dehumanized, living, as Thoreau said, "a life of quiet desperation." Psychoanalytically, we know that all too many men have not been able to resolve their feelings of hostility and have buried them. The immature man easily loses what little sense of freedom he may have achieved, as well as whatever self-respect and confidence he has had a chance to develop. He is more prone to give in to his desire to be the child he once was than to become a mature, secure man. There is safety and some sense of security in being taken care of by a powerful father, a strict father, perhaps even a harsh, brutal father, but nevertheless one who will take care of a child if the child will merely submit to him. There is a need to be cuddled in everyone, and symbolically as man surrenders to a leader, he regresses into the role of the child. And that is how man loses his freedom. His lost sense of masculinity is restored through the party emblem, the army he has joined, the symbol of an almighty power of which he is now part and from which he believes he draws strength.

War, then, is the price mankind pays for its emotional immaturity. Though there have been wars fought in the name of independence, many wars aim to enslave, not to free people. And those wars will continue until man accepts the disturbing fact that he is often driven into them by the unconscious part of his mind, the part that knows only the emotions of greed, envy, lust, jealousy, murderous desire. Yet a friend of mine says (and I hope he is not right), "Man seems to accept that an unconscious exists at about the same rate he oozed his way out of the slime."

As long as man is driven in large part by unconscious emotions, he will not be free and responsible, for man can fight only an emotion of which he is aware. To be free emotionally means to accept responsibility for the self and to assume responsibility as a political creature as well. An immature, childlike creature demands that society assume responsibility for him, even at the price of his sanctioning a dictatorship, for he feels he as an individual is too fearful, too insignificant and too confused to assume responsibility for society.

The more advanced civilization has become, the more detailed in structure and the more sophisticated in human interaction, the more it tends to make man feel he has lost his independence and his ability to fend for himself. The animal cunning he once needed to survive in the caves and jungles and deserts, if not given a constructive outlet, may slide into a destructive one.

During a psychotherapeutic session with me, a young man from Tennessee said suddenly, with a mixture of sadness and repressed anger, "I was never taught to fight. Everything was done for me. I had everything I needed. But 'everything' meant only in a material way." His father, a Harvard graduate, and his mother, a Radcliffe graduate, were both independently wealthy and brought up their children in a life style that discouraged resourcefulness and ingenuity. Though it was not so much the life style that proved destructive to the son, but the passive personality of the father and the aloofness between two emotionally opaque parents.

Speaking of his mother and father he said, "They had little use for my sister or me. We were left to maids and governesses." He added bitterly, "I hate my parents for what they did to me. I want to be different. I want to learn to trust. I don't want to live with my depression."

He wrote a long letter to his father in which he demanded that his father pay for his psychotherapy. That was the least his father could do, he reasoned, since everything that had gone wrong with him was his father's "fault." This young man could not see himself as capable of being a grown-up, a twenty-four-year-old university graduate, who was economically "emancipated," in that he had been given a substantial trust fund. He was even bitter about this money claiming it had been given to him by his father for tax purposes, not out of love. He clung stingily to his money as the only "security" he knew, his security blanket, so to speak.

Slowly, he learned in treatment what true independence was, how to lead his own life and make his own decisions, and to lose his bitterness at parents who had done their best to raise their children happily. He had to lose the sense of dependency on his parents. There can be a hostile dependency as well as a too-loving one, because of the existence of ambivalent feelings. He had been kept over the years from expressing his hostility.

We depend today on thousands of other people in order to live in comfort. We, in these United States, give up a certain amount ot individual freedom to live in groups, and we find security in such groups, sometimes security in the leadership of another man.

To use what Kant called the critique of pure reason, we have to say that absolute freedom, in a social sense, is an illusion. We all depend on each other too much for that. We have to observe the laws, pay taxes, hold to speed limits and rules of courtesy (we are not allowed to kill someone who insults us verbally), and obey government orders on emergency measures or rules of rationing, if necessary. Just as a man and woman relinquish some of their individual freedom when they marry, in modern society, in order to gain comfort and security, we have to give up part of our independence, give up a certain amount of joy, in order to get along with others.

In his play *Small Craft Warnings,* Tennessee Williams presents the philosophy that half a life is better than none. I do not share this philosophy. I think life can be full and gratifying if man resists living like an automaton and can establish a workable balance between his forces of aggression and inhibition. This requires assuming responsibility for himself and releasing his energies toward goals and activities that are meaningful and enjoyable. But, of course, a person must be capable of giving of himself.

Civilized man has never been truly free within himself, nor has he gained emotional freedom for the most part. Political systems and religious doctrines have enslaved his soul—if I may borrow that term. Yet there can be freedom of expression, at least in the Western world. There can be freedom intellectually. Artistically. Scientifically. But emotionally, man has remained, for the most part, a child. Society has given him security in the daily routine of life. Much blood has been shed over the centuries in many parts of the world so that the average man is no longer a serf. In the Western world, at least, he is more free politically; he can seek the job he wants, the house he covets. A man and woman can marry, unfettered by economic, religious or racial factors or class or caste.

But such freedom may make a man feel more isolated and alone than ever. In early days, as serf and slave, man took it for granted another man would be responsible for him almost totally. Today he is expected to assume full responsibility for himself—economic, social, sexual, mental and emotional— and this may be beyond the capacity of some people. There is the great lure of giving up responsibility, of not having to worry about a thing; that is why some people join the armed forces, become seamen in the merchant marine.

For many men, the sense of isolation, or alienation, and the feeling of being overwhelmed by responsibilities become a burden so intolerable that they prefer to escape into new dependencies and submissions. And this can lead to the desire for a father figure to take over and guide their destiny. Many a man is willing to give up some of his independence for this security, and that has led to an ever-bigger government. In America the government controls our life by guidelines and at the same time keeps a close check on us. We are all numbered, computerized, have secret symbols and if we, the citizens who want freedom and independence, do not stay on guard and reverse the trend, we might well end up by slowly allowing a police state to develop.

Facing a harsher and tougher economic squeeze with an increased world population, we can almost estimate when the world's resources will become inadequate. My professor in obstetrics, an aristocratic man who delivered the kaiser's children, speaking about abortion said, "It's a difficult issue, gentlemen. The King wants his soldiers and the church its souls; that is why the state will consider abortion illegal." Today's world calls for planned parenthood, hopefully on a worldwide scale, possibly through the UN, or we will be negligent and leave the problem to the next generation or the one after, and man will have no recourse perhaps but to cut down the population by war.

We have been living under threat of atomic war, and that has added to the feeling of individual helplessness and pervasive fear. While there have always been wars, the possibilities of destruction have now increased to the point where all life on earth could be destroyed. Though the threat of such war is seemingly less acute, it still hangs like a Damoclean sword.

The possibility of "mass insanity" through nuclear war differs from the "temporary insanity" of one individual who kills another, in that when one person, after his bloodletting, recovers, he regains sanity and goes about his daily life, while a nation that lapses into "temporary insanity" may be destroyed or if it regains sanity may find nothing but ruins, or may feel committed to war without being able to return to peace.

Therefore, if the human race wants to survive, it must believe that its destiny is to move towards a higher development. "Temporary insanity" for nations must never occur and the question is how to guard against it.

Wars can be prevented only if leaders are emotionally healthy, stable human beings, if they are carefully chosen, if they act as guardians chosen to execute the will of the people, and if they do not continue to usurp more power than is inherent in their office.

To treat citizens as if they were children too young and inexperienced to know what the stamp "Top Secret" conceals is arrogant usurpation of power. Our representatives in the House and Senate have not always acted responsibly and courageously enough. They could be more assertive in representing the interest of all the people, which is peace, and not supporting the "little wars" that hostile-aggressive agencies like the CIA and the military have designed for us.

War must be stripped of the big lie: that it is masculine and glorious and necessary to the security of a nation. If leaders cannot negotiate peace, they should be replaced by others who can talk to the "enemy" not merely from a position of strength, but from a position of humanity. Let us be strong; let us not be part of the herd that follows the signal to slaughter. Let us also realize that war is not only savage and unworthy of the creative potential of man, but a sick act concocted by sick minds.

V

Psychopolitics

THE LEADER, the father figure, the ruler, the king, the dictator, the fuehrer or the President—whatever his title and whatever the political entity he represents—cannot be understood psychologically as an entity in himself. He does not float in midair. Even a meteor is related to time and space and the dynamics that determine its fiery course.

Similarly, the personality of a leader, his own inner mental and emotional functioning, depends on and is greatly influenced by at least two basic factors. The first is the composition of the group, the fabric of its culture, the socioeconomic conditions, the mentality of the people, and the existing political structure or power struggle around him. The second is the specific time in history, the sequence of past national events, and the nation's relationship to the structure and life of other political units.

The first factor has some similarity to a German school of thought called gestalt psychology. This school emphasizes and interprets the wholeness of a being rather than analyzing the higher nervous activity. What matters is the total perceptual configuration of separate units or experiences and their inter-relationships. A whole is not merely the sum of all its parts, nor do the sum of all its parts make up the whole.

The Germans use the term Zeitgeist to describe the second factor, the spirit of the time. Napoleon would not have had a chance as a leader had he been born a century earlier. Nor could the American Revolution have occurred had not a fresh wind of freedom begun to blow from Europe, accompanied by a growing refusal among men to tolerate the abuses of tyrannical rulers. There was Rousseau's impact on French and English thinking—his theory that man by nature is good, but corrupted by civilization. And the increasing belief that some punitive laws had been instituted to consolidate the power of the oppressors over the oppressed. The ideologies of Im-manuel Kant, the greatest of German philosophers, spread and inspired others to think in terms of the rights of man. His proposal two centuries ago for a pacific-minded federation of nations and a plan for "Eternal Peace" among men has be-come the dream of the brotherhood of man, one that inspired Beethoven's Ninth Symphony, "Be embraced thee nations," (using a poem by Schiller) and led, after the horrors of World War II, to the founding of the United Nations, succeeding the ill-fated League of Nations after World War I. Thoughts of freedom from oppressors stirred the minds of thinkers in Western Europe, England and America, inspiring the draft of the Declaration of Independence.

Movements, be they cultural or political, run in cycles, like the Renaissance, or, before that, the Golden Age, the first of four mythical periods when peace, happiness and innocence reigned.

Germany—the disturber of the peace and instigator of the

two world wars—a troubled nation nearly in the heart of Europe, struggled for about one century, from 1848 to 1933, trying to mature politically. Having gone through the period of the Second Reich, after Bismarck's unification of the four kingdoms and the nearly two dozen principalities, the King of Prussia, Wilhelm I, was crowned "German kaiser" (not kaiser of Germany) at Versailles in 1871. The struggle ended after Germany's defeat in 1918, when it became a shaky republic. It stayed that way from 1918 to January 31, 1933, with a population that, in its political immaturity, deluded itself by never accepting the reality of its military defeat, an attitude of political discontent that prepared the fertile soil for the Third Reich of Adolf Hitler in 1933, a *government he proclaimed would last for a thousand years.*

The aftermath of World War II tumbled monarchies and kingdoms and ignited revolutionary movements that took a zigzag course in people's search for freedom and democratic reforms, usually ending with dictatorial imperialism of the left or the right. Individuals emerged as leaders, or leaders fermented mass movements. Mass discontent is endemic; rebellion can spread like a contagion, arousing the minds of fiery youth and of hungry and desperate men. Aggressive feelings cry out for action. Mass movements snowball. The prospect of more power produces pleasurable or uplifting sensations. This attracts the more violent combative or radical left- or right-wing movements who want change by force. They are opposed by two more moderate groups, one that advocates progression and the other that resists change. The latter group is held back by rigidity, unrealistic fear of the new, by complacency and the wish to turn the clock back; it resists progress, and calls its stand conservatism. The moderate, the democratic, the middle-of-the-road group desires progress and opposes violence and injustice but wants change to occur at an evolutionary, not a revolutionary pace.

Thus political regimes or philosophies are born into existing systems. They grow, mature and die, as do the people in their individual or collective existence. There are cycles of brilliant creativity and cycles of violent unrest. There are times of fierce progress and times of stunted growth or regression. There are manic periods and depressive periods. *"Panta rei,"* the Greeks said: Everything flows.

Even epidemics seem to run in cycles, perhaps because of a global proneness to mass excitement and mass depression. The influenza epidemic of 1918, after World War I, affected 500 million people, 15 million of whom died. The victims were mostly young people who should have possessed a higher degree of resistance to an infectious disease called the Spanish influenza. Why were these young people the victims? Was it mass guilt that followed the manic lust for shedding blood? Was it a wretched realization of how low civilized man had sunk? Society had returned to a sober and shameful reality. It was suffering not only because it had to absorb men who, at its behest, had become murderers, but also because it had to learn how to cope with an economic depression. Now both the victors and the vanquished were counting their dead, fencing off futility and facing their great guilt at the unrestrained destruction and shameful acts of inhumanity they had unleashed.

Great destructive episodes have reactive phases of depression, apathy, widespread discontent. Our own generation has undergone an agonizing example of human failure. The ending of the American armed intervention in Southeast Asia has not brought a sense of joy or any real satisfaction in having concluded a war of "survival." Whose survival? Because of the doubt that survival was a real issue, the war came under severe criticism, especially by the young people who were asked to give their lives. They became polarized, rebellious, angry and delinquent, and they still are confused and searching for new, more truthful and more meaningful values.

There is a general feeling of misery, rage, anger, and frustration. If the concept of law and order has been mocked by men in power, how can those who are powerless accept a double standard of values and live with any sense of security and trust? We have seen a vicious circle: the people blindly following the leaders of their choice, and the leaders trying to shape the people in their own corrupt image.

There is a live interaction, not always on clear conscious levels, between an age in the history of people and their political life style. A leader is not only the product of an era but also a man who knows how to take advantage of existing needs or an existing mass psychology. Hate, as stated earlier, is the first uniting bond of a group, and a skilled leader knows only too well how to take advantage of inner hostility to incite people, to make them angry at failures of the past regime so that he can then promise radical changes and help and inspire a new mass movement.

A political leader who aspires to the position of the presidency invites the question of what motivates his particular drive for power. Is it just a need for raw power or does he really feel he has a mission to fulfill? What historical leader is *his* ideal? Did he dream of wanting to be a Genghis Khan, a Caesar or an Abraham Lincoln? Is he possibly being put up by a political machine that intends to use him for its own gains, or is it the military, the big business or money interests who are backing him in order to use him for their own purposes?

We, the people who are about to elect a political leader, rarely know the man in depth. Often enough he himself may not know who he really is. I do not share the old slogan that all power corrupts and absolute power corrupts absolutely; I rather believe the corruptive element has existed all along in the depth of an individual and becomes more evident as he gains more power.

Actually, it is in the trusting sanctuary of the "magic room," as one patient called the office in which his psychoanalytic unfolding has taken place, that the carefully guarded deeper feelings of a person's love or hate or greed, or ambition, hostility and frustration emerge and then become a conscious reality.

I had a patient who was unaware of the depth of his own ambition. Thom was a thirty-four-year-old lawyer who was trying to decide whether to enter politics. He came to me for therapy because of two problems: one was his personal life; the other was a crisis in his career. As to the first, he wondered why, at age thirty-four, he had not gotten married and more so, why he could not maintain a satisfactory relationship with a girl for any length of time.

Thom had little difficulty meeting women. He could be charming and attentive and persistent in his pursuit when he felt "turned on" by a woman. "I am eager to get her into bed and if I succeed sex is generally great. But then comes a letdown. I lose interest. Sex is bad, even if I like the girl."

Discussing his psychosexual dynamic interplay with women, he realized that he was out more for a quick conquest than for a serious relationship. As soon as a woman gave any evidence of caring or being in love with him, he found excuses to terminate the relationship. Another problem with women was his insecurity as a man: if a woman liked him, she could not be worth much since he himself lacked self-worth.

Thom's other problem was his career. He was with a good law firm, but was unhappy there and did not know what the difficulty was. He thought the two senior partners were picking on him—partly because he just could not write up a case on time; his casework was always late. He concluded that he was lazy. By lazy, he meant it bored him to study a case as intensely as he should. "I always got by by my wits. I don't kid myself. I know I lack real knowledge of the law."

Thom's arrogant facade broke when he admitted that he had been given a last severe warning by the head of the law firm that he would be fired if he continued to arrive late every morning. "But I just cannot make it on time," said Thom, "no matter how hard I try." Somehow, he would turn the alarm off in his sleep.

Thom's office behavior was often undiplomatic. One day he told me how dismayed the senior partners had been the day before when he interrupted a discussion of theirs. Thom was well over 6 feet tall; they were both short. It must have been a grotesque scene when Thom literally pushed his big head between those of his superiors and towered over them like a curious, arrogant giraffe. When they indicated their displeasure, he replied not grasping the reality, "By listening to you talk, I just thought I would learn what goes on."

Thom was fired, but he reconciled himself by deciding to avoid any further such humiliation by opening his own office.

Luck was with him. He handled a few cases successfully and after a few months could cover his expenses. He debated a partnership with another lawyer, but resisted because he feared, and rightly so, that he would depend on the other man who was conscientious, meticulous and knew law.

Thom learned that his confidence in himself as a lawyer was as insecure as that towards women. He avoided total commitment. He would make just enough of an effort to fulfill his needs and to secure a comfortable life style. He became very depressed.

One day, he mentioned that a judgeship would come up at the next November election. He had a deep interest in politics. "If I run for that position, I'll be the youngest judge on the bench and always have that title, even if I go back to the practice of law." His home was in Westchester, in a heavily Republican district. "What is against me," he said, "is Watergate, and though I am Catholic I cannot as a Republican count on Catholic support."

I jolted him by a question: "What is it you want to get out of life?" And his answer came as quickly as a pistol shot:

"Power—I want power." At that time, he was not thinking in terms of happiness or of love with a woman, or of having a family. Outwardly, he was lazy and uncommitted—to women, law, or career—but deep within him power was his goal and a political career was the way of attaining it. It would be up to the voters to decide whether his ability matched his charming veneer. Fortunately for them, Thom is now determined to gain a true understanding of himself and to become a mature man.

The process of self-examination, desirable or exciting as it may be, is unlikely to be sought out by most political leaders, at least not for some time to come. We, as people, must therefore use every other means at our disposal to sharpen our understanding and ability to appraise the deeper motivation of a politician through his actions, his ideas, the projection of his personality, his candid or deliberate responses in a TV debate, his casual remarks or even the inflection in his manner of speech. Another thing we must learn is to examine not just the leader but ourselves, the psychodynamic interplay between a leader and his followers. What is it that attracts us in a leader or repulses us, and why? What causes our feelings of like or dislike for a man and what are the inner reasons for that? Some of this we do already know to some degree, but it is necessary to develop more protective measures until one day, hopefully, we may adopt methods, as we shall point out later, by which we can secure mentally healthy and morally strong leaders who possess the clarity of judgment to put the interests of a nation above their own power drive.

A number of people, intrigued by Richard Nixon's complex and contradictory personality, have written prolifically about him, but few really know the man the way he is when he is alone with another man he fully trusts and respects. Most writers, including psychiatrists who have written books about

President Nixon, analyze his behavior and thereby diagnose symptoms on which they build their pro or con, mostly con, evaluation of his personality.

Except for my *Look Magazine,* 1969 article, "The Mental Health of Leaders," which Professor Bruce Mazlish calls his best source of information, I have over the years resisted all attempts, direct or indirect, to obtain from me any professional information or impressions about Mr. Nixon. Throughout the rocky years we have maintained a friendly personal relationship. Because of this I can say that there are indeed few who know the man who is Richard Nixon. And there may be only a few, with the exception of his family and close friends, who have a chance to know him when he allows himself to lower his guard, displaying an image different from that so often seen on television. We all communicate on different levels with different people around us, and there are different degrees of objectivity, depending on the perceptive power of the observer. A close adviser may know intimately one side of his boss and not another side; a psychoanalyst may see things the patient's own family may not know. But, as I have stated many times, I have not analyzed President Nixon, I have only made my own observations. Some I must keep confidential and others can be shared because other people have reported on some of his attitudes. Whatever conflict may exist in the depths of him—and who is free of this?—he is a man who has a keenly aware intellect, is an intense listener, and asks for clarification of points of view.

The first time I visited Mr. Nixon, a couple of years after he had first come to my office for checkups in 1951, he was still Vice-President and we lunched in his office. At first we talked informally. He mentioned some bill that was pending, spoke of "The General," as he called President Eisenhower, hoping I could see him professionally, and then referring to the foundations of the Capitol building explained that the part of the basement facing the Washington Monument had originally been meant to serve as a fortress with gun emplacements. He pointed out some of the items in his office that were of cultural value, telling me what they represented and where they came from. Then world political events were brought up. I expressed, then already, my opinion of the futility of the cold war and my feeling that our encirclement of the Soviet Union would in the end make her stronger. I offered my appraisal of John Foster Dulles, then Secretary of State, as a basically angry and mentally disturbed man who kept the world in a state of jitters with his brinkmanship and who, if he could have his way, would seek military confrontation with the Russians. I also talked of the mental instability of Senator Joseph McCarthy in his early days and what harm I thought he was doing the country. This astounded Mr. Nixon, though he said he did not agree with the senator from Wisconsin. When I mentioned a political personality, he would ask how I had arrived at my interpretations, and I would explain. He never asked, and I never volunteered, how I would "diagnose" him. The difficult concept of peace was, generally, the main topic on which I expressed my beliefs, one I had written about as long ago as 1951 in the last chapter of *The Will to Live,* the chapter titled "It's Easier to Hate, But Healthier to Love."

Over the years whenever Mr. Nixon and I met, he was always pleasant, mentally alert and interested, and he always had a little anecdote to tell, or an interesting or humorous observation. Many people may be surprised at this, for they see only the facade President Nixon presents to a hostile world when he may feel self-conscious and on guard. These are general observations, not psychoanalytic ones, and may therefore be stated without infringing on the code of ethics.

There is nothing further I feel I can say at this time except that President Nixon, contrary to the many predictions by the press, including Gloria Steinem when she came to interview me, did not have a "nervous breakdown" in spite of the enormous pressure to which he was exposed. A question that has been asked a great deal is why a man who possessed enough vision and courage to end by one bold act nearly three decades of a miserable cold war could not have prevented the unhappy events and his own tragic role in the drama known as Watergate. But as I have stated, I am in no position to give an answer to that question. Still, I wish to express my hope that at some point in history all can be told, including my own anxiety as I watched helplessly from a distance the disastrous course that led to Nixon's resignation. And I hope that at some point in history there will be made available to all the people, a study of the personality of all our political leaders. Times demand that the public know more about the inner man, not only his voting record, his financial statement and the like. Finally, the evaluation of political leaders ought to include a study of why we, as voters, are attracted to one type of leader or to another, to examine what is right and what is wrong with *our* set of values.

The question of an individual's psychic survival often depends on how he deals with his inner (intrinsic) or outer (extrinsic) values. To the inexperienced, a facade can be deceptive. Forrestal's facade of charm and capability did not hide his underlying disturbances effectively or for long; his self-destruction confirmed the existence of a mental illness.

When I was a very young doctor, a young, very beautiful and brilliant woman, a leading figure in the new growing psychoanalytic movement in Berlin, came to my office a few times for treatment. Then one day suddenly she called on me for help, and told me she was confined to her home. By the time I arrived, she had committed hara-kiri. This was a terrifying eye-opener to me as to the mysterious depths of the human psyche. This young woman's schizophrenic state had been well concealed from the eyes of the inexperienced; her tragic death left on me an unforgettable imprint of the darker side in all humanity.

Voluminous reports are made and kept on the individual case history of every patient sent to a hospital, though his decisions in life be of no importance to anyone except himself. But when it comes to a political leader, whose decisions may have a worldwide effect, usually little is known or revealed about his background, physical or mental. Some people may argue the point of privacy. But the life of a nation's leader is not a private matter since it may involve the happy future or the slaughter of millions of men. If, in the words of Truman, a politician cannot take the heat, let him stay out of the kitchen.

Let us assume we had a chance to know what fantasies of grandeur or revenge or violence may have governed the life of a man and driven him to seek power as a leader. Would we, the people, support a man we know is ready to lead us into an accelerated arms race, an economic depression or even war? We can, for instance, only guess now at the hidden, fathomless hates of a man such as Hitler, hates that any capable physician living in Germany could have predicted at the first display of paranoiac rage. With nothing to stop him, the blood baths that followed were inevitable. But even if a doctor could have predicted insanity, would he not have been lynched by a nation in a state of mass hysteria?

A democracy has constitutional guarantees, but has a Congress or a House of Deputies really stopped a leader on the march? Has our Congress stopped our involvement in Southeast Asia? When men preached sanity, they were called traitors and when both sides finally talked, there was death and destruction and the realization that a military victory was unattainable. Could not what was accomplished in Paris in the way of ceasefire in 1971 have been accomplished in 1954 after the partition of Vietnam—if there had been leaders of greater strength, more wisdom and humanity?

Harold D. Lasswell, more than forty years ago in his classic book, *Psychopathology and Politics,* pointed out the close relationship between a man's political thinking and his psychological makeup. Lasswell also stressed that what we call "logical thinking" is not enough to explain a man's acts, that "our faith in logic (even where logic is adroitly used) incapacitates rather than fits the mind to function as a fit instrument of reality adjustment." And, most important, he said, "The supposition that emotional aberrations are to be conquered by heroic doses of logical thinking is a mistake."

The so-called "logical" mind, the mind that coerces others to act because "it is in your best interests," or "it is in the best interests of the nation," may actually be dominated by fantasy, illogic, hidden desires of revenge or paranoiac persecutions. A child may struggle against impulses to kill or damage a mother who strikes him, but whom he also loves and fears to hurt back. He resolves the conflict in part by projecting his hate and desire for revenge upon a fantasied ogre. As an adult, if he is still full of unresolved hate and desire for revenge, the fantasied ogre may become another person, a racial group, another nation.

In my book *Love and Hate in Human Nature* (1955) I quoted the words of a four-year-old boy singing happily while being given his bath. Here are some of the lines his mother wrote down:

He will do nothing at all. He will sit there in the noonday sun.
And when they speak to him, he will not answer them.
He will stick them with spears and put them in the garbage.

"But let us imagine him," I wrote, "thirty or forty years later, a brilliant, forceful adult [who has not worked out his love-hate conflict]. Under the disguise of social betterment or patriotism or scientific or religious zeal [he might] fulfill his destructive desires. The results will be another Robespierre . . . [or as history has presented] a fascinating array of . . . sadists parading as saints or patriots or statesmen."

As early as infancy we learn to give up, or at least curtail, many of our primitive drives and forms of gratification in order to be loved by our parents.

I had an acute example of the love-hate between parents and child with one of the first patients I treated after I had changed my practice from internal medicine to psychotherapy. It was a case nobody wanted—by which I mean that several psychiatrists stated that the patient could not be treated in an office, but required immediate institutionalization. She was a twenty-year-old Columbia University student whose acute break with reality manifested itself while she was searching for warmth one January. She had boarded a train for Florida. The conductor watched the girl—who looked more like sixteen than twenty—in a motionless position, her head buried in her arms, and took her to his home, from which he notified the Children's Aid Society. Her frantic parents flew to Florida to fetch their daughter.

The parents had gotten my name from the wife of a cardiologist in New York City. When they called me, disturbed and intensely anxious, they did not tell me that they had already seen several psychiatrists about her. I asked to see the girl and the father brought her.

I first talked to the girl alone. There was no conversation, for she was holding her head in both hands, her eyes closed, replying to none of my questions. I kept on talking while I tried to figure out what to do with this catatonic girl. To send her to a mental hospital? I thought of the scar this would leave in her mind forever. I continued to talk, asking for nothing more than a nod or a simple yes.

Finally there was a quick glance. She looked at me, then closed her eyes again, but in that second when our eyes met, there was something, perhaps not communication, but an awareness that she understood. Not knowing the problems I would encounter, I decided right then that I would take on the girl as a patient.

I asked her to go to the waiting room and then took her father into my office. As soon as I closed the office door behind us, he jumped up to open it. "Please close the door," I said firmly.

"No," he said, "I have to watch her; she might run away."

"She won't run away," I said. "If you don't close the door, you may just as well leave and take your daughter with you." The man had no choice. "I will see your daughter," I went on to say, "under one condition. She must not live with you. You must get her an apartment in New York nearby."

He was startled. "Alone, in New York? She is helpless, she needs attention."

"I know she does, but that is my condition."

"She could harm herself, she could run away again," the man protested.

"There is a risk in everything we do. Think about it and let me know."

"No," the man said. "I'll do what you say." We made another appointment.

I consulted with Dr. Lothar Kalinowsky, a psychiatrist friend of mine, who had brought electroshock therapy from Italy to the United States. He was the authority on this new treatment of depression. He was pessimistic. "I can give it a try, it probably won't work—"

Mary had three electroshock treatments, which had little effect. Moreover, she did not want to go back. We had no effective medication against this type of depression at that time.

Mary began to talk. "Why did you leave home with no luggage?" I asked.

"I couldn't stand it at home—I wanted to be where it's warm."

No wonder, considering the cold, uninvolved personality of her father. She constantly referred to his lack of affection for her.

Mary moved into a furnished apartment two blocks away from my office. She was both glad and frightened. It was the first apartment she had ever had. She finally agreed to go for one more shock treatment.

Both parents tried to call every day to get information. I

tried to stop them. "Your daughter will stop coming if she knows I talk with you." Then I added, "You have had her for twenty years. Now let me have her for a while; just have a little trust."

Two weeks after her first visit, Mary came in with a smile. "I feel wonderful, confident—I could play the piano."

The next day Mary felt guilty for having felt happy for a day. The weekends and the days she did not see me—I saw her three times a week—were difficult. She knew her symptoms of feeling isolated, restless and very sleepy. Sometimes she would regress into sessions of silence. All in all it was rough going, and I spent many anxious weekends, for the possibility of suicide still existed.

After a few months I had a battery of psychological testings done on her. In one card (of the TAT-thematic apperception test) that commonly depicts the psychotherapeutic situation she wrote, "Oh, this is horrible. This is like the mad scientist and the young girl is dead and he's doing all sorts of experiments. He's going to make her—talk."

Mary's main problem was her inability to communicate with her father and therefore with men in general. He was cold, void of feelings and overly committed to his business. He was a Wall Street man and even went to the office on Saturdays. Her distrust of him became evident when she said, "I bet he goes in just to change the books."

One day, after her twenty-first birthday, she came in, angry, eyes flashing. "My father," she said. "It was my birthday and what do you think he did? Did he kiss me or congratulate me? No. 'Mary,' he said, 'It's your birthday. I bought you half an oil well.' "

Three years later Mary got married, to a lawyer, a politician. "What the stock market is to my father, politics is to my new husband—" It was a most elaborate wedding. Here is how she answered my congratulation:

"I hardly know how to thank you for your beautiful letter,

except to say that I treasure it. I have never forgotten your faith in me, your kindness and all your great help at a time when my life was black and my need was very great. You gave me courage then—"

We must constantly strive to strike a balance between our love and hate conflicts. This requires that we develop the part of the self that carries out the demands of society as opposed to our own inner pressures, wishes and selfish needs. The demands of society are handed to us through our mother and father or parent substitutes, who force or coerce or bribe or wheedle us into accepting these demands. In that way we develop our own particular "conscience." As we grow up we learn the control of excretory functions and the control of murderous impulses. We learn "sublimation" of our powerful sexual and aggressive drives and the fusion of opposing ambivalent feelings.

The gradual acceptance over the years of the requirements laid down by society upon the personality does not always proceed easily. Nor does overt acceptance do away with our deep seated primitive psychological demands and our early reactions to them. The imprints remain in the form of a powerful "forgotten" first conditioning. The way we resolve early conflicts forms the basic pattern of our later behavior, and though we think that we have resolved many early conflicts, we may learn perhaps later in life that all we did was to cover them up, deny them; suddenly, triggered by some event, we may find ourselves plagued by buried feelings. Much of the energy in people is spent blocking or repressing the emergence of hidden, primitive impulses, or in their expression, their acting out.

Leaders too may become the victims of their repressed primitive impulses at times and consequently may act out to the detriment of others, be it a nation, or the world. Professor Lasswell pointed out that political movements derive their vitality "from the displacement of private emotions upon public objects," and says that "political crises are complicated by the concurrent reactivation of specific primitive motives which were organized in the early experience of the individuals concerned." He puts it, "political acts depend upon the symbolization of the discontent of the individual in terms of a more inclusive self which champions a set of demands for social action." At the present time, there is no way other than the psychoanalytic process to reveal a political leader's inner feelings and the nature of his drives. We can only agree with Lasswell's hope that the preventive politics of the future will be intimately allied to general medicine, psychopathology, physiological psychology and related disciplines.

It is also important to learn the mood and the motives of voters. Dr. Theodore I. Rubin, author and noted psychiatrist, urges that there be a study of the conscious and unconscious motives of voters and why they elect a particular leader. Dr. Rubin poses such questions as: What kind of character structure identifies with authoritarian symbols? What parties are appealing to people of particular character structure? To what extent do sexual psychodynamics play a role? What kind of person votes the way everyone else votes? Do people in fact "dare to actually *choose* a candidate when so many are obviously *constrained* and even paralyzed in making choices in all other areas of life?"

These are some of the excellent questions Dr. Rubin has presented, and they should be asked of the individual voter. But without wishing to diminish the importance of such a study, I suggest that it is of even greater importance to know the personality of the man for whom the individual citizen is voting. How much, we may wonder, do we know about another man? How did we see President Johnson, or how would we rate General MacArthur or James Forrestal, our first Secretary of Defense? Certain actions or words can be so dramatic that they reveal the existence of psychopathology in a person without the need for prolonged observation, as was the case with Senator Joseph McCarthy, for those who wanted to hear or see.

Though I take into consideration the mentality of the people as a group or nation, my area of interest focuses on the personality of the political leaders, for, once their talent or good fortune has put them into the desired position, they possess the power to shape a nation's destiny. When the American people elected Lyndon B. Johnson President, it was because of his platform of *peace in Southeast Asia,* and yet as the Pentagon papers proved, in the depth of Johnson's mind, his decision to wage a wider war had already been made. Brainwashing has become a political tool. Advertising and a skillful bombardment by the press and TV may confuse the voter to the point that he cannot distinguish the chaff from ᵗhe grain.

While the people and public opinion may play some part in the making of our foreign policy it is, at least in the American system, decided by the President who thereby guides our lives. He who emerges as the supreme leader possesses an unparalleled power inherent in his lofty office. In spite of the assumption that Congress controls his actions, it is the President who determines our foreign policy, our socioeconomic existence and the security of all of our lives, as well as that of generations to come.

We, as voters, have experienced the difference between an impression gained about a leader and his performance via the news media and that of the picture given by those who have known him personally. Here again there is a difference between someone's power of perception, or psychoanalytic awareness in evaluating a leader, and that of his colleagues or consultants who may know only the tip of the iceberg, so to speak, and can only guess about the deeper, more complex and often contradictory behavior. Also, the perceptive power of a layman, regardless of how brilliant he may be, differs radically from person to person. Then, too, evaluating a man's political decisions or actions is one thing; appraisal of the very heart of a man's inner motivation is another.

There is nothing more important to world peace than the mental stability, the clarity of thought and objectivity in decisions of the leader. Let us assume a leader is paranoid (suffering from delusions of persecution and monomania, that is, pathological preoccupation with one issue). Such a leader's view and decisions will be distorted, as were those of Senator Joseph McCarthy, an emotionally unstable and vicious man who tried to push a powerful and civilized nation back into the dark days of the Middle Ages—and who nevertheless managed to evoke a charged response in large parts of the population. He had only to give the signal and the Communist witch-hunt was on. He cast a spell of suspicion and defiled the Fifth Amendment.

When McCarthy ran out of Communists, he began to concentrate on homosexuals in government. A cultured, attractive man in his mid-thirties came to see me because of acute conflict. He had served with distinction in the State Department for years but now was confronted with the demand that he give the names of homosexuals in the department to the McCarthy committee. Only by turning witness against his colleagues could he escape prosecution. He chose to resign —another career wrecked by McCarthy.

Returning to the grimmer topic of war and peace, let us attempt to see its reality in a calm, dispassionate way by considering what powerful principles govern both leader and followers at a given time. Our mind selects and organizes a variety of data impinging on us in such a way as to construct what to us is a coherent image of the external world, including the interaction of independent countries and the political personality of their leaders. That "variety of data" includes the sum of our emotions as they relate to our childhood experiences of love and hate and our early judgment of good and bad.

Psychoanalysts know that images based on one's past emotional experiences are too often fallacious. For instance, we may harbor a stereotyped image of a Japanese that stems solely from our feelings about the United States being stabbed in the back at Pearl Harbor. This may not be a true image of today's Japanese man or woman. Often the "enemy" is the enemy of childhood—a punitive mother or father, a parent in a state of uncontrollable rage or alcoholic stupor who spoke sharply, or slapped, or whipped, or mistreated us, sometimes when we were "bad," and sometimes when the parent hated the image of himself as it appeared in us—which has little to do with the reality of the current "enemy."

At least today there is an effort to know our leader better, not to accept him on blind faith. There is, as we said, the powerful influence of television which makes for a more enlightened public. There have been many attempts to extract from me knowledge about President Nixon and, most recently, President Ford. (In Mr. Nixon's case, the pressure by the news media has led me to place the President's file and papers in a vault for safekeeping.)

My appearance before both houses of Congress may be the first time in history that a doctor's testimony played a part in or even helped influence the confirmation of a Vice-President of the United States: psychiatric opinion was sought, if not obtained, in regard to a political leader.

The "need to know" is not only evident but understandable. People intellectually accept the fact that a physician must keep the trust of his patients and not reveal confidences, as Chairman Rodino acknowledged, and yet some who should know better kept trying nevertheless to extract statements from a physician as to the mental health of a leader.

It was Freud who discovered there was a way to ease the fear and rage within a man so he would not unleash it on the world unless he was criminally insane. And even these cases yield to treatment.

Since this new knowledge, as powerful in its own way as perhaps a nuclear device, belongs to our age, why do we not use it? Why do we not take advantage of the knowledge we possess for more constructive living, for overcoming the destructive impulses that lead to an obsessive drive for power and to war?

Paragraph two of the charter of UNESCO states: "Since wars begin in the minds of men, it is in the minds of men that defenses of peace must be constructed."

In the light of such reasoning, and feeling we can no longer delay the psychological study of our political leaders, I suggested the new concept of psychopolitics in an article I wrote for the November 20, 1973 Op-Ed page of *The New York Times*. (*See* Appendix.) In it I said the leader should be evaluated before he attained power or, if that were not possible, as he was about to assume a position of power. I also suggested that leaders be allowed to obtain psychiatric help if they wished, while in office.

Psychiatrists should examine a potential leader in order to establish the state of his mental health. This examination could help guard against a possible mental illness that might lead to fallacious judgment or destructive action. I had seen evidence of the fear people had of having a leader who might go mad and push "that" button, leading to an all-out nuclear holocaust.

An important point considered by this writer and others is how a psychoanalyst who is to serve a President would be chosen. There could be a list of psychiatrists, chosen in secret ballot by psychoanalytically-oriented psychiatrists from all over the country and from leading psychoanalytic institutes and universities, perhaps even representing both political parties. Those psychiatrists who received the highest rating by their colleagues would then appear before a board, also chosen in secret ballot, to determine which one is best qualified.

Such a physician should not be a cold intellectual but a man able to establish a warm, secure rapport with a patient. Especially important is the rapport between such a physician and the specific man he is to serve, the future or current President. Perhaps there should be preliminary meetings with three doctors and the one with whom the leader feels he can communicate best would be considered the nominee. Later on, once the stigma of seeing psychiatrists has disappeared, a political leader if he wished could choose his own psychiatrist as he would his personal physician.

After long thought and in accordance with democratic principles, but also in order to avoid any semblance of governmental controls or any doubt about what kind of doctors would be in a position to determine the mental stability of a political leader, I suggest that perhaps the simplest way would be for *major political parties to have their candidates certified by at least two psychoanalytically-oriented psychiatrists before they ran for office.* This would eliminate most points of criticism as to who selects the doctors. It would become the responsibility of the political party to choose candidates who are mentally and physically healthy, who have integrity in financial and other matters.

A further suggestion is the testing and examination of candidates by psychoanalytically oriented psychiatrists, determined by Congress in conjunction with the medical profession.

Psychopolitics would make available to a leader and his staff a physician or physicians for consultations in times of stress, men who had experience in psychodynamic principles in both therapeutic and preventive areas. Political crises, decisions of confrontation or wars usually involve misperceptions, prejudices or distortion of the realities in the intentions, capacities and responses of other leaders, other nations.

Some main issues involved in my concept of psychopolitics are:

1. The study by qualified psychiatrists and/or psychodynamically oriented physicians of the mental health of potential political leaders.

2. The right of leaders to obtain psychiatric or psychoanalytic help if they feel they desire or need it.

3. The use of psychodynamically oriented physicians on the staff of leaders to advise them on the conscious and unconscious motives of their own staff members, counsellors and advisory personnel.

4. The use of psychodynamically oriented physicians to advise a political leader on unconscious human aggression, his own and that of other political leaders or hostile groups, and possibly how to ease tense situations.

5. The establishment of a liaison office between the executive, the legislative branches of Government and the medical profession, in order to further peaceful interdepartmental interactions aimed at diminishing international tension and preventing violent political philosophies or rash decisions (such as the Gulf of Tonkin Resolution), so that negotiation can be considered before confrontation is set in motion.

These are some initial points that, if adopted and executed, would greatly reduce the chance of war, corruption in higher places of government and bungling international episodes. Some of these points probably need to be revised and others added. But as they are, they would help to inhibit impulsive actions or reactions not in the interest of most of the people. They would also help us secure as leaders the choice of more aggressive-adjusted personalities, those capable of objective evaluation of acute problems, those who can act with a minimum of anxiety or anger, those who will not be carried away by momentary inflammatory provocations or acute political crises.

The application of psychopolitical principles will also greatly reduce corruption, because a healthy mind will resist temptation of power or greed. A mature political leader will resist the pressure of lobbying industrial power groups, especially the Pentagon and ammunition manufacturers, and he will recognize, and consequently not tolerate, advisers who are corrupt or unbalanced or who have obsessive-compulsive power drives of their own.

The staunchest opposition to my psychoanalytic approach to human problems comes, I have found, mostly from mentally disturbed people and religious dogmatists. Some cynics responded quickly and sharply to my suggestion of a psychoanalyst on the President's staff. Paranoia was evident in some who saw in such a physician a sinister, Rasputin-like figure who would secretly guide, or rather misguide, an American President. Such fear not only resembles the anxiety of mentally disturbed people but reveals a complete lack of understanding of the role of a psychotherapist who, as a doctor, *does not advise* a patient, does not rebuild a patient's shattered psyche in his, the doctor's image, but helps a patient to mature so he can make decisions of his own. The doctor helps to clarify existing confusions, doubts, conflicts or self-destructive trends in a patient's mind, and then helps the patient create a better, more secure, healthier image of himself. The role of the doctor, then, is that of a guide for a patient who wants to find his place in the world, to create a more effective career, to have a more self-fulfilling, happier role in life.

A doctor's concern is a patient's health, be it physical or mental. Throughout the centuries most plagues have been brought under control by physicians. Physicians today are at work studying how to heal the plague of mental illness. But prejudice, superstition and fear are still rampant and they are enormous handicaps. A great deal more public enlightenment is necessary to insure further progress in this area. And now there is the new challenge for the physician—to assume responsibility in helping to select physically and mentally healthy political leaders.

Even if we advance to the day when a political leader can see a psychoanalyst without public condemnation or anxiety, his physician will have to maintain confidentiality. This means the general public will learn no more as to the characteristics or mental stability of a leader than it does today—unless the leader himself is willing to disclose these facts.

But far more important is that there be an air of freedom in the *selection* of our leaders so that the public is not left in the dark, merely guessing as to what kind of man they may be ready to elect. Knowledge of what a man is like would protect against our electing an inadequate American President. Because we are a functioning democracy, we cannot have quite the incompetence of a leader like Czar Nicholas II, for his was an autocratic monarchy and his word carried as did his decision to enter World War I, a tragedy triggered by a shallow, blundering German emperor, Wilhelm II.

What we physicians have to cope with are the dogmatists and fanatics who deride medicine and ridicule psychoanalysis or who hate psychiatry outright because they fear it. When my proposal that psychiatrists examine and serve a President was published in *The New York Times,* it was answered by a most disturbing editorial (from the point of prejudicial judgment) by a man who presents himself as an objective intellect and great liberal but who, nevertheless, revealed the same prejudice shown by other biased people. He indicated a deep hostility to psychiatry because of an unfortunate personal experience. He blamed psychiatry for not having prevented the suicide of his son. In his case, he may have been well justified in his opinion, because there are indeed cold, uninvolved or even incompetent psychiatrists. I think of a highly respected professor of psychiatry who told a twenty year old college student and her parents that she would have to stay in a psychiatric hospital for the rest of her life. Yet, a few years later, after the young woman had worked hard in her sessions, this professor, giving a lecture on TV, remarked to the young program assistant how attractive and efficient she was. She did not dare say, "I am the girl you said would never leave a psychiatric hospital." The writer in point has had an unfortunate experience but that does not entitle him to condemn a whole profession. Yet he wrote that the dependent relationship in which a President might find himself with a psychiatrist could ultimately project the question of which one was running the White House. This is a projection of that editorial writer's own deep distrust of psychiatry which he now tried to instill in his readers. It is this type of personality who slows down reform and progress in the field of psychodynamic psychology.

The majority of psychiatrists are, however, without question concerned human beings who in their dealings with patients are nonjudgmental, maintain a clear, objective view of an emotionally charged situation, and are largely free from unconscious prejudices. Consequently, a psychoanalytically oriented psychiatrist will not be carried away in matters of foreign policy by his own drive for power, for we can assume that he has successfully sublimated it, or by slogans based on political might, and will have enough control and courage to resist intense pressures and overreactions of hotheads, aggressive advisers or leaders.

Such a psychoanalyst will be supportive not only of a President under stress, and his advisers, but will be aware at all times of the needs of the people. He will help a President, as we say, to keep his cool, just as the President's physician tries to keep the blood pressure on a normal level. For a man to remain cool, yet firm, and to be aware of all the consequences in the face of danger, shows inner strength and the rare quality that is wisdom. Dr. Jonas Salk has mentioned "survival of the wise," and perhaps today that is more true than the biblical "meek."

To speak for a moment in ideal terms, the ability to care about human beings, mental maturity, the vision and the ability to feel love, should be as important as the ability to make decisions and to act. These should be prime demands in our choice of a leader; otherwise we will perpetuate the destructive paths of the past. Remember that it is not the people who create international conflicts; it is, as a rule, their neurotic leaders. And human concern, reverence for life, control of impulses and inner strength, should belong to the policy-making group of presidential advisers as well as to the leader. If in recent years the advisers had been mentally healthy and emotionally more mature, there probably would never have been armed intervention by this nation in Southeast Asia and there would not have been a Watergate.

In his book *Human Dilemmas of Leadership*, Abraham Zaleznik, professor of organizational behavior at Harvard University's School of Business Administration, says that the main source of the dilemmas leaders face

is found within themselves, in their own inner conflicts. . . . Dealing more intelligently with knotty decisions and the inevitable conflicts of interest existing among men in organizations presupposes that executives, at least the successful ones, are able to put their own houses in order. It presupposes that the executive is able to resolve or manage his inner conflicts so that his actions are strongly grounded in reality, so that he does not find himself constantly making and then undoing decisions to the service of his own mixed feelings and to the disservice and confusion of his subordinates.

He stresses the tendency in a human being to project personal feelings, to place conflicts that really lie inside himself upon the outside world, to take an attitude of his own and attribute it to someone else, to project his own anxieties on others. It is crucial for a leader to be able to "separate" the conditions within himself from those existing on the outside, states Professor Zalesznik.

More than twenty-six years ago, I was called on in an unofficial capacity to advise a world leader. By a sheer accident I happened to play a role in the birth of the state of Israel.

I had met Dr. Oswaldo Aranha, ambassador plenipotentiary and former foreign minister of Brazil, before he was elected president of the emergency session of the UN General Assembly, which was meeting to decide the question of the division of Palestine; it was the first crisis to face the new UN. The United Kingdom had decided to give up its mandate of Palestine, and the question at hand was whether to divide Palestine into two independent states, one Arab and one Jewish, or to establish one federated country.

On April 7, 1947, when I was still practicing internal medicine, I was asked to see Dr. Aranha, who had come to New York to attend this emergency session of the United Nations. The president of the session was to be chosen from a country other than the five permanent members of the UN Security Council (the United Kingdom, the United States, the Soviet Union, France and China). Each year a different continent was to offer a candidate, the first, Paul Henri Spaak, having come from Europe (Belgium). This year's turn was South America.

Dr. Aranha was rumored to be the favorite, but his prospect of being elected president now seemed in doubt because of the seriousness of his illness.

Dr. Aranha had dismissed his two former physicians who had told him he had pneumonia—he told one of them: "You are a very good man and one day when I want to commit suicide I shall call you"—but my examination confirmed that diagnosis. Dr. Aranha asked what his chances were of attending the opening session less than two weeks away. Penicillin had just become available and I said that, with proper rest and if assured of his full cooperation, I could probably prepare him to attend the meeting at Lake Success for a few hours. "How sure are you?" he demanded. I said it depended largely on how well the proud and somewhat unruly gentleman would follow my orders. He paused, thought for a moment, then asked, "When do you begin?"

"Right now," I said, having brought with me the medication as well as the equipment.

The medical treatment continued over the next two weeks, early in the morning and at night. At Dr. Aranha's invitation I attended the meeting of the United Nations on April 23, at Lake Success. The majority of the fifty-five United Nations were ready to support and elect Dr. Aranha. Backed by the Latin American republics and the United States, Dr. Aranha still had not given his formal consent to his nomination as president of the session because of his severe illness. According to *The New York Times*, he was "expected to receive the support of the Arab League members." The Soviet Union also supported him.

Dr. Aranha was elected president at that session. Thereafter in the course of my twenty-eight visits to the Waldorf Towers suite where he was staying, I had many discussions with him about issues both personal and political. By the end of May, when the session ended, a committee had been formed to determine the future of Palestine, and Dr. Aranha and I parted as friends.

In September, just before the regular sessions of the General Assembly were to start, he called me. He said he wanted to talk to me and to have me prepare him medically, through vitamins or whatever was necessary, for the stormy sessions ahead. Dr. Aranha often detained me so that I could meet some of the foreign diplomats who were trying to get his ear: "You wait a little," he would say, "and then you tell me what you think of *him*."

On a Saturday morning early in November, I received a phone call from Ambassador João Muniz, Dr. Aranha's most trusted deputy. Could he see me? I was puzzled as to why on a Saturday, and even more puzzled when he added, "But not in your office."

Punctually, at the designated hour of 3 P.M., Dr. Muniz rang my bell. We decided to take a walk in Central Park, two blocks away. Suddenly the Brazilian career diplomat stopped. We stood face to face. He said, "Let me come to the point. Dr. Aranha," he called him the "minister," "wanted me to talk to you. It is about the division of Palestine. We Brazilians have no feelings about the matter, one way or another. We want to do the right thing. Dr. Aranha is being heavily pressured from all sides. He has great respect for you and your judgment. He wants to know how *you* feel about a division of Palestine."

I was stunned. Why would he want my opinion? I was not a politician, not a diplomat. But neither was I a psychotherapist at that time, and therefore there was no restriction on my speaking freely to his deputy—as one man to another.

I paused and then said hesitantly, "I think, all in all, it is a bad solution. It is now two and a half years after the war. There are still concentration camps. Nobody wants the people who have been brought there and left to rot in the camps. Foreign governments keep their doors closed. As I see it, it is not a political but a humanitarian issue. I therefore see no other solution than a division of Palestine." It was clear to me that if the decision was made for one federated state of Palestine, the Arab majority could block the Jewish immigration and the concentration camp immates would have no place to go. Dr. Muniz thanked me and we resumed our walk, talking about his favorite subject, philosophy.

On Wednesday, November 26, 1947, the General Assembly was moving to a vote. President Truman supported the division of Palestine, as did Gromyko of the Soviet Union. But President Truman was out of the country and General Marshall, Secretary of State, secretly favored the Arab side because of oil and military interests. I watched Dr. Aranha's seemingly unconcerned yet incredibly masterful tactics that aimed at a postponement of the vote that would have brought certain defeat to those who favored a partition.

After bitter wrangling and because of Thanksgiving the fateful session was set for Saturday, November 29. In the meanwhile, the friends of the partition had reached President Truman, who ordered full support. My wife and I accompanied Mme. Muniz and her two beautiful daughters to the Assembly Hall at Lake Success. The air was charged with excitement as Dr. Aranha, before addressing the delegates, received a standing ovation. Starting with Guatemala, the roll call began. The tension rose to a painful climax as the votes were counted. When the decision was announced—the division of Palestine into two states, one Jewish, one Arab, had carried—a roar of applause arose. "A new reality, wrote *The New York Times* the next day, "is rising in our days to which we must impart the spirit of the United Nations, the only conception capable of insuring peace, solidarity, dignity and equality for all people."

Over the ensuing twenty-five years, I have often asked myself why a statesman of Dr. Oswaldo Aranha's stature would have wanted to listen to his physician, or even why my opinion would count at all. The answer was simply that he must have shared that opinion. I was not being consulted as a physician but as a friend. But it took twenty-two years for me to get some confirmation. In July 1970, I received a communication from his son-in-law, Sergio Da Costa, at present ambassador from Brazil to the United Kingdom. He had referred a friend of his to me as a patient and I had written to him. He answered from London on July 7, 1970:

I can hardly tell you how pleased I was to receive your letter of June 18th, with a flashback to our first meeting and to your relationship with Oswaldo. Ours (Zasi's [Aranha's daughter] and mine) are very general and centered in the instantaneous affinity of soul and mind he felt for you . . . he went on describing you and your first conversation and the apparent ease with which you shifted from psychosomatics to international politics. He certainly detected the potentials of your well disciplined mind, of your acumen and quick grasp of the significance of events.

He was then deeply involved in the Middle East problem and the impending birth of Israel. Right after the historical session which created the new State, I drove with him from Lake Success to the Waldorf Towers. In the lift, several Arab princes were fuming with rage, hands gripping their daggers. As we walked to his apartment, he commented that such Arabs were quite unaware of the real, long-term consequences of the partition of Palestine—an unsuspected turning point in Arab history. *Nothing would operate the miracle of awakening the Arab world from their secular lethargy except that Israeli thorn imbedded in its side.* [Italics mine]

I did not know—but it does not surprise me, that Oswaldo was keen to hear your opinion, your forecast regarding events then still in the making. This shows to what extent he valued your judgment, your reasoning and ability to assess without passion and draw logical conclusions.   With fondest regards

Later that Saturday, after the historic session at Lake Success, I did send a telegram to Dr. Aranha to congratulate him on what I thought was his personal victory. When I saw him on Monday in his suite at the Waldorf Towers, he thanked me for the telegram and said he had been severely attacked because of the war that had just broken out. With his gentle, sophisticated smile, he commented, in his Brazilian-English drawl, "When you perform an operation, a little blood must flow." We talked; he too needed what Freud called an abreaction . . . an emotional release. He would not need me anymore.

The course of history has borne out my apprehension about the consequences of a division of Palestine, and yet in retrospect, and in view of the circumstances as they existed then —the indifference of the European countries to a human tragedy of unimaginable dimension—it seemed the only possible humane and civilized solution. If my word has had any meaning at all, I feel fortunate and glad to have been able to have presented my thoughts to Dr. Aranha the way I did at that time.

Thus a footnote to history ends, but if it contains any lesson, it is the hope that in the future a political leader with the vision of an Aranha might be able to ask openly a physician he respects, who has psychological and psychopolitical awareness of the behavior of man and of nations and yet has no political ambitions of his own, what in such a doctor's opinion is the best course to take in decisions that may be far-reaching.

So far, political leaders depend only on the advice of "experts," many of whom think in terms of power and lack experience in the field of human behavior—lack also a humane, compassionate, understanding view of mankind. Availing himself of a qualified psychoanalyst's or psychopolitical counsel would indeed be a giant step forward in the life of a political leader in whose hands may rest the destiny of millions of people. To attain this is one of the aims of psychopolitics.

VI

The Making of Violence

MAN'S POWER to conquer the violence in nature only underscores his seeming inability to conquer the violence within himself. Even the wisest of men are not free of a feeling of violence in their hearts from time to time, though they may possess the strength to control it.

Man's innate capacity for violence differs from human to human and is triggered by different signals, at different times and with different intensities.

The capacity for violence is part of our early instinct for self-preservation. It enables us to fight for our very life. Merely to survive in an everyday existence requires the use of our aggressive energies, but it also requires coping with violence once it erupts by learning how to control it.

When rage is on the rampage, when the passion of fury does not relate to threats that are real but is felt in reaction to an imagined menace, it becomes dangerous and destructive. An assassin who kills a political leader usually has neither a personal nor a realistic reason for the murder; he is driven by a rage so violent as to want to do away with the internalized image of a threat that has become intolerable to bear. The rage may be rooted in the distorted belief that through the killing the assassin will actually do a good deed, become a liberator, or a hero who delivers his people from evil. Rage has slumbered in the depths of his mind for years, stoked by hate, until suddenly aroused by some signal or image, as with Sirhan Sirhan, the killer of Robert Kennedy. The target, real or imagined, is generally a substitute for the parent or surrogate parent he had wanted to strike in infancy.

Long before some of today's behaviorists came up with theories of their own on aggression, Pavlov, in his laboratories, demonstrated both the making and the undoing of rage and violent behavior. True, he worked with dogs, and they do not have what he called a second signaling system, that intricate system of uncounted millions of conditioned reflexes which develop as a result of thought and speech and leave their imprints of images in the billions of cells in the two hemispheres of the brain that, in large part, governs our conscious thinking.

But Pavlov was careful and modest in his conclusions, something that cannot be said of some of our contemporary scientists. Konrad Lorenz, for instance, introduced a theory on aggression which seems to me to be a dangerous jump from the behavior of fish and geese to that of human beings. He defines aggression as "the fighting instinct in beast and man which is directed against the members of the same species." He states that human beings "in a state of highest violent aggressive feelings" usually attack the person who elicits that emotion, which means that generally it is a member of the family or someone who has been loved, rather than a stranger.

Lorenz has been hailed by some people with such enthusiasm that I wonder whether their praise has not come in part from a need to replace Freud's theory that aggressive feelings are caused by the frustration of the erotic instinct. It seems to me they embraced Lorenz's scientifically questionable theory on aggression without examining or testing its objectivity.

The instinct theories of scientists are based on close observation of animals. Lorenz particularly studied geese and their built-in behavior of "imprinting"—the process by which baby birds recognize and respond to their mothers. He showed that, under proper conditions, goslings can develop a permanent attachment to humans, or even to cardboard boxes. Lorenz stated that people can become imprinted by "demagogic leaders" who trigger almost irresistible inbuilt tendencies to violent aggression, threatening the survival of humanity. It might perhaps be possible that leaders could imprint "their demagogic views on people who, as children, had been 'imprinted' with similar views by emotionally immature parents."

In his work on fish and geese, Lorenz proved that they would fight for their "real estate," or breeding ground. Commenting on "how furiously the brightly colored coral fish fight their own species" in the waters of Florida, Lorenz reported in his book *On Aggression* that he began to study these reef fish in the aquarium. First, he asked why the necessity for their brilliant color and what "species-preserving function" could have caused their evolution. He made an unexpected discovery, he said, when he put several members of the same species into a tank. Vicious fights ensued within a short time and only the strongest fish lived. Peaceful coexistence occurred between two of these same species only among those that lived in a permanent conjugal state. But when only one of each species of a variety of fish was put into the tank, all lived peaceably together.

Lorenz theorized that in the sea the principle "like avoids like" is upheld without bloodshed because the conquered fish flees from the territory of his conquerer who does not pursue him far, whereas in the aquarium there is no escape and the winner often kills the loser or claims the whole tank as his territory and so intimidates the weaker fish.

He concludes that his observations in the aquarium, confirmed by his sea studies, "prove the rule that fish are far more aggressive toward their own species than toward any other."

Lorenz applies this to human beings, explaining that this principle exists to preserve the species, that

the environment is divided between the members of the species in such a way that, within the potentialities offered, everyone can exist. The best father, the best mother, are chosen for the benefit of the progeny. The children are protected. The community is so organized that a few wise males—the "senate"—acquire the authority essential for making and carrying out decisions for the good of the community. Though occasionally, in territorial or rival fights, a horn may penetrate an eye or a tooth an artery, we have never found that the aim of aggression was the extermination of fellow members of the species concerned. This of course does not negate the fact that under unnatural circumstances, for example confinement, unforeseen by the "constructures" of evolution, aggressive behavior may have a destructive effect.

The judges who awarded Lorenz the Nobel Prize in 1973, have a "plumber's view of human nature," according to Dr. Peter Breggin, director of the Center for the Study of Psychiatry in Washington, D.C. He criticizes those scientists who treat people "as if they were objects in the physical universe to be manipulated very much as one would manipulate an automobile."

Dr. Frederic Wertham is a distinguished New York psychiatrist and winner of the Sigmund Freud Award of the American Association of Psychoanalytic Physicians; his books including *Black Hamlet,* have earned him recognition as a crusader for psychiatric treatment of violent criminals. As a critic of social and psychic causes of violence, he declared that "To give the Nobel Prize to Lorenz does unspeakable harm to my mind. Millions of people will die for that reason." He called Lorenz's ideas "distinctly Nazi theories" developed in the intellectual climate that led to the killings of 275,000 German mental patients by their own psychiatrists. He pointed out that Lorenz had been the head of the department of psychology at the University of Köningsberg in East Prussia, "the most Nazified university" at that time. Wertham also said that while he was doing research in Germany for his book on mass violence, *A Sign for Cain,* he discovered a paper Lorenz published in 1940 advocating "race-hygienic defense" and the *"extermination of ethnically inferior people."*

Wertham objected to Lorenz's use of the term "aggression" as unscientific. Wertham had concluded that "human violence is always due to negative factors in the personality or in society—and therefore these factors are *"remediable and preventable."* Widespread acceptance of Lorenz's theories, he felt, "makes it easy for people to say of a murderer, "his instincts got the better of him—he can't help it."

Lorenz stretched his theory based on low animal behavior to unscientific deduction about the behavior of human beings, to the point of supporting Nazi racial ideologies, couching it in scientific language. He stated: "Socially inferior human material is enabled . . . to penetrate and finally annihilate the healthy nation. . . . The racial idea as the basis of our state has already accomplished much in this respect." Was it arrogance or ignorance on his part? Or, like so many weak-minded people, did he try to please the new men in power at the time? And what to Lorenz is socially inferior human material? And what is a healthy nation, or how healthy is a nation if it can be annihilated socially by "inferior human material," material which must be in the minority or there would not be "a healthy nation"? Did deliberate or unconscious prejudice run away with this scientist? Dr. Leon Eisenberg, professor of psychiatry at Harvard Medical School, challenged the idea that human behavior is largely based on instincts. "Lorenz's scientific logic," wrote Dr. Eisenberg, "justified Nazi legal restrictions against intermarriage with non-Aryans." Dr. J.B.S. Haldane, the late British biologist, as long ago as 1956 referred to Lorenz's Nazi sympathies. Margaret Mead, the American anthropologist, was shocked at his pro-Nazi ideology. She was quoted on Lorenz in "The Sciences" (Vol. 13, No. 10, December 1973);

> I've heard him say that unfortunately you can appeal to human beings in the name of the thing they value most to do things that are terrible. . . . One of the traps of idealism and patriotism is this appeal. I've seen him stand up and take the position that a male goose takes when it's defending its nest, and say that this is the way human beings become involved and caught—and this, he feels, is the greatest weakness in human beings.

Lorenz is presented here only because he is a prime example of men who have used the robe of science to promote subjective, deranged ideologies as valid scientific theories, theories that have led to the destruction of uncounted millions of innocent lives. A politician bent on self-promotion can be understood, if not forgiven, for his inexactness, but not a man who demands acceptance from the scientific community and who violates the basic principle of science—the search for truth based on knowledge of facts and exact, critical and objective observations. We may ask again: What was wrong with the men who considered Lorenz worthy of sharing the Nobel Prize?

The key word here is integrity; without it, it is questionable whether a man can be a true servant of science.

Pavlov, a scientist who turned to psychiatry at the age of eighty, doublechecked his own experiments painstakingly and then had them checked by assistants in different laboratories who were kept unaware of the professor's findings. He was able to create in dogs conditioning that resembled human schizophrenia, and he learned how to cure these conditions, hoping to apply his methods to humans. These methods still form the basis of Russian psychiatry.

Pavlov wrote a most moving letter to the young scientists of his country in 1936, shortly before his death. He referred to the letter as his "Last Will and Testament."

It read:

What would I wish for the youth of my fatherland who devote themselves to science?

First of all—Consistency. I can never speak without emotion of this most important condition for fruitful, scientific work. Consistency, consistency, and still more consistency. From the very beginning of your work train yourselves to be strictly systematic in amassing knowledge.

Learn the ABC's of science before attempting to ascend its heights. Never reach for the next step without having mastered the preceding one.

Never attempt to cover up the gaps in your knowledge by even the most daring conjectures and hypotheses. No matter how the colourings of this bubble may please your eye, it will inevitably burst leaving you with nothing but confusion.

Train yourselves to discretion and patience. Learn to

do the manual labour in science. Study, compare, and accumulate facts.

No matter how perfect a bird's wing, it could never raise the bird aloft if it were not supported by air. Facts are the air of the scientist. Without them you will never be able to soar. Without them your "theories" are useless efforts.

Yet, while studying, experimenting, observing, try not to stop only at the surface of facts. Do not become an archivist of facts. Try to penetrate the mystery of their origin. Seek persistently the laws governing them.

Second, modesty. Never think that you already know everything. No matter in what high esteem you are held always have the courage to say to yourself: "I am ignorant."

Don't allow yourself to be overcome by pride. On account of pride you will be stubborn where it is necessary to be conciliatory; you will reject useful advice and friendly assistance; you will lose your sense of objectivity.

In the group which I am called upon to direct, atmosphere is everything. We are all harnessed to one common cause and everyone furthers it to the best of his strength and ability. Frequently we cannot distinguish what is mine and what is thine, but through this our common cause only gains.

Third, passion. Remember, science requires your whole life. Even if you had two lives to give it would still not be enough. Science demands of man effort and supreme passion.

Be passionate in your work and in your quests.

Our fatherland opens broad vistas to scientists, and we must truthfully say science is being generously introduced into the life of our country. Extremely generously.

What is there to say about the position of a young

scientist in our country? It is perfectly clear. To him is given much, but of him much is demanded. And it is a matter of honour for the youth, as well as for all of us, to justify those great hopes which our fatherland places in science.

Aggression, in a psychological sense, is a normal, healthy forward drive necessary for our survival, especially in a society as competitive as the United States. Since the term "aggression" has been so frequently associated with unprovoked attack in a military sense, or with ruthless overbearing behavior in everyday social life, I have often used, in order to avoid confusion, the term "assertion" or "self-assertion" to indicate a positive, self-starting approach and healthy action in dealing with the demands of modern living. But I do use and accept the term "aggression" as normal behavior. Its opposite is a helpless, evasive, passive attitude that ranges from inertia to the more severe pathological conditions of depression or catatonic states, or catalepsy, a diminished responsiveness or complete immobility.

Inhibition, that powerful negative force that represses activity and human spontaneity, is at one end of a wide semicircle that ranges from such passivity to healthy aggression to, at the other end, the acting out and violence that comes from loss of inhibition.

Notwithstanding genetic factors, still inconclusive at this time, the difference between aggression and violence appears to be one of degree. Uninhibited, more or less fully unleashed aggression aims to destroy. Its target may be an object, as in the case of acts of vandalism, or it may be directed at a life. People in big cities have become bewildered about the spread of a plaguelike rule of terror and what is often called senseless killing. The awareness of this seemingly new rise of destructive and homicidal terror has led to fear, confusion and the anxious question: What is the cause?

People have blamed the era of permissive upbringing of children in this country, denouncing, for instance, as overly tolerant Dr. Benjamin Spock's attitude toward children—indeed an oversimplified answer. The problem goes much deeper, of course. Permissiveness is one thing, uninvolvement and not caring about a child is another. The child needs discipline and wants it, if applied caringly. My formula of discipline is *firmness, kindness and consistency.*

Freud at first related aggression to the sex impulse, stating that aggression was aroused when the pleasure principle (the avoidance of pain) was blocked and the frustration that ensued became intolerable. Later Freud postulated that there was a death instinct as well as a sexual and aggressive one. Erich Fromm, among others, disputes the idea that there is a death instinct, but I have wondered how many of the opponents of Freud's death instinct have stood at a bedside watching patients die or observed their determined behavior to destroy themselves.

Animals die when they are injured or cannot fend for themselves by refusing to eat. In man, I accept a death wish as an unconscious negative force that, caused by guilt, worthlessness or hopelessness, is carrying out a policy of self-destructiveness: consider the psychosomatic illnesses, accident-proneness and other acts that injure the life force short of outright suicide. All of these are aggressive acts against the self committed by people who would rather hurt themselves than others.

Whether we call a man's wish to injure others or to be destructive a neurotically compulsive drive—it is not an instinct, though Freud talks about a death instinct—this powerful urge exists in many. Many men deny they possess the wish or the capacity to destroy when provoked or utterly frustrated, but that does not mean that the rage or the power to act out violence does not exist in depth. It is a matter of control or of displacement of feelings; the woman who breaks dishes in a rage at her husband may be displaying only a fraction of her feelings or fantasies of violence in depth.

During many years of clinical experience, I have learned to accept with increasing conviction Freud's concept of a death wish. I wrote a chapter about it, "Man Dies When He Wants to Die," in *The Will to Live*.

I had just watched my mother die and eleven months later, my father, who thus almost deliberately avoided the trauma of facing as a widower the anniversary of their fifty-six years of marriage. It was an evident and deliberate giving up on his part because life had lost its real meaning and had become too difficult to bear.

My thoughts on death—there was almost no medical literature on the subject at that time (late 1940s)—evoked the interest of many, among them a psychologist, Herman Feifel, Chief Psychologist of the Veterans Administration and Clinical Professor of Psychiatry, University of Southern California School of Medicine. He set up and invited me to participate in a symposium on "Death and Dying" at the yearly convention of the American Psychological Association in Chicago. Out of the papers of this symposium Dr. Feifel edited a book, *The Meaning of Death*, published in 1959 by McGraw-Hill, with contributions by Carl Jung, Paul Tillich, Herbert Marcuse, Herman Feifel, Curt Richter, fourteen others and myself. (The title of the paper I read at the symposium was "Personality Factors in Dying Patients.") A flood of studies and literature on dying followed, and the Foundation of Thanatology was established with an Archives, of which I am listed as a member of the Professional Advisory Board on Psychiatry.

The death wish may express itself in subtle or not so subtle ways. There may be an accident through carelessness, or a phase of morbid depression, or a series of strange maladies. Living sometimes means to question the meaning of life or the harshness of the daily struggle and, especially after a painful and significant loss, a half-serious flirtation with death. There may be unconscious guilt about the lost one and often a powerful unconscious longing to be reunited with the person one has loved and lost.

Recently the Foundation of Thanatology asked its board members to write a new definition of "anticipatory grief" for a convention in conjunction with Columbia University, Department of Psychiatry. In my paper I said that anticipatory grief was a profound emotional response to an impending and irreversible loss through death. Because of its element of absolute finality, the anticipation of the loss of a beloved person may arouse a heightened sense of anxiety, pain, regret, fear or depression, depending on the intimacy and meaning of the threatened relationship.

Anticipatory grief may be felt by both the dying patient and his survivors. The dying one may feel the pain of parting and anxieties about those he cared for (a spouse, children, close friends). There may be feelings of regret and guilt at perhaps not having provided well enough for surviving dependents. Also, there may be a sense of unfulfillment, of not having finished his life work, or the bitter sense of failure at not having used his potentials and thereby wasted his life.

Then there is, of course, a cold fear of death, of grieving about the cruel reality of having to die, just as there exists on the other end of the scale, a wish to die. As a rule, death is desired when a longing for final peace outweighs all other emotions and when the daily battle for survival becomes too burdensome and tormenting to be endured.

Anticipatory grief may vary in depth and intensity, for at no time does the total personality reveal itself as fully as in the face of death. An immature man may die in anger, and one whose personal life has remained unfulfilled may die with a curse on his lips, whereas a mature man may meet death with acceptance and feel at peace because he feels fulfilled. He may outwardly display little sadness in order to make the parting less painful for those he loves.

Anticipatory grief in survivors at losing a cherished companion is often mixed with the fear of losing a source of security, of protection. There may be an upsurge of love never fully displayed before. Or there may be fear, panic and depression. Or there may be a Freudian "sympathetic response," a pain that physically resembles the one of the dying patient and that emotionally causes anxiety and a purely neurotic anticipation of one's own end: a dying a little bit with the person who is dying.

Independent of but frequently mixed in with anticipatory grief is conscious or unconscious guilt. Conscious guilt often stems from a feeling of not having done enough for the dying person. Unconscious guilt has its basis in ambivalent feelings toward the dying person or it may be rooted in the religious concepts of some people's anticipatory judgment by God. Anticipatory grief heralds a trying time for both, the dying person and those left behind.

In view of earlier criticisms of my idea that premature death is an unconscious act of suicide—a search for the peace which the turbulence of life prevented—it brought me special satisfaction that in November 1973, twenty-two years after I first developed Freud's concept by my own clinical observations, psychologists and cardiologists working at the Harvard School of Public Health reported that the incidence of "sudden fatal heart attacks" was related to emotional stress. The researchers, significantly, were using Pavlovian methods combined with American technology to prove their point that "unexpected sudden death strikes people in the prime of life with such frequency as to make it a major public health problem throughout the world."

The men I had seen dying from heart attacks were hostile, aggressive men, regardless of how well they defended themselves against such hostility. They were unfulfilled perhaps in their need for affection: some who overload themselves with responsibility are seeking praise and love. Some cannot really give of themselves in order to be loved. They display a mask of outer friendliness and concern to mask their anger. In everyday life, these men may be known as the kindest, most considerate human beings, yet may rage with inner turmoil. In the last analysis, a heart attack is an act of violence against the self, especially in people who have displayed an overcontrolled, often driving yet overly conscientious behavior with rigid repression in the area of sexual satisfaction. The conquest of the next mountain top may not bring such a man the inner peace and warmth of love he has been hoping to attain. "I have never known a man who died from overwork," said Charles Mayo, the American surgeon, "but many who died from doubt."

Fromm draws a distinction between aggression—a defense against a threat to a person's vital interests, such as his children, his food supply, his territory—and destructiveness. He calls destructiveness a lust in cruelty and killing which, and I agree, is not biologic but social and cultural. But to blame the destructiveness in America on the logic of machinery and on the excess of material things beyond the necessity of life which numbs Americans to the point where they are indifferent to violence, is to enumerate evident factors or symptoms, but not to explain the deeper, motivating destructive forces, the illness itself.

The violence we see in many people today is a complex phenomenon. It demonstrates an inability in a person either to understand life or to cope with it, or it is an angry protest against the injustices of a society, our feelings of exploitation or the withholding of the fair share of happiness a child in America so often grows up to believe he is entitled to.

Television has sharpened the conflict. Television has shown the poor, the disadvantaged, the hungry, how the rich live. It takes the poor into living rooms of luxury, painfully pointing up a lack of equality that seems to conflict with the rights guaranteed by the constitution. It brings into sharp contrast power and helplessness, overabundance and poverty, thereby arousing in many the feeling that they are entitled to take by force what an unkind chance has withheld. There are many who are impatient or who realize that their chance to advance themselves in a competitive and sharply hierarchical society is slim. The whip of violence drives them and they put themselves above the law in order to get what they want.

Bewildered by today's glaring show of violence, many dream about the good old days and want to turn the hands of time back. This is as impossible as the wish to return to the safe, parasitic life in the womb. Our life style can never be that of the Victorian era. American creativity, ingenuity, fermentation and growth mitigates against going backwards. Though we build on the past, we cannot regress to what was, in spite of or because of a restless and threatening present. We must go forward. If we equate building with creation (an application of the creative instinct) we cannot, while we are building, be destructive. We may commit individual destructive acts, even collective ones, but as though we are passing through a depressive phase, a slump, or a blue Monday, we pick up and go on. Most people do this and, the more mature the person, the easier the picking up and the rarer the slumps. We, as individuals, all possess a certain amount of energy. We can channel this energy into creative *or* destructive pursuits. It is the same with a nation. As long as a nation is building and creative it fights off degeneration, depression and self-destruction.

The young people I see strike me as outstanding examples of renewal; they move ahead, examining with devotion and honesty the structure to which they have fallen heir, and at the same time trying desperately to rid themselves of bigoted and rigid judgmental beliefs. These young people are searching for new values that are less materialistic, more sincere and humane. They are searching for inner independence and self-esteem. They want security built on self-worth for themselves but with consideration and respect for others. They truly believe in live and let live. They struggle to be more civilized and emphasize a greater reverence for life. And that is why I say to many of them that I do not believe in a generation gap—but a communication gap.

But while this process of fermentation and reevaluation goes on in some, violence still reigns in others. In regard to the latter we must try to answer the two questions every physician asks himself of an illness: What is the etiology (the origin or cause)? What is the therapy (the treatment that will produce a cure)?

I mentioned the belief of Freud and other thinkers that the generating force that ignites people to violence is a shift from a controlled drive for power—a drive to gain a position within a system governed by law—to an uncontrolled drive to take by brute force, regardless of the law, what belongs to another man. Violence is power in the negative and is destructive.

Some psychoanalysts believe that narcissism is at the root of man's drive for power. That is to say that when a person feels narcissistically threatened, he will become enraged and strike out at those he feels have injured the beloved or flattering image of himself. Perhaps we can differentiate between the infantile feelings of narcissism, the self as the center of the world, and the mature feeling of self-esteem—a sturdy, integrated ego. Such an ego cannot easily be injured by others because of its strength. A man who has confidence in himself and his own abilities allows neither praise nor criticism nor abuse to induce him to lose control.

It is the child in the grown person who is narcissistic and stirred by the drive for power, causing fantasies like "I will show you how powerful I am, how I can strike back at you and those who have been so heartless and have dared to hurt me." One boy, the son of a patient of mine, acted out his anger by stealing out of the house in the middle of the night to puncture the tires of all the automobiles in the neighborhood. He demonstrated his power by preventing the wealthy, powerful business and Wall Street men from catching their trains or driving to their offices in the morning. Another boy, twelve years old, proved *his* power by forcing his father to buy a new car. He rose quietly during the night and set fire to the family's garage, making sure the colonial brick house in the small New England town would not be in danger, and then went back to bed and slept peacefully. He pretended to be astonished the next morning when he heard the dreadful news that the garage, with the family's car, had burned to the ground.

The emotionally immature youngster, who has difficulty controlling his hostility and who lacks the ability to build or create, sometimes can satisfy his drive for power only by acts of overaggression and destruction.

He may turn his hostility against himself; then we see the angry, rebellious adolescent—or, worse, the silent hater, the dropout, the confused, depressed youngster who is so absorbed by inner hate that he cannot share, cannot concentrate on learning or on pleasure.

How does a child learn control? Only a mother who knows how to control her own feelings of rage can instill control in a child, and this should be done early in his life. A father who displays self-discipline and restraint can also teach his child by example as well as by taking an interest in the control of simmering violence. The examination of the childhood backgrounds of murderers usually shows the parents to have had violent tempers, either openly expressed in acting out behavior or rigidly repressed with just occasional explosions.

It is not necessarily the underprivileged child who grows up with hostility, though poverty contributes to feelings of deprivation and lack of self-esteem. All children will experience anger in the process of adjusting to the demands of authority or of learning to live with frustration. Sometimes they want to test their strength of knowledge but choose a destructive way, as did two thirteen-year-old youngsters who manufactured a bomb just to see whether it would work. They put it into the mailbox of an old lady and it worked so well that when she opened the mailbox the bomb nearly blew off her arm. The youngsters when caught told the police they were only testing their technical skill. They were not conscious of their repressed hostility—both had new stepfathers and were furious at their mothers for remarrying—but only of experiencing the victory of success and temporary omnipotence mixed with a dreadful but exciting fear of danger.

Because destructive feelings involve the display of power and the exhilaration that results from a sense of omnipotence, they hold an excitement that is often contagious among young people. Hostility begets hostility, evoking an echo of rage, especially in the inwardly angry, frustrated or bored. Then the competitive race is on as to who is most ingenious or most powerful (which means beyond the power of the father—the most godlike). To be above the law, to see victims as utterly helpless, or to make them tremble by holdups and hijackings, to outrace or to outgun a police officer—all these acts constitute a display of power. There may be some fear but the dominating drive is one for power. A moment of utter excitation and omnipotence seems well worth risking one's life for, if that life seems uneventful, drab, empty, boring and hopeless anyway. "Nothing ever happens," complains a youngster who believes excitement comes from without, because a joyless existence has desensitized his inner feelings of aliveness.

To fight what they feel is the lifeless, deathlike existence they lead, many men use their aggressive drive to excess, sometimes to a point that borders on violence, yet still keep it within socially acceptable situations like automobile racing. These men may rise to the top of the business, financial or political world, sometimes "stepping over bodies" on the way up and, once on top, don the vest of respectability (leaders of organized crime have done this too). Such men seek the fulfillment of the American Dream, not realizing the psychological price they pay for it: they may be respected, but are not loved.

Power and violence can be used for breaking a human heart without any evidence of breaking a law. The scene is the bedroom in a townhouse on the Upper East Side of New York City. The patient, a pale, red-haired, green-eyed woman, has just had her fortieth birthday. She had been one of Hollywood's great beauties, but her dream of fame and independence had come to an end nineteen years ago. That was when she finally yielded to the relentless barrage of her mother and the suitor she married because, as mother said, he had "saved" the family and Emily had to be grateful.

Emily had been almost dragged to my office by a close friend of hers (a former patient of mine), who was worried about Emily's increasing depression and withdrawal from people. Emily was frightened and tense and very reluctant to talk. But at the end of the hour she said, "I'll come back and tell you the whole story—it's silly what I'm doing."

I learned about Emily's ambitious mother who forced the girl at age four to take dancing, and later singing lessons. While other children played, Emily sat with her mother in agents' offices to get little jobs. They moved around a great deal and there never was money.

Bill, the man she eventually married, was around all the time. He helped out with money, bought food and clothes, and was more like an uncle than a man a young woman would dream of marrying.

Nobody knew where Bill got all the money from. Later I learned that he had been with the Internal Revenue Service and discovered that a corporation had a serious tax problem. He told them he could settle things, and when he left his government job it was for a partnership with the company.

Emily never loved the man and when she discovered the ruthlessness under his facade of an ever-ready smile, her life became intolerable. Nevertheless, she had tried to bring up her children as well as she could, without the pressure she had had as a child.

One day I sat at the bedside of Emily, because she was too weak to get out of bed. She said quietly, "Why don't you let me die? He will never let me go. . . . I'll never have a chance. . . . He will bribe any lawyers, and judge—it's his way. And if it isn't money, he has the political power to get what he wants.

"I trust you," said Emily, "and therefore I'll be honest with you. He knows how I feel. He's like the Gestapo: there is not a pill I have he doesn't know about. I have not had any food for two days, and I'll refuse to eat. . . ."

When I met with the husband, he pretended an easygoing joviality, and he greeted me by saying "All a man needs is a good doctor and a good lawyer. . . ."

"It's a little more serious than that—" I answered, and instead of explaining her condition I asked bluntly, "Why don't you let her go?"

There was a debate about his belief in the freedom of an individual, of his love and the welfare of the children. Bill did not like to be interrupted.

"Your wife is going to die, and there is nothing you can do about that. If you don't leave her alone I'll have to take her to the hospital. She needs to feel secure and be protected."

His smile was gone. "I'll come to your office," he said.

When he came, he talked about the hard life doctors had and noted that most of them were not practical. It was a subtle prelude to a bribe.

I apologized for my rudeness in interrupting him again, but I told him I had asked a colleague of mine to take his wife to the hospital and informed him that she had just been admitted.

He was furious but answered with a broad smile, while pointing out that it was customary for a doctor to consult with the husband.

There was no display of anger or harshness. I simply asked for his cooperation in doing all I believed was in the best interests of the patient.

I saw Emily that evening in the hospital and she promised she would take some food. But later that night she called frantically. Her husband had appeared at the hospital, pushing aside the night nurses by representing himself as a doctor who had been called by the physician in charge. He had warned Emily that what she was doing wouldn't do her any good and that she better be a good little girl and come home.

Since she was convinced that there was no lawyer Bill could not eventually get to, I suggested my own trusted attorney, a man I knew to be impeccable.

As a personal favor to me, he visited her in the hospital and offered his help. She retained him and he confronted Bill with the reality that his client was determined to have a divorce and that they had better concentrate on a settlement.

Bill moved out of the house.

A few years after their divorce, my wife and I were on vacation and were having lunch at a restaurant when I pointed out that a man we had passed on our way to the table had been the husband of a patient I had had a great many problems with, and I was glad he had not seen me. At least so I thought. But when we were almost ready to leave the restaurant, he got up and marched straight to our table and asked to sit down. What followed was an incredible scene. Hardly looking at me, he let loose a barrage at my wife. He told her that he had acquired a large estate in Southern California for the union of which he was now an officer. The estate was to be used as a research center. His problem was to find a physician with vision and integrity and enough stature to run such a place, for it would be heavily funded. For an hour and a half, without a stop, he outlined the magnitude of the project. Then he abruptly got up and left.

My wife was in a state of utter exhaustion; she complained of a violent headache from the drilling effect of his tirade. And, in all innocence, she asked me what he wanted of her.

He wanted to lure me into a trap in order to gain control and possibly vengeance.

The lack of love is of course at the bottom of the lack of self-esteem. It is in a general sense the feeling of being unloved or of being unworthy to be loved that causes humans to feel empty, bored, hopeless and destructive—and may give them a need to show their power by making those in power powerless.

VII

The Imbalance of Power

THE DRIVE for power, the dynamic force of man's aggression, plays a decisive role in man's finding his place in the world and determines how he strikes a balance between his basic will to live and his unconscious wish to die.

The will to attain and to hold power demands self-confidence, a clear objective and a pouring out of aggressive energy, rooted in or fed by a healthy will to live. But it may also be motivated by an unconscious wish to die and to have others die as well—if a man's mind is sick, if his ego controls are weak, if his thinking is impaired and if his goals are unrealistic and essentially destructive. Some men have such an exaggerated, narcissistic and paranoiac sense of self that they want the whole world to go up in flames when they die (Goetterdaemmerung). A man who has reached great power can think and plot in terms of war—if not in reality, in fantasy.

There are men who stave off crippling states of mental depressions by creating high-pitched activities, ruining careers, breaking up relationships, leaving in their wake a trail of destruction, the ultimate of which is murder.

I recall a man who, years ago, was sent by J. Paul Getty to Acapulco from London to find out and report back to Mr. Getty why his luxuriously built hotel, the Pierre Marques—a place he has since sold—was losing money. At the time my wife and I were in Mexico on vacation, Sloan Simpson, a beautiful lady and a friend of ours, who worked at the hotel, asked us to join her and some friends for drinks; we were in turn joined by this man from London.

Slightly drunk, he began to make anti-Semitic remarks, such as, "I would like to kill all the Jews," pointing at people sunning themselves on the beach and drinking on the terrace.

Sloan was stunned, visibly upset, not knowing what to do. No one said a word. He kept on raving.

Finally I asked, "Suppose you had the power to kill all the Jews, what would you do next?"

He hesitated a moment. Then he muttered, "I would kill everyone in Mexico."

"And then?"

His violence mounting, he said, "All! I would kill all! They are nothing but pigs or rats."

I leaned over and whispered something in his ear. He turned crimson. Then he stood up, mumbled an apology, and left the table, as though he had quickly sobered up.

"What were the magic words?" everyone at the table demanded of me.

I would not tell them, except for Sloan, to whom I later said, "I told this man, 'How you must hate your own guts! What keeps you from killing yourself? Isn't this really what you want to do?'"

After this episode, the man followed me around like a little dog, begging me to talk to him, inviting me for drinks though

I ignored him. He must have felt a sense of terror because I had detected the self-hate and violence within him. I told Sloan that I would not be surprised to learn sooner or later that he had killed himself. Two years after, he committed suicide in London.

A scientific meeting devoted to a study of death was held on the day of the Cuban missile crisis. As the world waited in fear for the Russians' response to President Kennedy's ultimatum, one psychoanalyst reported what he thought was a telling incident. He had a patient who, for years, talked about his terrible fear of dying. But that afternoon the patient seemed cheerful, almost free from anxiety. "You know," he said to the doctor, "I really feel good. Until today I couldn't stand the thought that the world would go on enjoying itself after I died, but with today's crisis, I feel a sense of relief. I am actually happy. If the Russians don't give in, we all go up in smoke and, with nobody left, I won't be any worse off than everybody else." We all laughed at this weird kind of to-getherness.

What holds true for an individual holds true for nations as well. A nation that starts an aggressive war believing it is fighting for freedom against injustice or for some other noble cause, is showing an unconscious wish to kill and then to die—at least on the part of the leaders and the greater part of the people who follow the leaders. It may well be that those who live by the sword die by the sword, sooner or later, in one way or another. The psychodynamics of groups are no different from those of the individual. Groups follow the same pattern except that in a group the force of violence multiplies. Members of a pack or a gang join together for the sake of getting power so they can overcome an individual sense of insignificance and inferiority by a collective display of strength. In their use of terror and killing there is an unconscious wish to die, again to take with them as many people as possible.

Killing is the ultimate sense of power. Murder is a show of ultimate omnipotence, superseding the rule of God, who is supposed to be the supreme judge over both life and death. Gang killings give the members a sense of violent power, but it is a power born out of a sickness that carries with it the seeds of each one's eventual destruction.

Gangs differ in the intensity of their violence and their stated goals. In the New York area marauding teen-age vandals destroyed stores and threatened the lives of innocent people unless they were given a playground. Recently a more sophisticated, sadistic wave of kidnaping has emerged, carried out by left-wing or right-wing so-called "armies of liberation." Some of these "armies" kidnap for political reasons; others for their own gain. For "General Field Marshal Cinque" of the Symbionese Liberation Army, it was a case of living by violence and dying by violence. We may wonder whether it is the rise in violence and wish to kill that seeks a cause, or a supposed cause that is fabricated in a sick mind, if not to kill then to demonstrate supreme power.

Violence in America and other countries sees the manhunter on the loose with his Saturday-night special. There are not only trigger-happy hunters but trigger-happy cops—or trigger-happy National Guardsmen who fired at innocent students at Kent State University. The trigger-happy people are men with a control so fragile that the slightest provocation brings an uncontrollable urge to see blood. When we consider the relative helplessness of governments, local or Federal, to stem this plague it may be as Halldor Laxness, the Icelandic Nobel Prize winning author wrote what he had learned in his Jesuit School—that "Mankilling is the King's Game" and that "war as a man's glory" is the unadulterated moral of our good Icelandic classics.

We do not have to accept either this nordic mythological or Freud's psychoanalytical explanation for the reason why one man kills another man, but what other explanation is there?

How does anyone explain murder in cold blood, such as Hitler's storm troopers lining up old men, women and children and then mowing them down after they had dug their own mass graves? Or, in our own back yard, the case of First Lieutenant William L. Calley, Jr., convicted of killing, "wasting," he called it, not less than twenty-two Vietnamese civilians in a ditch east of My Lai South Vietnam during the assault on the hamlet which took place March 16, 1968? Witnesses at Calley's trial testified that his personal slaughter of South Vietnam civilians in the ditch went on for an hour, with group after group of men, women and children shoved into a trench by soldiers, then shot by Calley. One witness, Thomas Turner, a member of Calley's platoon during the assault, testified that Calley had shot down a Vietnamese woman who ran toward him with her hands in the air, pleading for mercy. Other witnesses testified he tossed a child into a ditch and shot him and that he also killed a Buddhist priest. Others told how he paused between shooting the groups thrown into the ditch, "some screaming and crying," to insert a fresh clip in his M-16 rifle.

It is one thing to take an enemy village under orders but quite another to callously murder helpless villagers and children. Calley's feelings of primitive violence got completely out of control; he dismissed his accusation of the murders by the words "no big deal," showing what he thought the value of a human life—his own as well as others. We can only guess the fury and horror that had been stored in his twisted mind over the years since childhood, hidden under a mask of expressionlessness, and the insurmountable hatred he must have had of everyone who lived. He had the power inherent in the wearing of a uniform and the bearing of a gun, a power that gave him permission during a time of war to open up the emotional valve and release the explosive rage stored within. It was a rage far beyond that of a hungry animal, a rage that came out of Calley's "far country," which is what Freud called the unconscious.

And what about his superiors, the generals? Who gave the orders to defoliate the Vietnam countryside, who ordered the making and the buying of the chemical herbicides? A report of the Academy of Science said it will take over a hundred years before the country is restored. And who covered up and falsified reports on unauthorized bombings in neutral Cambodia, lying so they could continue playing the deadly game of murder? Shall we shrug our shoulders, sweep things under the rug and say, "That is war"? And give the generals a medal for bravery? Actually, if we uphold the moral lesson of the Nuremberg trial, where is the difference ot principle, except that the American generals were in a position of unquestionable power in a small country in Southeast Asia?

Endless are the examples, different and bizarre in their execution but not in their motivation, that illustrate man's need to gain power through violence and murder. There is a steady increase in books and scientific papers written on violence, and symposia held by psychiatrists and men in related fields to explore its origin and its dynamics—all in the hope of coming up with a better understanding of the causes and with concrete suggestions on how to cure this growing cancer in the live organism of society. The *World Medical News* in its November 23, 1973 issue published an article called "The Mind of a Murderer." It began:

> The ranks of murderers include a physician who advised his wife to vigorously massage the lump she found in her breast; a farmer who killed his wife with a rifle after she served him a meal of cabbage and scrambled eggs; a young man who stabbed his mother, whom he loved, right after stabbing his father, whom he hated, because "I did not want my mother to know her son had done it. She was sick, she had a bad heart, and if she found out, it would have been pretty bad on her"; Albert Anastasia, a gangland figure, who, after Arnold Schuster had pointed out bank robber Willie Sutton to the police, saw Schuster on

television and snarled to one of his henchmen, "I can't stand squealers. Hit that guy"; a fifteen-year-old boy who confessed, "I just wondered how it would feel to kill grandma"; a nephew who murdered his uncle because the uncle, with whom he shared a bed, would not move over; a man who murdered his estranged wife after she had charged birth control pills to his drugstore account; and a dentist who killed his father-in-law for insurance money by filling a cavity in his tooth with aconitine.

More recently, a twenty-four-year-old Air Force veteran [in New Jersey] shot and killed his parents over a weekend, then got into his Volkswagen, drove 100 yards to the next neighbor, killed her, invited a former classmate to visit a mutual acquaintance, wounding her as she got out of the car, mortally wounding the two-year-old baby she was carrying. Each was killed by one shot in the head with a .32 caliber automatic pistol. Then the man surrendered to the police.

In the summer of 1973 in New Jersey four women and a six-year-old boy were found knifed to death in a two-family home in Newark. Four of the dead represented four generations of the same family. The year before, in June 1972, a former Pinkerton guard, thirty-three-year-old Edwin James Grace, entered an office building in Cherry Hill, New Jersey, and deliberately fired at male employees as he walked from room to room. Six men were killed and six others wounded within seven minutes, then the gunman shot himself in the head. He died the following month of his injuries. The previous April, a nightclub shoot-out in Atlantic City left three young women and a millionaire heroin dealer dead, and eleven persons injured, including five struck by stray bullets. In December 1971, a woman, her three teen-age children and her mother-in-law were found shot to death in their decaying nineteen-room house on a quiet residential street in Westfield, New Jersey. The man of the family, who had disappeared, a shy, bespectacled accountant, forty-six-year-old John E. List, was indicted as the sole suspect in the five deaths.

The killings go on and on, day after day, no matter what the state or town.

According to Dr. Michael G. Kalogerakis, psychiatrist at New York Medical Center, "We are in desperate need of sorting out from the many troubled individuals in our society those who will be the murderers in tomorrow's headlines." Both Charles Whitman, who shot forty-one people from a tower in Texas, killing seventeen, and Richard Speck, who killed eight student nurses in Chicago, had committed acts of senseless brutality before they murdered, points out psychiatrist Frank R. Ervin of the Neuropsychiatric Institute of the University of California at Los Angeles. If these murderers had been identified as potentially violent and treated before it was too late, the reasoning goes, their victims' lives might have been saved.

The nearly 20,000 homicides and other acts of violence in the nation prompted President Johnson to appoint a commission headed by Dr. Milton Eisenhower to study causes and prevention of violent crime.

Dr. Karl Menninger in his book *Man Against Himself,* an impressive and penetrating study of man's drive to self-destruction, was, I believe, the first in this country to point out the ravages of hate. He wrote:

It is nothing new that the world is full of hate, that men destroy one another, and that our civilization has arisen from the ashes of despoiled peoples and decimated natural resources. . . . We have come to see that just as the child must learn to love wisely, so he must learn to hate expeditiously, to turn destructive tendencies away from himself toward enemies that actually threaten him, rather than toward the friendly and the defenseless, the more usual victims of the destructive enemy . . . I believe that our best defense against self-destructiveness lies in the courageous application of intelligence to human phenomenology. . . . To see all forms of self-destruction from the standpoint of their dominant principles would seem to be logical progress toward self-preservation and toward a unified view of medical science.

He dedicated his book, "To those who would use intelligence in the battle against death—to strengthen the will to live against the wish to die, and to replace with love the blind compulsion to give hostages to hatred as the price of living."

How does the average person cope with the violent feelings in his own life? As in the case of any onset of an illness, first by becoming aware of what it is and then knowing how to fight it: in this instance, by becoming aware of the buried feelings of violence deep in his being. One must become conscious of feelings of simmering hostility, rage and outright hatred that may have existed for the greater part of a lifetime.

Awareness offers at least a chance of learning how to control feelings of violence. Without awareness, there can be no control, and hatred may linger on like a time bomb and then erupt, as it did with Calley and a long row of murderers.

We are brought up to believe that anger is not a "nice" feeling to have and that hate is sinful. We are trained to believe we must not even *feel* anger, nor must we feel hate even when we are deeply hurt. But to *feel* and be aware of these explosive feelings does not mean to *act out* anger. We can learn to channel our rage or anger or a fury, or any physical labor serves as a release of our hostile aggressive feelings. We may not at first understand the deeper unconscious nature of our anger, nor even the specific signal that triggered our angry mood. But if we try to relate our feelings of fury to a specific disturbing situation, and if we avoid denial or rationalization we can learn to gain an awareness of cause and effect.

If we learn to accept the reality that it is normal and human to react with anger when provoked, and cease to deny or repress the anger, we will be healthier and happier and will never need to act in passion, to flare up in violence.

When President Truman referred to General MacArthur as "a dumb son of a bitch," he was angry. He had good reason to be angry. He did not ever come near violence, but he expressed his feelings of anger and he could act, when he had to, without vindictiveness.

If we write down a scene of distress, humiliation or outright provocation, we will not only gain relief but turn amorphous churning feelings into a creative act, regardless of the quality of the creation. If the description is an honest reflection of the event, it is creative. Even telling a friend of our anger is helpful. Or we can take a long walk, we can garden, we can seize a clump of clay and give it form—any raw work or act that requires the release of physical energy will serve as a release. Thus by realizing that we no longer need to repress the corrosive force of anger, we can develop our own technique of turning hate into love.

As one patient, a young woman lawyer, told me after months of therapy, "I can feel the anger in my bones now, at long last. And that's enough. I don't have to let it out on my husband and child."

She no longer had to hurl her angry, childish (and childhood) feelings on innocent targets. She was becoming more peaceful within herself; she did not have to look for a target or make war on the world.

Because it illustrates what happens in many a family, to greater or lesser degree, I present in detail the case of one young patient who learned to accept that he could be angry at times with his mother and father, and also that it was his deeply buried feelings of violence that had made him feel his life was futile.

In the early sixties a frail, young, blond Ivy League graduate came to see me because of a variety of nervous symptoms, primarily headaches. Several extensive physical examinations had revealed no organic cause. I sent him to a neurologist, a friend of mine at the Neurological Institute of the Columbia Presbyterian Medical Center and the examination, including an electroencephalogram, proved entirely negative. The report declared he had fully recovered from a concussion he had suffered and "his present complaints are based on anticipatory anxiety."

This young man was plagued by two overriding anxieties: one that he might one day go mad, and the other that he might possibly have homosexual tendencies. He had never had a homosexual experience, though there had been the traumatic threat of a homosexual man making advances to him when he was in his teens. His homosexual fears had been temporarily eased by an opera singer, a woman older than he, with whom he was having an affair. Sex with her was superb. She had helped him overcome his anxiety and develop a more confident sexual image of himself as a man.

A few years before his visit to me, he had suffered a head injury when on a freedom ride in a southern state when he took part in a peaceful demonstration which the police called illegal. He was roughed up and beaten hard over the head by the police; he suffered deep wounds that required several stitches, and he was jailed for six weeks. The only thing that eased his pain, he told me, was the act of informing his father, a conservative oil executive with refineries in the Middle East, that he was in jail.

Both his father and mother flew at once to bail him out of prison. Angered at his son for having joined the civil rights movement, the father threatened to kill him if he dared make a speech in his father's home state denouncing the racial bias of such concerns as the ones owned by the oil executive. But the father also had guilt and fear about his son's future, and both parents tried to talk some "sense" into their son.

My patient likened his father's attitude to that of the marines who "shoot first and ask questions later." When he had misbehaved as a boy, his father had first punished him, then demanded an explanation. He had recorded his feelings in a diary which he showed me from time to time.

My father punished me by spankings, when I was probably too young to understand why I was being punished. Let us assume that such punishment occurred mainly between the ages of two and five. After five I am sure that I had learned why and when I was being punished, so that I could generally be said to have punished my own self willfully after that age by committing acts which would bring about flagelation. Thus my tortures could be said to have been masochistically self-induced, using my father as an agent who automatically whipped me when I provided the proper conditions.

My mother was cast in the role of a shield from these blows. She could be manipulated. Though my mother did spank me, I doubt that she spanked me until I was past the age of four or five. Then she used a willow switch, which was considerably less painful than the belt I recall my father was using.

Through this early conditioning, I was taught that (a) my father (authority, god, society) was a thing to be feared. And (b) the way of authority was the Right & Good way, to be imitated and followed and (c) my mother was identifiable with my own fear and weakness. My weakness sought her as a shield, but because I despised my weakness in me I also despised her, thus all women (for all women represent that which was the only woman in our lives at such an early age).

What shall I consider as motive behind my adolescent

revolt and denial of God? Clearly, God was my father
. . . Thus I denied the inherent right of my father to
induce pain upon me. I denied also that the ways of my
father were necessarily enviable. . . . The dream of
heaven had never been a reason for my belief, so I did
not greatly miss that promise when it was removed. It
had always been the fear of hell that had kept me in line,
and this fear I had now removed. Yet the fear of hell was
no more than the fear of my father's punishing hand, and
had I removed that? I think not, because I feel that I
clearly had not resolved my scorn for women.

He wrote how he felt about women in a very eloquent,
perceptive fashion.

It is important to consider the attitude toward women that
was professed by my immediate society. Women were
"screwed," "fucked" and "had." An attitude of mutual
satisfaction in the act of sex was extremely minor or
nonexistent. A successful seducer of women was referred
to as a "cutter," a phrase that envisioned the penis as a
knife and the entrance into a woman's vagina an act whose
meaning was equal to ramming an icepick into her belly.
Come to think of it, "ram it into her" was another current
phrase. Sex was to me a way of punishing women. I
believe it still is. I have never brought a woman into a
successful climax without the conscious strong will to
make her scream. Women do imitate great pain sometimes when they near a long-awaited climax. They seem to
enjoy it more. At those times when I sought only release,
only release was achieved and no satisfaction was provided
to the woman. I look back on all such encounters with
embarrassment and shame. To be loved despite this failure is mortifying, it makes me feel like a child being
forgiven by his mother. I am worshipped for my ability to

inflict pain, I am treated as if I were the child, she the
mother, and I was forgiven because I had not yet grown to
the state when I could achieve the sexual power that my
father already possessed. [The term "Oedipus Complex"
seems like a meaningless understatement here.]

As he faced his mother and father in jail, he could enjoy
their concern and helplessness. After he had been bailed out
by his parents, he refused a generous gift of money to take a
trip around the world. Nor were his parents able to prod him
into pursuing an academic or business career. He told his
father he would accept only a truck.

"I wanted the truck," he explained to me, "so I could explore Mexico. Owning a truck in a country like Mexico would
make it easier for me to find work." His parents, he said, were
very upset both by the idea and because they considered him
too weak physically for such work. But his father reluctantly
bought him the truck he had picked out.

Then followed a traumatic incident, one in which he repeated the experiences of childhood. While driving to Mexico
City, he picked up a hitchhiker, a man in his early thirties. As
they talked, my patient learned the hitchhiker was a pimp,
who spoke proudly of the ten prostitutes working for him in
Mexico City. The trip took several days, during which they
slept by the side of the road in the truck.

As he spoke of this, my patient paused, then his voice
changed as he said, "What happened next—it's all my fault—I
brought it on myself." He mentioned the small diary he carried with him, filled with dates and poems he had written,
which still bore bloodstains from the head injury he had suffered during his freedom-ride encounter with the police.

He went on, "I had lost a lot of weight and I still felt
weak. It was only a few hours more to Mexico City but as
we drove along it was getting dark and I suddenly felt

very tired. I was also too embarrassed to say I wanted to stop because I felt tired and weak. I felt this would be confessing my inadequacy as a man."

Then he said, "I set it up for this man. To explain why I wanted to stop, I invented the story that I had a brain injury and was very sick. I said that I would die young, could, as a matter of fact, die at any moment.

"So we stopped once again to sleep in the truck for the night, planning to arrive in Mexico City the next morning. I fell asleep quickly. When I woke, I found myself in a hospital. I had been unconscious, they told me, for several days. Finally, I figured out what had happened. After I had fallen asleep, the hitchhiker had beaten me over the head with some blunt instrument. He believed he had killed me—I had told him I might die at any moment."

He paused, then continued, "He had mentioned how nice it would be to have a truck like mine, then he could go into some other business than being a pimp. He had taken my money, since he thought I was dead, but fled without the truck because he did not know how to drive it. Though the police wanted information from me, I would not tell them anything about the hitchhiker. I did not want him to be punished. I thought it was all my fault. If I hadn't felt too weak to drive on to Mexico City, if I hadn't made up that silly story, he never would have been tempted to violence."

He seemed somewhat shocked at his masochism, his passivity, for he was now capable of getting an inkling about the deeply repressed feelings of violence he had turned on himself, asking always to be beaten, from the time he was a child. Even with the police, he was now once again beating himself, refusing to help them catch the man who had acted so violently toward him. Such behavior could only come out of his own feelings of guilt at wanting to beat up other men and escape punishment.

During his third visit to my office he related a dream in

which he said, "I was machine-gunning southern whites. A friend killed a man. I was reprimanded but not punished. I was injured by mistake by one of my own men. I woke up but went back to sleep. Then I was escorting Nazi prisoners. One was a general. He was injured. He was in the desert fighting. Enemies. Nazis, Arabs. I felt great enjoyment at the sight of killings, the death of enemies."

The dream clearly revealed his great inner rage and desire for violence. His being injured "by mistake" related to the assault by the police, by the hitchhiker, and, originally, by his mother and father. The injury was symbolic of castration, the theme of his life, his feeling he was not a man. He was always the victim—the victim of his father, the police, and almost the victim of a homosexual assault by an older man early in his life. But in his dream he reversed roles, showing his deeper wishes. He was in charge of Nazi prisoners, which put him in a position of power. The Nazi general represented his father and the general's injury was his deserved punishment for his cruelty. The overall theme of the dream was killing—the enjoyment of killing, the seeing that enemies—Nazis, Arabs (working for his father), the general, his father—got what they deserved.

Our talking of the existence of his inner feelings of violence helped this young man understand some of his contradictory feelings. One day, for instance, he spoke of the wish to push, then slug an old lady when she blocked him as he walked down the street. His associations led him to mention a feeling of always being "blocked" by his mother. He now sensed his anger at his mother and how he had repressed it, then felt guilty and turned it on himself. He had been very dependent on his mother, a woman who spoiled him, but hated her because he thought her weak, like himself, and easily manipulated. He said, "She shielded me from my father, which I considered being unfaithful to father. Because of her, I had scorn for all women."

He was able to understand that he was capable of love and great sensitivity to a woman but had difficulty in the act of sex because of his unconscious unwillingness to give and his wish to punish women, rather than to be tender to them. He held back his own orgasm for both these reasons, fear of hurting and unwillingness to give—pleasure or semen or a baby.

The relationship with the singer became more and more stormy as he became more assertive. He decided he would not marry her because she could not have children. His headaches, which had left him during treatment, returned as her pressure to get married increased. He told me, "So far in life I have lost all the battles. But now I have decided to grow up on all fronts—work, women, human relationships."

In the past, in the office where he now worked, he had asked several times for a raise but, as he now realized, in a very meek way. His superior always knew how to brush him aside. But one morning we talked about self-assertion and he said he was determined to practice it: defeating his boss would mean defeating his father. Strengthened by our discussion, he marched straight into the office of the President of the firm. He was stopped by the secretary in the outer office. When she asked what he wanted he said, "It's very personal and I have an appointment." As he told me later, "Though I hate lying, and never do it, this time I had to."

The President's personal secretary tried to stop him but he told her the same story and walked right into the President's office. The latter, who was on the phone, looked astonished, then frowned because my patient had not been announced.

My patient just stood there, staring at his boss, waiting for him to end the conversation on the phone. For a moment he felt in a panic, then told himself, "I must be self-assertive," and threw himself into a chair facing his boss.

When the President finished his conversation, he hung up, said sternly to my patient, "Who are you? What do you want?"

"I work here and I want a raise," my patient said quietly. Though the President seemed outraged, suddenly my patient had no fear.

"You have to go through channels. Don't you know that?" demanded the President.

"I have tried—five times," said my patient, in a firm voice.

The President looked more intently at the thin, attractive face of my patient. Then he asked what salary he was getting, inquired about his past experiences. After listening carefully, he buzzed for the manager, introduced him to my patient, and arranged that they talk things over, saying to his manager, "We have to place this young man where he belongs. He is superior material."

Whereupon, surprising even himself, my patient said quietly, "I thank you, sir, for what you have done. But I now realize, to be honest with you and myself, that I want to quit this kind of work." The firm was in the computer business.

This new confidence and what it had achieved had led to the decision to seek the kind of work he really wanted. Propelled by his new courage, he called a leading public relations firm and, after interviews there, got a job at almost double his former salary. He also ended the relationship with the singer and met a girl three years younger than himself whom, he felt, he could love.

"The world may be in a mess," he told me, "but I feel pretty good." He was taking pleasure in his work; he no longer felt sex was a sin; he could enjoy tenderness. He could admit he was entitled to feelings of violence, but that this did not mean he had to act on them, against others or against himself.

He had learned the futility of violence—the torture of suffering physical pain and the debilitating effect of the repression of pain. As he faced up to his long-repressed drive for power and began to use it increasingly in more constructive ways, instead of punishing himself for feeling weak and ineffective, he experienced a new sense of confidence and self-esteem. It made him feel good when he stated the discovery that he wasn't too bad a guy and that life could be fun. The imbalance of power with which he had lived had shifted to a controlled, productive use of it.

VIII

Can Violence be Prevented?

I F LIFE is to have any meaning at all it demands that beyond making use of our potentials, we stand up for our beliefs lest we sink into a mass of passivity. Cynics don't build a better world; men with imagination do.

It has been always a handful of people who have moved this world forward against the cohesive resistance of the frightened and the many of little faith. Equally, it has always been a handful of fanatics who have been able to arouse the slumbering violence in man though perhaps none to the degree of that individual who started by writing anonymously because " . . . people must not be allowed to find out who I am" and who finally fulfilled one of his predictions that "we will carry half the world into destruction with us. . . ." Adolf Hitler, author of these statements, did not originate violence, but he masterminded its annihilative force and forged it into a heretofore unimagined holocaustic power.

After World War II, America did not build Wendell Willkie's One World, but heeded Churchill's policy of the I-on Curtain. Fear, poor judgment and an obsessive need to seek military rather than political solutions prevented a settling down to a peaceful state of coexistence which inevitably led to two American wars in Southeast Asia. The use of force had its repercussions, for it polarized our nation and bred more violence and angry opposition by the youth of America. Many young men opposed the war in Vietnam on grounds of conscience and morality. Many fled the country not out of cowardice, but because they did not want to become murderers.

Deeply disturbed by the escalation of this unfortunate war, the killing of a peaceful population and the burning down of Vietnamese hamlets, and by the reactive violence in the United States, I felt I had to take a stand.

I was concerned about violence not only in the streets of America, but in the minds of men in authority, the men pursuing a national policy of force from behind polished desks. With great reluctance, I decided to make use of my twenty-year personal relationship with President Nixon to formulate an appeal that would constitute an indirect plea for peace. I did not wish to abuse a privilege. I felt I had no right to ask to see the President in order to express my disapproval of the way he was running or "winding down" the war. But I felt I had to talk to him, as one small voice against the roar of the hawks, to try to interest him in my dream of a Department of Peace.

With a somewhat heavy heart, on October 22, 1969, I wrote the following letter:

Dear Mr. President:
   Since it has been my belief to cherish and not to abuse the privilege of our personal relationship, I have re-

frained from writing to you earlier. The reason for my doing so now is to ask whether you would consider giving me some 15-20 minutes of your time, knowing only too well what in the life of a duty-bound President even that short span of time may mean.

I am preparing another magazine article dealing with the problems of human aggression. I do not intend to turn our meeting, should you grant me one, into an interview to be used for the article. But being motivated by my conscience and watching what is in the making on the political horizon, I believe that the time has come for someone to take action which is necessary to deal with the rising drive to violence on a world wide scale and to channel it into creative pursuits. I do not wish to refer to the war in Vietnam (although I had thought—some time ago—that a cease-fire would have had a tremendous impact and build up of prestige for your administration as well as our country). But as I told you back in 1956: Peace is more than the absence of war just as health is more than the absence of illness. I therefore believe that the end of the war would be only one step, a great step forward toward a larger task.

To build world peace in ways other than [on concepts of] power would be such a task. But I am realistic enough to know that it would take more than an agency like a Department of Peace to bring this about; and yet such an agency could be turned into a most important and effective pilot project and at the same time serve as a symbol of hope for the many discouraged and frightened people all over the world. *We need an education for peace.* And we need a mobilization of all the energies, physical and psychic, which are inherent in man and which need to be led out and into productive channels for the benefit of our nation and of mankind as a whole.

In your hands lies the golden opportunity to give this

last third of our century an imposing historical significance. You could open the road to the achievement of at least one of man's ancient dreams besides the conquest of hunger and disease, to conquer the curse of war.

The thoughts I would like to present to you are not really that of a dreamer. I think they are practical and realistic enough to be heard by the man the whole world looks up to in solemn hope.

Respectfully and with warmest personal regards,

The answer came in less than three weeks, in the form of a telephone call from Rose Mary Woods, personal secretary to the President, who told me the President would like to see me. She gave a date, and asked whether this would be convenient. Of course it would, I answered. This was at a time when Mr. Nixon had reached a position of unequaled power and prestige.

I went to Washington one day before the appointed time, on a Sunday, and walking through the National Gallery thought over the salient points I wished to make. The next morning, December 1, 1969, I went to the White House and was met at the South Gate. I passed along various checkpoints, before I reached the office of Miss Woods.

She was warm and friendly and we chatted for a little while. Then came a signal and she stood up and led me along a corridor to where an apparently unarmed guard stood, his hands behind his back. She nodded and he must have pushed an invisible button, for a sliding door suddenly opened.

I was walking into the Oval Office. The President came towards me; both hands cordially shook mine. Before we sat down, as if in answer to my question as I looked around the beautiful room, he explained that Pat had decorated it, choosing the colors of the room and the enormous blue, oval-shaped carpet with fifty gold stars woven in it, to represent the fifty states of the Union. There was one picture on the wall—the landing of the first American astronauts on the moon.

The President was relaxed and seemed pleased to see me. He inquired whether I was still working around my country place, as I had told him I did, nearly fifteen years before, when he asked whether I played golf. As we sat down, he pointed to the enormous, shiny desk, explaining that President Wilson had brought it to the White House.

Not wishing to lose any time, I plunged right into the topic: a Department of Peace. I knew beforehand that the President was not in favor of such an idea, and now he replied that some people (not saying but meaning himself) considered the Department of State and Department of Defense to be departments of peace.

I challenged this point and questioned whether the leaders of these departments, men such as Forrestal and Dulles, could ever be champions of peace because of their temperaments (I called them hostile-aggressive types of personalities). I may have worded my thoughts differently and may have mentioned others I considered angry men, but in essence I expressed my belief that such personalities, when under stress, because of their low threshold of tolerance, would tend to react aggressively—that is, in favor of violent confrontation rather than patient negotiation. What I was proposing was an agency that would present counterbalancing points of view and seek nonviolent solutions to acute international tensions.

A short but lively debate followed. The President expressed concern about setting up another bureaucratic agency and about the expenditure. I was prepared for such an answer and suggested readily an "Agency for the Exploration of the Dynamics of Peace," whose function would be the study of the psychological aspects of aggression and the presentation of a coordinated program based on education for peace. I envisioned such an agency as being given the chance to voice an opinion in matters of international conflict. It would constitute a forerunner of a Department of Peace. (I was willing to settle for half a loaf.)

The President listened with great intensity to my suggestion. He then leaned back and, closing his eyes, nodded a few times; then in a low voice, as though speaking to himself, he said, underscoring his words with another nod, "It can be done."

My heart jumped with joy. It was like a quick waking dream. I felt a moment of triumph at the thought of initiating a humane and civilized way of handling international tensions and their prevention. It could promote a peace built not on the power of the sword and missiles, but on the greater power of the human mind to understand the fallacious reasons for making war.

As our hour drew to a close, the President asked if I had seen the Milton Eisenhower Report. I replied that I had read something about it in the newspapers. He pressed a button, a secretary appeared, he asked for the Report, and gave it to me when it was brought to him. It was his own first copy.

"Would you read it," he asked, "and let me know your thoughts about it?"

"Of course, Mr. President," I replied, not knowing then of the difficulties this was to create for me.

He walked me to the door. There came a brief moment packed with an emotional upwelling as I said, "Mr. President, you may never know how I feel this very minute, a foreign-born who came to America in search of freedom, now received by the President of this great country." To me it was now my turn to give back to the country that had welcomed me all I was capable of giving. He seemed touched, we shook hands, and the solemnity of the moment ended.

On the plane to New York, my mind flashed back to a meeting I had had with another President, the first President of West Germany, Theodor Heuss, back in 1955. I had been in the President's villa in Bonn and we had talked about psychosomatic medicine. *"Bitte nichts politisches,"* nothing political, please, the German President said.) He had read or knew the gist of some of my writings. It was a pleasant, animated meeting, but I had not been emotionally touched by it. When I had left, I had realized how estranged I had become from the country I had grown up in and I now realized how American I had become in feeling, thought, involvement and concern.

I picked up the Eisenhower Report, a twenty-two-page book. Fortunately, it did not have statistics, which I have always hated, but was packed with facts. I was determined to make my reading of the report a thorough study. Still in a state of exhilaration, I began to think how this terrible problem of crime could be met. The President knew of my strong interest in prevention of illness and was now interested in what ideas I might have for the prevention of crime.

The next day, after reading the report slowly and carefully, I considered two choices. One was to make a thorough study of the problem on my own and then write a detailed report. The second choice was to present as quickly as possible a reasonable approach to the problem, one that could start, with almost immediate steps, to attack crime in America. My ideas would, of course, run parallel to, or be in conjunction with the Eisenhower Report, which advocated the curing of slum conditions. This was a necessary but very costly program and one that would require at least a generation of reeducation and reconstruction. It had to be done, but I felt we did not have the time to wait a generation or so, while crime mounted.

After consultations with child psychiatrists in New York and Boston, and finding out what methods of early detection of criminal tendencies existed, nine days after my meeting with the President, I wrote the following fateful (as it proved) *provisional, confidential report,* in order to keep the President's interest alive. Since my plan was, a few months later, "leaked" to the press in a distorted version, I do not hesitate now to present it in its original form.

On December 9, 1969, I sent my report directly to the President:

This is a provisional report on the "COMMISSION STATEMENT ON VIOLENT CRIME" under the chairmanship of Dr. Milton S. Eisenhower.

The report is an excellent and explicit presentation of the causes of crime, the disturbing national rate of increase of violence, the seeds of violence, the frequency of violence among the age group of fifteen to twenty-four, the breeding ground of violence in the predominantly black ghetto slums and other pertinent data.

The report makes valuable recommendations in regard to the *prevention of violent crime* like increased, interracial police patrol, low-cost treatment of addicts, restrictive licensing of concealable hand guns, etc.

The Eisenhower Report concludes that "violent crimes are chiefly a problem of the cities of the nation, and that violent crimes are committed mainly by the young, poor, male inhabitants of the ghetto slum."

The report states further that "in the slums increasingly powerful forces are generating rising levels of violent crime which, unless checked, threaten to turn our cities into defensive, fearful societies." And finally: "An improved criminal justice is required to contain the growth of violent crime, but *only progress toward urban reconstruction can reduce* the strength *of the crime-causing forces* in the inner city and thus reverse the direction of present crime trends."

THE PLAN

While the basic value of the Eisenhower Report in regard to the Profile, the Causes and the Rise in Violent crime is beyond question, I do not believe that *"only"* progress toward reconstruction can reduce . . . and reverse the . . . crime trend. No doubt there is a desperate need for Urban reconstruction, but I would like to suggest another, direct, immediate and what I believe effective way of attacking the problem at its very origin, by focusing on the "criminal mind" of the child. The aim is to *prevent* a child with a delinquent character structure from being allowed to grow into a full-fledged teen-age delinquent or adult criminal. The longer a child is permitted to live with his criminal tendencies in a criminally charged environment, the harder becomes the core of his antisocial conditioning and the wider grows the gap between his disturbed, angry inner world and the society at large. By the same token, the sooner this destructive trend is recognized and reversed, the better the chances for the prevention of crime and the cure of the individual. The rationale presented here is similar to that practiced in medicine which is not to wait for an epidemic to break out, but to prevent the possibility of an epidemic from destroying a population. In medicine we seek preventive measures: We vaccinate, we quarantine, we immunize. There are already studies in existence which indicate that future delinquent tendencies can be predicted in nine out of ten cases, even at the age of six. This means that a drive to violence and crime can be discovered as early as the age of six. Rorschach and other projective tests of the eight-to-ten year old children can show evidence of homicidal trends. (We may remember Lee Harvey Oswald, the killer of President Kennedy, who at the age of eleven showed violent tendencies and whose mother was strongly advised to have the boy treated at Bellevue Hospital in New York. The mother, a nurse, refused and moved to Texas. Treatment could have prevented that tragedy.)

The Eisenhower Report states that "violent crime is

found in all parts of the country . . ." and that "crime rates are not racial, but the result of conditions of life in the ghetto slums." It also states that poor, uneducated individuals with few employment skills are more likely to commit serious violence than persons higher on the socioeconomic ladder.

The child that is exposed to the "pernicious influence of the slums" emulates the destructive emotional behavior around him. Consequently, the child learns young to be unhappy, discontent, rebellious and angry, or he can become depressed and hopeless. The child watches violence in the streets and watches violence on television. The environmental forces shape the personality of the child. He reacts to all the stimuli to which he is exposed, be they physical or emotional. Depending on the rigidity of parental care or the absence of it, overdiscipline or the lack of it, the deprivation of affection, neglect, disinterest in his development, feelings of rejection, or injustice or believing to be a burden to his family, he forms specific patterns of behavior. These traumatic experiences, causing him despair and a sense of failure, influence deeply the development of the young child's mind. They produce compensating reactions:

1. One type of child may develop a drive to power in order to "show them" (*them* meaning the parents or their substitute—society at large).

2. Another type, violent, raging turns his aggression outward, determined to seek vengeance on those he believes have forced him to a life of disadvantage and with little opportunity. As he grows older he becomes more determined to take by force what he feels life has denied him. We now have the future criminal who commits acts of robbery, sex crimes, assault, homicide and other antisocial acts.

3. Still another type gives up the battle and by turning

his churning anger and aggression against himself, becomes weak and overly submissive. He seeks escape and he becomes an addictive personality (alcohol, drug addiction).

4. The child whose spirit has been broken by an unrelenting harshness of his parents, or by neglect escapes into fantasy and we then have the mentally sick, the vegetating individual who represents a heavy burden on society. This type has a tendency to commit suicide (a turning of aggression inward), but can, under certain provocation rise to action and commit murder, and then suicide.

SUGGESTION FOR THE PREVENTION OF CRIME

1. The Government should move to improve the already existing day-care centers of the three-to five-year-old children and increase their number and quality, especially in the slum areas. By sublimating the aggressive energies of these young children toward pleasurable and constructive pursuits (like playing games, dancing, singing, exercises etc. under qualified and caring supervision), they can learn to develop healthy habits and overcome, at least partially, feelings of rejection and unhappiness. This may prevent a considerable number of children from becoming delinquents.

2. The government should have mass testing done on all six-to eight-year-old children. There are various tests (Rorschach, the Sheldon-Glueck Prediction Test and others: the author needs to have more research done in this area in order to determine the most effective and least costly method). These tests could help to detect the children who have violent and homicidal tendencies. Corrective treatment should begin at that time.

3. There should be special "After School Programs" for the young children under the guidance of counselors, possibly graduate psychology students—in order to re-

duce costs—for all those tested children who show delinquent tendencies. There will be available many intellectually superior young people with ideals and enthusiasm who would be eager to serve a great cause and to serve their country.

The after school programs should be improved and extended for the eight- to twelve-year-old children. For these and the older boys up to sixteen there should be added educational courses and activities to channel aggression and to teach them skills. The more disturbed, the more angry, rebellious, undisciplined and disruptive boys, especially those who show criminal tendencies, in addition to treatment should be given aptitude tests to determine areas of interest which should be carefully encouraged. There are Pavlovian methods which I have seen used effectively in the Soviet Union.

[And now comes the fatal paragraph:]

For the severely disturbed, the young *hard-core criminal*, there may be a need to establish camps with group activities under the guidance of counselors, under the supervision of psychologists, who have empathy (most important) but also firmness and who can earn the respect of difficult adolescents. By governing themselves, these boys would learn the meaning of responsibility and of adjusting to life in a group.

4. In order to execute a crash program, the government should extend loans to a large number of students to enable them to become psychologists or psychiatrists. These graduate students could repay the government by devoting time to help rehabilitate America's endangered youth and at the same time restore a sense of security to the frightened communities. Also, to make available quickly the manpower necessary to put such a vast program into operation and to reduce the costs for these projects, "psycho-medics" could be trained within a few

months to assist the psychologists, psychiatrists and social workers, a process that would be similar to the medics in the army in case of war.

Disturbed, antisocial and violent adolescents need a kind, firm, male figure they can respect and emulate at a time when they make their final adjustment to an adult life. This process of *Identification* is of utmost importance and its need has been recognized and stated in the Eisenhower Report.

The above-stated suggestions for a mass program of Prevention of Crime could begin almost immediately, without the need to wait for the slow, agonizing process of improving living conditions and the elimination of hunger. With the aid of the National Institute for Mental Health, the local chapters of mental health all over the country, and the psychiatric clinics in Urban America, a wide scale program could be set into motion as soon as approved and funded. [Here my report ends.]

In the meanwhile, I continued my search for effective means to detect as early as possible tendencies to delinquent behavior in children, consulting not only the medical literature but talking with more child psychologists, psychiatrists and psychoanalysts.

It had been a stroke of good fortune that I mentioned my quest for effective means to detect delinquent behavior in children to a friend, Dr. Robert S. Hartman, professor of philosophy at the National University of Mexico and the University of Tennessee. He told me that his work in the special field of axiology (the theory of values) for more than twenty years had led him several years before to the development of a method that could, without error, determine tendencies to delinquency or other antisocial behavior.

"*Mensch,*" he said in a Berlin-German accent, "you have come to the right place."

He then described his *Hartman Value Profile*. He felt that life for all of us could be reduced to three realms: the personal or spiritual, the practical or situational, and the theoretical or normative.

The personal or spiritual refers to the intrinsic nature, the essential and the authentic, the unique equality or "unsubstitutableness" of a person.

The practical or situational refers to what happens in everyday life, all the experiences we capture through our senses—the concrete, tangible and material things that we classify in time and space.

The theoretical or normative is comprised of the world of ideas and abstractions created by the human mind—concepts, rules and theories, norms and systems that claim both external and internal validity. They put into play our sense of order and perfection, both in the directing of others and the disciplining of ourselves (our "moral sense," so to speak).

Each of these three realms is determined by specific values that enable us to judge and manage it. The values for the first realm are called "intrinsic," for the second, "extrinsic," and for the third, "systemic."

These values correspond to distinct internal capacities, which we must develop throughout our lives. To the degree that we develop them, we will live in harmony with the world and with ourselves. To the degree we do not, we shall live under tension, for either the internal world or the external world, or both, will appear confused and meaningless.

The scores obtained in the test devised by Dr. Hartman to judge a person's values, and hence his behavior, correspond to the capacities he listed. In the following description of the test, they are qualified in descending order, as excellent, very good, good, fair, poor, very poor, extremely poor.

THE HARTMAN TEST

In Dr. Hartman's words: "The Hartman Value Profile is a test of the human personality. It is based not on psychology but on axiology (theory of value): it measures the value capacity of people. The capacity to make value judgments is a special talent which is similar to the musical talent, consisting of the intellectual organization of feeling components. For this reason, the test gives indications both of the existence of emotional problems and of intellectual capacity. Various validation procedures have confirmed the accuracy of the test. Factorial analysis has confirmed its logical structure.

The test applies methods of mathematical logic to the measurement of value judgments. It is completely quantified and can be applied to any kind of group, showing both the value pattern of the group itself and the value pattern of the individuals of the group. An individual of an abnormal pattern, that is, one with *a tendency to commit crime or violence diverted against others or himself, sticks out like a sore thumb* (italics mine) from the normal pattern of the group. Groups themselves can be compared as to their patterns, which means that a violent group can be distinguished from a nonviolent or less violent one.* The test is fully computerized. Every test takes a computer about 10 seconds to calculate, and the printing of the results takes about 1 minute. (The cost of each test is estimated to be 50 cents a test.) The test is self-administering. It takes between ten and twenty minutes, which is a fraction of the time used by other tests. Being completely quantified, it can be applied to any number of people in groups. The results of any number of groups can be averaged, so that a value pattern of a total population, of a country, a city etc., can be produced on one single sheet."

*Because of its mathematical structure, there are no two tests alike. Theoretically the possibilities of different individual readings go into the quadrillion range, an inconceivable concept considering the world population [footnote mine]

The Hartman Value Profile

Part I

The procedure of the Hartman Value Profile is to order 18 words or phrases in such a way as to list "1" the phrase that represents the highest value to the person concerned, "2" is the second best, "18" the worst.

Do not judge the expressions by the importance but only *by the goodness or badness* of their content.

A good meal
A technical improvement
Nonsense
A fine
A rubbish heap
A devoted scientist
Blow up an airliner in flight
Burn a heretic at the stake
A short circuit
"By this ring I thee wed"
A baby
Torture a person in a concentration camp
Love of nature
A madman
An assembly line
Slavery
A mathematical genius
A uniform

Part II

Write the number "1" on the line in front of the quotation you *agree* with most—that is, the one which has the highest (most) value in your life.

Write the number "2" in front of the quotation with which you agree next most (second most).

Number *all* of the quotations in the same way, to show

the order of their respective values to you. Use a *different* number for each of the 18 quotations (3, 4, 5 and so on). The number "18" should be in front of the quotation that has the lowest (least) value in your own life—that is, the one you *disagree* with most.

Decide quickly how you feel about each of the quotations. There is no time limit, but most people are able to complete numbering all the quotations in about ten to twelve minutes.

"I like my work—It does me good."

"The universe is a remarkably harmonious system."

"The world makes little sense to me."

"No matter how hard I work, I shall always feel frustrated."

"My working conditions are poor and ruin my work."

"I feel at home in the world."

"I hate my work."

"My life is messing up the world."

"My work contributes nothing to the world."

"My work brings out the best in me."

"I enjoy being myself."

"I curse the day I was born."

"I love my work."

"The lack of meaning to the universe disturbs me."

"The more I understand my place in the world, the better I get in my work."

"My work makes me unhappy."

"I love the beauty of the world."

"My work adds to the beauty and harmony of the world."

After collecting further data and information, on January 9, 1970, I sent another letter to the President, that read:

In my search to find more effective and inexpensive methods of how to remedy the problem of "Violent Crime," I have met with a professor of philosophy at the National University of Mexico who had developed a new "Axiological testing" (the measurement of values). According to the Social Security Administration of the Mexican government, this testing method of personality features has proven to be so effective that this agency, after having used it for several months, is now going to make a psychological census of the whole country, in their words: "like a thorax census to detect tuberculosis."

This surprising and revolutionary undertaking by a government has a striking resemblance to my own suggestion to have the total young population in this country tested, proving that new needs require new steps of action. The new test, I had it done on myself, has easy applicability, it is swift (10 minutes with the use of computers) and it can be applied to a large number of populations. Its cost is estimated to be 50 cents.

Since I had been assured that a future delinquent "sticks out like a sore thumb," I am now comparing the "axiological" method with those used in the United States in order to determine the most reliable and most economical method, possibly a combination of tests for different age groups (of course it could be later on used for the older population as well).

The program, as outlined in my preliminary report, is in no way meant to replace the Eisenhower Committee's recommendation but ought to be looked upon as an augmentation of it. The approximate cost of my program will be a fraction of the Eisenhower Committee's estimated 20 billion dollars.

It is my hope, Mr. President, that you may give my project your kind consideration and since Mexico seems to be on the move now, put our country in the forefront of not only curing a cancerous social illness, that of violent crime, but to pave the way of preventing other debilitating problems as well, such as the high rate of drug addiction, of dropouts, of unwillingness to work and of aimless rebellion.

The worldwide importance of a government attack on so much misdirected human aggression on a grass-roots level is self-evident and could indeed amount to another "giant step for mankind" if I may borrow the beautiful words of our astronauts.

With warm personal regards, etc.

After further studies, I sent still another letter to the President, on March 10, 1970:

Today I write to you as a friend rather than as a concerned citizen writing to his President. Your suggestion on December 1, 1969 to submit to you my opinion on how our crisis of violent crime could be solved, by means other than an increase in law-enforcing agencies, has led me to a further study of the problem. The only solution that holds out any promise of success lies, I believe, in *the earliest possible detection of future delinquency* and which can be done successfully (and will show up emotional disturbances as well) at the age of 6-10.

The Harvard people who developed the Glueck Prediction Test responded with enthusiasm and willingness to cooperate with me, although I avoided mentioning our meeting and your personal interest in this subject. Through them I learned that the prediction test will be done soon in the Phillippine Islands and I reported to you already that the Mexican government is conducting a census of the whole population by applying the Hartman Value Test. Both Mexico and the Philippine Islands are poor countries, and I feel that the United States, the richest country in the world, must not fall behind.

It is for this reason that I write to you for should there be little likelihood that—because of priorities or other reasons—you could not consider accepting a plan of early detection and treatment of future delinquents at this time, I would like to set up a pilot project myself, on a modest scale of course, to prove the validity and worth of detecting future delinquency and of treating at an early age violent tendencies by channeling these complex aggressive drives into creative pursuits.

However, before moving toward such a goal, I would like to ask your permission to use the basic material which I have submitted to you and also, I would like, if I may, to refer to your personal interest in this problem because you deserve the credit for having directed my attention from the wider aspects of an Agency of the Exploration of Peace toward this related, but more detailed, social illness.

The President responded positively, I am pleased to say, by sending, on March 23, 1970, his counselor, Dr. Daniel P. Moynihan, a Harvard professor, later Ambassador to India, to see me. A man of polished affability, he did not inquire about the test, but merely remarked that the President "just wanted me to talk to you." We spoke for quite a bit longer than an hour and parted after agreeing to hold a joint meeting with Dr. Stanley Yolles, director of the National Institute of Mental Health.

Then on April 3, I received the following letter from Dr. Moynihan:

THE WHITE HOUSE
Washington

April 3, 1970

Dear Dr. Hutschnecker:

That was an extraordinarily interesting conversation. I have related it to Stan Yolles, Director of the National Institute of Mental Health, who is doing some staff work for us. I should be hearing from him in a very short while and then you will be hearing from me.

Sincerely,

Daniel P. Moynihan
Counselor to the President

Three days later, April 6, proved to be one of the most extraordinary and upsetting days in my life. It began at 7 A. M. with an overseas phone call announcing, "This is the BBC in London. Are you Dr. Hutschnecker? We want to talk to you about your idea of testing children. We here are very excited about it. We want to learn more." One voice was that of a man, the other that of a woman.

I was stunned. I said, "That was supposed to be a confidential report."

The voice from overseas continued, "It was sent to us." Sensing my doubt, he began to quote from what was unquestionably the original report. Then he added, "Perhaps it was leaked." But as he spoke, he seemed to convey a tone of happiness at the fact that "your Government, thank God," was taking steps to combat violence and crime.

Indeed, in a letter written to me on May 21, 1974—four years later—by the Secretary of Health, Education and Welfare, Caspar W. Weinberger, I learned that "—No material of any kind related to your proposal was released from this Department and we have no way of knowing the source of the material which did appear in the press on April 6, 1970." So, my report was leaked.

There were London calls again within the hour, this time from several newspapers, all seemingly excited and pleased and then there followed phone calls from various American newspapers and syndicates, including United Press International, and radio and television networks, all asking about the report and the "tests." There was also a call from West German television and, ominously, one from the African press. This latter call was very significant in the light of what followed.

There was no question that my report was leaked with a malevolent intent, as evidenced by an uproar in the press with bitter attacks on me and cynical remarks and ridicule of my supposed plan to set up "detention camps" for delinquent six- to eight-year-old children. I was dumbfounded and completely in the dark about the allegation that I was discriminating against the blacks in advocating the establishment of "detention camps." Since crime was chiefly a problem of the black ghettos, it was assumed that the plan was aimed at discrediting the black population, a preposterous distortion of fact. The plan *must* have been circulated in its falsified version.

Perturbed by this sudden turn of events and concerned about its possible negative effect on the President, I wrote to Moynihan, who replied promptly on April 8, 1970:

THE WHITE HOUSE

. . . Being all too familiar with documents finding their way into the newspapers, I can well sympathize with your concern. Please be assured that from our point of view there is no problem whatever.

I expect that Dr. Yolles of the National Institute of Mental Health, will be in touch with you about the Hartman test and related matters shortly.

Sincerely

Daniel P. Moynihan
Counselor to the President

No call ever came from Dr. Yolles. I learned later that Dr. Yolles had resigned on June 2, 1970, after unsuccessfully battling against drastic cuts in funds for mental health.

I started to get some clues as to what had happened when a story appeared in the *New York Post* by Robert C. Maynard, datelined Washington, which read:

A proposal to the White House that all of this country's 6-year-old children be psychologically tested for their criminal potential has been deemed unfeasible by the Dept. of Health, Education and Welfare.

HEW said its view of the proposal, made to President Nixon last December by Dr. Arnold Hutschnecker of New York, is "most unfavorable."

Rep. Gallagher (D.-N.J.) was informed of the HEW rejection of the proposal yesterday by a White House official. Gallagher had informed HEW and the White House of his intention to hold hearings on the Hutschnecker proposal.

White House staff members reached last night would only confirm the report that HEW has rejected the proposal sent on Dec. 30 to the agency by John Ehrlichman, the President's assistant for domestic affairs.

Details of the rejection were also unavailable from HEW, which was asked by Ehrlichman to advise the White House on the "advisability of setting up pilot projects embodying some of these approaches."

The approach of Hutschnecker to the problem of urban crime is to test all children between the ages of 6 and 8. Those children found by the tests to have a potential for crime would be treated through a massive psychological and psychiatric program.

"The hard core," Hutschnecker said, "should be confined to camps where they would learn more socially acceptable behavior patterns."

Psychiatrists and psychologists have denounced the plan as "ridiculous," "ignorant" and "Frankenstein fiction." HEW had remained silent for the 10 days since Hutschnecker's memorandum to President Nixon came to light.

I did not know until I received the above mentioned letter of May 1974 from Secretary Weinberger, to which was attached the official "briefing letter" of HEW to John D. Ehrlichman, that stated ". . . some of Dr. Hutschnecker's suggestions are indeed feasible and worthy of being tested through pilot projects . . ." which makes me assume that an influential faction of a then restive HEW—under an ineffective Secretary Finch—must have given out, unofficially, the above-printed derogatory opinions as well as a distorted version of my report. Mr. Weinberger's letter to me did not mention rejection of my plan.

Then Jack Nelson of the Washington Bureau of the *Los Angeles Times* called to ask if he could come to New York and interview me, and though I had not been granting interviews, I thought perhaps if I saw him I might learn more about how my plan had come to be distorted. He told me, and stated this in the story which appeared in the *Los Angeles Times* on May 3, 1970, that HEW did not officially release the report but copies of it were "leaked to the press earlier this month by someone who identified himself as 'an interested black HEW employee.' " He said further, "Also leaked was a copy of a

Dec. 30, 1969 memo from presidential aide John D. Ehrlichman to HEW Secretary Robert H. Finch saying, 'The President asks your opinion as to the advisability of setting up a pilot project embodying some of these approaches.' "

While in my office, Mr. Nelson pulled out of his pocket a small piece of white paper on which was written the following:

> This memo hasn't reached the press as of today—April 3; it smacks of Nazi Germany. We haven't determined if Finch has replied to it yet, but others have copies of this memo in their hands and we expect it to break by the end of this week.
>
> *Do what you can with it.* [italics mine]
> An interested black HEW employee.

The story written by Mr. Nelson had as headline:

EX-NIXON DOCTOR UPSET
OVER REACTION TO PLAN
Hutschnecker Shocked at Row Created by Idea
of Mass Testing for Crime Tendencies

In his story Mr. Nelson quoted me as saying, "I didn't know what had hit me," and reported I called the news reports of my plan "close to a smear."

Mr. Nelson sent me a letter on May 4, enclosing a Xerox copy of the "memo" quoted above. He said, "The note was taken down on the phone from a guy who received it and a copy of your report along with a copy of Ehrlichman's memo."

As I said, the *New York Post*'s Robert C. Maynard had reported on testing six- to eight-year-old children and confining the "hard core" to camps, and that point was emphasized by Secretary Finch, when he appeared on the David Frost show one day after I had. He stated he had rejected the Hutschnecker report because "We don't want to send six- to eight-year-old children to camps." Nowhere in my report was there any reference to sending six- to eight-year-old children to camps. This then was a portentous misstatement of fact. Because of the hostile response I encountered, I wrote a letter to Secretary Finch on May 23 (with a P.S. "I am sending a copy to President Nixon") asking him to retract his false statement. He replied saying he regretted his misinterpretation, but by that time he himself had resigned as Secretary of HEW.

As to the plan itself, it may not have been the best or most adequate—improvements could have been made, no doubt—but at the time I wrote it I was not aware of a better one. Moreover, in the light of the spreading crime rate, I find the way the plan was killed unfortunate. And what was most unfortunate was that from that time on my plan has been judged on the basis of a viciously distorted version.

I heard from Dr. Hartman, writing from Knoxville, Tennessee, saying:

> The news I heard on the radio was a distortion of our plan . . . As far as I understand it . . . there was to be first a detection of unstable and potentially violent and/or criminal youngsters with, secondly, a psychotherapy program. There was nothing of detention of hard-core youngsters for, naturally, if a person has not committed any crime he cannot be called a hard-core criminal. Rather, this was to be a prophylactic program. Like chest X rays, with the therapy indicated by the test(s). No test can predict the actual behavior of a person, that is, whether if there are criminal tendencies, he would actually become a criminal. But it can show the need for therapy. My test very clearly shows the instability of a person as well as the nature of that instability and therefore the course that a therapy should take. Thus, as one of the enclosed sheets says at the end, the aggressive

drives of the young people could be directed into creative channels. This is all the program can and should do, and this is its value. Somehow on the way it has gotten the wrong slant. Thus, what Finch objected to is not what we had in mind at all.

Incidentally, how close the plan had come to being implemented could be seen from an incidental inquiry sent to me by Dr. Peter R. Breggin, director of the Center for the Study of Psychiatry, Washington, D.C., on January 29, 1974. Dr. Breggin, a psychiatrist who does not know me personally, stated in a letter, "I have heard a considerable amount about your proposal on the prevention of delinquency and I am told that it was considered for possible funding on very high levels. Can you tell me how far you got with it before the publicity interfered with it?"

Dr. Breggin, incidentally, is a leader in the movement to halt the growing practice of psychosurgery on criminals and violently disturbed mentally ill persons. I, too, am against this. I think psychosurgery is itself a subtle example of violence by physicians, under the guise of healing. Neuropsychiatrists who indulge in indiscriminate psychosurgery, operating on the brain and destroying vital memory connections, claiming this reduces the "violence" in a man, do not understand that they are taking away from a man his full capacity to think, to remember, to feel, reducing him, in many cases, to a vegetable. Who gives these scientists the right to mutilate other men, to violate their human rights? If we want to decrease the violence in a man, it should be done in the spirit of the physician, the healer of the mind. The aim of a physician loyal to his profession is to help the wretched man ease his violence, first by medication, then by physical work and then by therapy so that he can understand his fantasies, his repressed motives and distorted needs, and no longer needs to be violent.

As to my plan, the press had been quick to pick up its distorted version, dramatically headlining it as the idea of the "President's former doctor" who was recommending the establishment of "detention camps" or, as some papers put it, "concentration camps." We live in an era of computers and labels and once a falsity about a person has been fed into the computer it becomes part of his personality, his way of thinking and of his record, as far as the public is concerned.

The stigma started by Finch, perhaps without his knowledge, and his department of HEW was sticking effectively, as evidenced in a letter written to a lay inquirer on November 13, 1970 by a research specialist, Division of Research and Evaluation, Children's Bureau of HEW, Office of the Secretary. Perpetuating the falsehood, it stated that "as a voluntary public service he [Dr. Hutschnecker] sent a proposal to the White House. . . . This proposal suggested that *young boys* who are potential criminals should be identified through the use of the Glueck's prediction scales and/or the Rorschach and they should then be sent to *special training camps* where treatment and education would be used to prevent their development into criminals."

What a clever mixture of fact and evil fiction! It went on to say that scientists had rejected the proposal because it would have required a "police state."

I felt it necessary to write the new secretary, Elliot Richardson—to ask his help in preventing further dissemination of a falsified plan.

July 21, 1971

PERSONAL
CONFIDENTIAL
Dear Mr. Secretary:

It has come to my attention that the "Division of Research and Evaluation, Children's Bureau" of your department has given out information about myself and "A

Plan for Prevention of Violent Crime" that is so grossly distorted that I am obliged to ask you kindly to have the points of misinformation corrected.

In order to facilitate the necessary changes, I enclose a copy of my original report to President Nixon as well as an editorial I had written at the request of *The New York Times* and in which I attempted to set the record straight. Yet, in spite of my efforts, your department, so it seems continues to give out information that is not only incorrect but defamatory. I have in my possession an original letter written to an inquirer by the above mentioned division which contains some of the points that are untrue and contrary to the facts.

Your department's letter reads:

1. " . . . As a voluntary public service, he (I) sent a proposal to the White House . . . etc." This is incorrect. The fact is that at a meeting I had with President Nixon at the White House, he asked me to let him know my opinion on the Milton Eisenhower Crime Report. My above mentioned proposal, later on leaked out by HEW, was my reply and is contained in the enclosed copy.

2. ". . . young boys who are potential criminals . . . should then be sent to special training camps. . . ." It is this part that is not only fraudulent but that has inflamed the news media to a point of referring to my proposal as having suggested to the President to send six-year-old children to training or "concentration camps." My original report does *not* contain any such statement. The only reference to "camps" in my report is on page 4 in its last paragraph: "For the severely disturbed young hard core criminal, there may be a need to establish camps. . . . etc." The emphasis is on "hard-core criminal," that is, adolescents who *have already committed a crime or crimes*. Therefore, the two other statements in the HEW letter, the one: " . . . we cannot put such individuals in special

treatment camps *before* they have committed any crime" and the reference to a *"police state"* are baseless and irrelevant assumptions aimed at giving my original report a destructive and prejudicial slant.

As to the opinion of your scientists and their recommendation for a rejection of my plan I have no quarrel with it, though their points of view may be wide open for a critical debate. In a scientific paper I read before the National Convention of the American Society of Psychoanalytic Physicians, I have questioned their objectivity and corrected points of doubt. If you wish to continue to give out the information that my proposal to President Nixon has no scientific merit, that is your privilege, and it has nothing to do with the purpose of this letter to you.

The purpose of my letter and my concern is to see the perpetuation of the false information by HEW being stopped. It is therefore, Mr. Secretary, that I appeal to you to have this slanderous distortion of fact corrected as soon as possible. I am aware, of course, that all of this happened before you, Mr. Secretary, became the head of HEW, but now since you are its official head, I have no choice but to turn to you for help to clear up a regrettable situation as it has caused me enormous harm. Would you be good enough to let me know what steps you plan to take?

Respectfully,
Arnold A. Hutschnecker, M.D.

The Honorable Elliot L. Richardson
Secretary of the Department of
Health, Education and Welfare
Washington, D.C.

Secretary Richardson sent a letter of apology and said he would correct the facts. But as so often happens, the press "forgets" corrections when a sensational charge has been made.

I summed up my impression of the whole matter in a letter I wrote Herb Klein, Director of Communication of the Executive Branch, on October 8, 1970. I said that when the report was leaked in the HEW memo I had found it incredible "that a government agency, the Department of Health, Education and Welfare would not only allow to leak out a confidential report to the President but issue a distorted and vilifying statement to the press. It was clear to me, from the very beginning, that the attacks against me were concealed attacks against the President." Or, I thought, it was meant to steer the President away from a political matter which the White House staff did not approve but did not dare to oppose openly.

The response to my original report by the news media had been overwhelming, yet I could detect a division of opinion between theorists and those in the field, between the so-called "experts" working with statistics, and those in direct contact with people and particularly with children in trouble. The first group questioned my plan, the second supported it.

The majority of those who supported my proposal were judges, probation officers, guidance counselors, psychiatrists, all in favor of seeing something done about crime. Dr. C.D. Marshall, psychiatrist of the Rutland Mental Health Service in Vermont called it "a glow of hope for this country." Judge Nanette Dembitz of the Family Court of the State of New York referred to my plan in the following words:

His present explanation of his position is confirmed by studies of juvenile delinquency and by firsthand daily experience with juvenile delinquents in the Family Court. Interest by a presidential adviser in securing aid for neglected and delinquency prone children should not be hooted down for political reasons nor because of one's disagreement with other presidential policies.

Dr. Louise Bates Ames, associate director of the Gesell Institute of Child Development in New Haven, declared, "We've got to start trying to predict delinquent behavior. *This is one of the few chances we have to prevent it.*" (Italics mine.)

Another judge, Donald M. Habermehl, Judge of Probate, Alpena County, Alpena, Michigan, wrote in a letter to *Time* appearing May 18, 1970, that

> Dr. Hutschnecker's suggestion has a lot more merit than you ascribed to it. It wouldn't label these children pre-delinquent; it would only advise us that these are children in trouble, for these children are as likely to develop neuroses or psychoses as they are to exhibit criminal tendencies. The idea is not new. . . . Awareness of the emotional problems of the children in our court and attempts to help them have certainly shown results. . . . To recognize and treat these rejected, hostile children is our only real hope of reducing our skyrocketing crime rate.

A school psychologist, Victor M. Zike, of Perry, Iowa, wrote that he thought my idea had much merit and that "it is too bad that people in the powerful organizations and those in position to promote new ideas are so steeped in the traditional method of remediation that they can't understand the preventive approach to children's problems." He said that he had worked with more than four thousand preschool children over the years and with individual parent conferences and found

> a lack of understanding and absence of awareness of what is really involved in parent-child relationships. There is a

serious need for ways of creating parent awareness of parental responsibility. Without a grass-roots approach to the early needs of youngsters plus the predictiveness of those who need help, we can only expect to reap the results as we see them today and more so as time goes by. . . . It would be a wonderful experience if we could get the medical profession, the educators and other interested educational areas aware of what could be done if we would zero in on the problems and make a concerted attack.

One day in September 1970, Harrison Salisbury of *The New York Times*, a Pulitzer Prize winner, called me to suggest a meeting. He came to see me, an attractive, charming man with a keen sense of perception. He told me that there must have been more to the story of my proposal for testing children than appeared in the newspapers.

He also told me that *The New York Times* planned to invite outsiders, scientists, statesmen, writers, people who had something to say about current events, to contribute to the paper on a new Op-Ed page. Would I write my story? I did. It was published on October 2, 1970, one of the first articles on that new page, appearing under the title, "A Plea for Experiment."

I explained in a condensed form my original ideas. I also quoted Dr. John B. Train, president of the American Society of Psychoanalytic Physicians who said at a scientific meeting,

I take my hat off to Dr. Hutschnecker, who single-handedly went to Washington, stuck his neck out and got hurt. What have we psychiatrists done to help him? Has anyone of us stood up in support? No, we did nothing. The time has come for us to organize so that our voice can be heard in our urgent need to help the children in trouble and to work for the prevention of crime.

I ended the column by saying, "Officially the President has not as yet rejected my plan." Little did I know about the intrigue and power struggle within the White House staff and that, once condemned, any effort on my part was futile.

Whether it is my plan or another plan, whether the Hartman Test is the best test or whether there is a better one, I leave open to debate. But debate must be only an introduction to action. In an emergency doctors do not stop to quarrel about the value of a theory. They act, because human lives are at stake and because physicians are healers and doers and not dreamers or talkers. If at the present time there is no proposal of greater value than the one I presented, then it either ought to be supported or a better plan substituted. By the same token, if there is no test of greater accuracy than the Hartman Profile, then we should begin with that test. Begin we must, and on our way we can add improvements.

Some of the press reaction was unbelievable. One newspaper, the *Phoenix* (unknown to me), on April 30, 1970, printed a long article full of distortions as evidenced by its headlines: "A Little Shrink Shall Lead Them . . . President Gives OK to Pal's Plans to Label Black Youth 'Genetic' Crooks." And *The New Yorker,* on the opening page of "The Talk of the Town" on October 10, 1970, wrote of my "Op-Ed" article:

Last week, when we turned to the *Times'* new page for guest columnists, we expected to find the usual parade of presidential official advisers and ex-advisers, but instead we found, to our considerable dismay, two modern-day witch doctors performing a dance of death on the printed page. Actually, both of these men, if they are not official advisers to the President, at least advise him informally, and each was described by the *Times* as a "friend" of the President. One, Dr. Arnold Hutschnecker, is the President's former physician and the author of some plans for controlling crime, and the other, Dr. Billy Graham, is often mentioned as the President's spiritual mentor. That is to say, these are men who have looked after the body and soul of our President.

It went on to describe me as "a theorist whose field is the kind of thought control and behavior control that in modern times has had its fullest expression in the totalitarian states of Hitler's Germany and Stalin's Russia." Then it said that when my plan was leaked to the press it received unfavorable reactions which "seemed enough to consign it to the dustbin, where it clearly belonged." Evidently, a writer's mind went berserk.

The unusually stormy reaction to my plan invites a postmortem. It seems the fatal word, the one HEW used as a chief weapon of assault to kill the proposal, was the word "camp." To me, camp meant a pleasurable place filled with happy children, for I spent my first summer in America as a doctor in a children's summer camp.

My aim was *not* any uprooting of children, but rather the early detection of disturbed children and early treatment so they could function and learn to communicate with other children, regardless of how unfortunate their environment had been. By attempting to turn troubled children into happier children, I hoped to prevent them from growing up into angry and violent adults and criminals. Therefore nothing could have been more contrary to my intention than the allegation that I wanted to send six- to eight-year-old children to camps.

Reading over material I have collected, I am amused by my stubbornness as I note that on May 12, 1971, I sent another letter to President Nixon about the plan. I presented to him a renewal plea to consider the formation of an agency for the study of the dynamics of human aggression and for the prevention of war. I said that "our society's new message is that 'as men of science we must unite internationally (to assist political leaders) so that greater energies can be applied to constructive concepts assuring man's healthy survival.' "

I pointed out

History has taught us that military or political solutions, though they have their place, have nevertheless proven not to secure a lasting peace. Scientists on the other hand, when working as a team, have landed men on the moon. Scientists working as a team can teach people how to think and feel peacefully and how to channel, by sublimation, their hostile, aggressive forces into creative and constructive pursuits, for their own happiness and for the good of the country and the world.

I concluded the letter:

I realize that the innovation of any new idea, similar to the one I outlined, might be attacked as being overly idealistic and not practical. This has been the case throughout history. Yet Pestalozzi's one-room school has grown into universally accepted school systems all over the civilized world. What we need is a beginning and you, Mr. President, have the power to begin.

But then another incident occurred that only proved to me how hate begets hate and how quickly, and how far the ripples of hate reach. Once a man has been labeled a crackpot or antiblack, as was the case here, many people who have an ax to grind feel free to take a potshot. During the first week in November, 1972, a few days before the election, I received a call from R. Peter Straus, the president of radio station WMCA, in New York. He asked my opinion about a release he had just received, written on McGovern-Shriver stationery. It was headed "McGovern for President." The release was supposed to be a reprint of an article that appeared October 18, 1972 in *Psychiatric News*, the weekly newspaper of the American Psychiatric Association in Washington, D.C.

The article was headlined "PHYSICIAN CLAIMS JEWS ARE SCHIZO CARRIERS." The story reported that a paper I was supposed to have prepared for the *American Journal of Psychiatry* gave evidence that "Jews are carriers of schizophrenia." It stated that in a study entitled "Mental Illness: The Jewish Disease," I had said that "although all Jews are not mentally ill, mental illness is highly contagious and Jews are the principle sources of infection." It quoted me as saying that "every Jew is born with the seeds of schizophrenia and it is this fact that accounts for the worldwide persecution of Jews. . . . The world would be more compassionate toward the Jews if it was generally realized that Jews are not responsible for their condition." There followed more such incredible anti-Semitic statements.

I told Mr. Straus of WMCA that this was an incredible and vicious falsehood. I decided to ignore this unfortunate fabrication. When, one and a half years later, Staten Island Community College printed the release as authentic, it began to sound like one of Segretti's "dirty tricks." But, at my request, they retracted it after calling Robert Robinson, editor of *Psychiatric News* who called the article "an unfortunate hoax" some person or group had composed. He said there had not been an issue of *Psychiatric News* on October 18, 1972, and that under his editorship it would never publish an article of this type. He commented that the person or group responsible for the "hoax" had gone so far as to duplicate the type of the *Psychiatric News*, and had distributed copies of the article throughout the country.

Once again the letters came pouring in, including one from David Rosenthal, Ph.D., chief of the Laboratory of Psychology at the National Institute of Mental Health, who wrote on

May 7, 1973, that his name was included "in the diatribe in connection with a newspaper quote that distorted what I had said," and who asked me to write him a note to reassure him and his colleagues that "none of the calumnies in the article can really be attributed to you."

I answered him on May 10, saying that when I first learned of the article "I was stunned and questioned the motive for this vicious piece of work that could have come out of Goebbels's kitchen. I had a notion that it must have had something to do with the political campaign to hurt somebody. I could not learn who was behind this devilish plot nor its objective. I talked with some colleagues about whether to have the whole thing investigated, which possibly would give it the publicity its instigators wanted. I decided to ignore it though this left me with a sense of deep dissatisfaction.

"The fact that I had been a victim of the Nazi persecution may reassure you how disgusted I felt at that time and still feel about the 'article.' If you have any thoughts about who the masterminds behind this vilification could be, please let me know."

A year later, on January 24, 1974, I wrote Dr. Breggin, who had asked me what I knew about the article, that though I found it "terribly upsetting," the only thought I had at that time was that "because of my earlier relationship with President Nixon it was meant to somehow influence the Jewish vote" against McGovern.

I still do not know the reason for the unbelievably malicious hoax written on McGovern-Shriver stationery. Was an American Nazi group behind it? Or was it possibly one of the "dirty tricks" perpetrated by the "plumbers" group, for reasons unknown to me?

The lesson I have learned from these experiences—the above article, the HEW attack, the many personal attacks in the press—is not to allow myself to be sidetracked by acts of hate and get involved in little battles to defend my reputation, but to use my energies in order to make whatever contribution I am capable of. Some of my friends advised me, "If you stick your neck out, you'll get hurt." I replied, "If that means not to express ideas, I'd rather get hurt."

It gave me satisfaction when a reporter called just before Christmas and said, "Doctor, I want you to know, you have been vindicated."

"Vindicated from what?" I inquired.

"The Department of Justice has accepted your plan of testing children in order to prevent delinquency and crime." This was not quite true. The Department of Justice, I learned, has supported several pilot projects dealing with ideas similar to mine, which sprang up after my ill-fated plan had received such wide attention.

The United States Department of Justice replied (on April 26, 1974) to my inquiry about its support of plans for the prevention of violent crime that the Law Enforcement Assistant Administration, since 1969 has "provided support for approximately 1,000 projects aimed at the prevention of juvenile delinquency among preoffenders. Of these projects, approximately fifty have had as a major objective the early detection of delinquent tendencies in children, and fewer than ten have attempted the early identification and treatment of violent tendencies. None of these fifty projects has represented a major effort."

It would have been a boon if the enormous resources of the federal government could have been used. Perhaps one day, when we have more progressive, concerned, mature, and also more daring leadership, we, the doctors, may have a better chance to receive the support needed to cure not only man's physical ills, but the cancer of crime and violence.

IX

Sex and Power

W HEN LEE Harvey Oswald shot and killed President Kennedy, I discussed the deed with a few friends, and even some patients who wanted to talk about it. The general mental state, including my own, was one not only of grief but of bewilderment.

Why? Why had this strange, apparently estranged, if not deranged, young man killed the President? We all had a need to know. There is something about knowing the cause or causes that lessens the pain, at least intellectually.

My own first theory, that Oswald could be a political fanatic brainwashed by the Russians to the point of hating a symbol of bourgeois power, never quite sounded plausible to me. Was there a conspiracy? And if so, why Oswald? Who was he? But whether he acted alone or as part of a conspiracy, there had to be something in him that triggered a fury intense enough to want to carry out the assassination of the President of the

United States. Not only fury, but a special event, a special signal that set off the fury, a mental time bomb.

The first meager reports about Oswald—his search for a political identity, the apparent weakness of character, his preparations to smuggle the murder weapon into the Texas School Book Depository, reports of separation from his wife—all this indicated the desperate determination of a man with a mission. If there was no conspiracy, then Oswald must have been psychotic, driven by a need to prove his power in an abysmal negative way. The act of killing one's own President in cold blood indicated such maniacal blind rage in the killer that, no matter what his conscious motive, it pointed in the direction of psychopathology. He had to prove he possessed power—power enough to kill not just another man, but the symbolic father of his country.

What was the reason for the separation from his wife? Rejection? Unbearable sexual frustration? It was sheer speculation on my part that Oswald could be suffering from sexual conflict of some sort, possibly impotence. And if he was sexually impotent, there could be a misdirected, furious drive to display supreme power in an attempt to prove to his wife and the world his masculinity.

The reports of Oswald's restlessness, his enlisting in the marines because of a determination to leave an overprotective mother who babied him (who kept him sleeping in her bed with her until he was almost eleven years old), his flight to the Soviet Union, and what subsequently was described as his very violent relationship with his Russian-born wife, Marina, all added up to the picture of an unstable, weak, angry and mentally disturbed man who was begging for the acceptance of a woman, and, at the same time, basically fearing and hating all women. His feelings of inferiority and a deep sense of deprivation could create a ferocious hunger for power, with compensatory delusions of self-importance and grandeur, symptoms of mental pathology. And with this might go a need to be admired and loved by all women. The reports that came in, though scanty about his personality, indicated nevertheless that Oswald's ego was fragile and that the brittle pride of the child in him could not take a final rejection from an unsympathetic woman, his wife, at a time of acute inner turmoil. And his wife? Her rejection of him was bound to come eventually because of his uninvolved, unloving and brutal treatment of her.

Oswald's immediate murder by Jack Ruby prevented the world from gaining full disclosure of his personality, or learning the specific signal that triggered his plan to assassinate the one man who represented all he must have envied: the leader of the most powerful nation in the world, a man of wealth and social position, the idol of women, in short, a rich, powerful man and a famed sex symbol. And Oswald? A frail boy who did not belong anywhere, who could not give his ambition attainable goals in a world of reality. He had no conscious awareness of what it meant to feel secure, to be a man with self-confidence and self-esteem.

He was brought up almost totally by his mother, was the youngest of her three sons, a young man who turned out a misbegotten failure, possessing nothing but bitterness and an angry dream of the day he would show his power and make the world tremble. And, for one terrible moment indeed, the world did tremble and hold its breath because of the shocking way he displayed his power.

Oswald's father, an insurance agent, died two months before the youngest son was born. Oswald's mother soon married Edwin A. Ekdahl, an electrical engineer, but this seemed to have been an unhappy marriage from the start. She told the Warren Commission that there had been another woman in his life when she met him and it was only about a year after their marriage that she learned he was unfaithful. They separated several times before they were finally divorced. Oswald's own marriage was to repeat this very pattern in the same city, Fort Worth, sixteen years later.

Marina Oswald appears to have been quite frank in describing her lack of sexual intimacy with her husband. Mrs. Ruth Paine, who had two children and was separated from her husband, and with whom Marina was living at the time Oswald assassinated President Kennedy, testified that Marina had told her that she and Oswald had sexual relations "very seldom." Several of Marina's friends testified she told them her husband was "not a man." Marina described her husband to the Warren Commission, "This man is very unhappy, and he cannot love. . . ." She told how Oswald had beaten her, even when she was pregnant, flew into rages at such things as her forgetting to fill his bathtub, or smoking a cigarette, or wearing lipstick, or speaking English, which he forbade her to learn because he wanted to keep up his Russian. He would strike her if she argued back, or if she served dinner five minutes late. Once he slapped her hard, twice, across the face in front of company because he did not like the dress she put on. Numerous accounts of his brutality were testified to by friends, landlords and even by Oswald's mother, who said that she noticed that Marina had a black eye one day when she was nursing her first baby, June, and when she asked Marina how she got it, she said Oswald had struck her. As the Warren Commission Report put it, Oswald possessed a "capacity to risk all in cruel and irresponsible actions."

It seemed as if Oswald was behaving with his wife as ambivalently as he had with his mother, who had indulged him so extravagantly as a child. One moment he would strike Marina, the next, tell her he could not live without her. This is not the love one adult feels for another, and certainly not a love that combines tenderness and sensuality.

It was a violent need, rather than love—the need of a man who could not love because he had not learned to love and had therefore remained a frustrated, spoiled, destructive child, demanding affection of a parent who could not give it and who thus left the child in the man forever hungry, consuming, possessive. It is the need of a child throwing a tantrum, screaming to his mother, "You belong to me, to do with what I wish. You must love me even if I hate you, even if I wish you were dead, even if I kill you!"

Oswald ordered a high-powered cheap Italian-made war-surplus rifle, a telescopic sight and a Smith & Wesson .38 revolver in March 1962. On April 10, according to Marina, he fired a shot at Major General Edwin A. Walker, a prominent figure in the right-wing movement, as he sat behind his desk in his home. The bullet, fired from a range of between 100 and 200 feet, apparently struck a part of the window frame and glass, which deflected it, thereby probably saving the general's life. Slivers of the bullet's shell jacket tore into his arm, the general reported. Ten or twelve days after this, Marina told the Warren Commission, Oswald got dressed in the morning, took a pistol and said, "Today Nixon is coming and I want to go and have a look." She said she wanted to prevent his going out, fearing he would use the gun, so she started to cry and told him he had promised her not to leave the house with his gun. He told her "I am going to go out and find out if there will be an appropriate opportunity, and if there is I will use the pistol." But he finally gave it to her, took off his suit and stayed home reading a book; he was unemployed, as he was much of the time. She hid the pistol under the mattress but gave it back later when he demanded it.

Marina moved to Mrs. Paine's house in Irving, fifteen miles from Dallas, when Oswald decided to go to New Orleans to look for a job there. Mrs. Paine, then separated from her husband, asked Marina to teach her Russian in return for room and board. When Oswald got a job in a coffee-processing plant in New Orleans, Mrs. Paine drove Marina, pregnant again, and June, to New Orleans. Within two months Oswald was fired for disappearing from his job during the day. He decided to go to Cuba via Mexico to evade the American prohibition on travel to Cuba. Marina accepted Mrs. Paine's invitation to return and live with her, at least until after her second baby was born.

Oswald traveled to Mexico City by bus and visited the Cuban and Soviet consuls there. He told them he intended to return to the Soviet Union and asked for an "in-transit" Cuban visa to permit him to enter Cuba on the way. He was turned down by both the Cuban and Soviet embassies. He returned dejected to Dallas, facing the birth of his second child, jobless and penniless. He rented a room in Dallas at 621 Marsalis Street, calling Marina every day, but soon was thrown out because the landlady did not like him. She later told the Warren Commission she "just didn't want him around me." He found another room at 1026 North Beckley Avenue, and visited his family in Irving every weekend. After looking for work, he got a job at the Texas School Book Depository on October 16, filling book orders.

Two days later, on his twenty-fourth birthday, Marina and Mrs. Paine held a small party for him. Marina testified that he "was in a very good mood, since he had a job and was expecting a son." Two days later, his second child was born—another girl. Things seemed to go quite smoothly on the surface for about a month until he visited Marina in mid-November and said he wanted "to make peace" with her. She said he tried to talk to her but she would not answer him because she was very angry that he had had his telephone disconnected in the rooming house and she could not reach him. She testified, "Lee said that he was sick of living alone, that it was better for him to take an apartment [in Dallas] and to take me there. But I did not agree, saying that I would live a little longer with Ruth Paine, since she was helping me with the child and treated me very well." She also told him they were spending less money under this arrangement.

He stayed the night and in the morning when he left, he took with him his rifle, which he had hidden in Mrs. Paine's garage under a green and brown blanket he had brought with him from Russia. He also took off his wedding ring and placed it on the dresser, and left Marina $170 in a wallet. Marina testified, "When I got up, the television set was on, and I knew that Kennedy was coming. Ruth had gone to the doctor with her children and she left the television set on for me. And I watched television all morning, even without having dressed. . . ." She said that when she heard someone had shot the President she "turned pale" and "went to my room and cried."

Very early in life Oswald possessed a gun, and it appears as though he had an inordinate need to keep a gun with him. The man with a gun is not only a potential killer but symbolically displays the additional power of a penis. The symbolism is a combination of male strength and aggression so powerful as to instill fear, respect and accedence to a demand for submission. We might guess that Oswald, as a boy, felt both sexually threatened and sexually aroused. There was no loving father he could emulate and from whom he could learn to develop a sense of security and confidence as a man.

Psychiatrists believe that if a child sleeps in the same bed, or bedroom, with a parent, particularly the parent of the opposite sex, he will suffer deep emotional confusion. Such physical closeness to a parent arouses fantasies in a child's mind and makes it difficult for him, even more than for the normal child who sleeps alone, to break away from the parent. Every child is a sensitive, sensual little being whose simmering sexual feelings are all too easily stirred up. Any special sexual arousal may call for controls. Oswald's early rages, of which he had a considerable history, were undoubtedly related to sexual fantasies and frustrations connected to the powerful taboo of incest. His mother never taught him to control his temper but permitted him to take it out on her, just as she took hers out on his stepfather, screaming and throwing dishes at him when he angered her. Throughout his life, Oswald appears to have tried to repress a titanic inner fury which led to a mask of an impassive, rigid manner. And when his outer control finally broke under the pressures of marriage, children, economic responsibilities, failure to keep a job and lack of money, he hurled violence at his wife, as he had as a child done at his mother, his brothers, and later, his classmates, his fellow marines, and finally—at the President of the United States. Because of the absence of a caring father he could possibly have become a homosexual but was perhaps too frightened and seemingly too much in need of a protective mother substitute.

The connection between sexuality and guns was made incidentally by a patient of mine, a man from Texas, who spoke of the white Southern male's preoccupation with and fear of, black male rivals supposedly possessing a larger penis. He mentioned one Southern gentleman who always carried two loaded guns in the glove compartment of his car, just in case, he explained, of "communist aggression." But it was this man's own agitated, aggressive state of mind that caused him to need the two guns, rather than any fear of sudden attack by a mythical Communist in mid-America. The fact that "two" guns were needed, rather than one, may indicate not only the degree of his anxiety that one gun may not fire, which symbolically relates to his sexual self-doubt, but also the simmering violence expressed in the term of "overkill." We often read about a gangster scene in which an assassin feels compelled to keep on pumping bullets in the already dead victim (a concept that seems to dwell in the minds of some military men who are not content with an atomic arsenal that could destroy the world; their wanting still more weapons can have, it seems, only one purpose—to make sure that no enemy, that is, no human, survives).

How do sex and power interact? As we have said, at first Freud believed that man was governed by only one drive—the sexual. Man became violent only when he was sexually frustrated. In later years, Freud added the aggressive drive as the second of man's most powerful drives. He believed the sexual and aggressive drives were fused in the child and became separated as a man matured. If he did not mature, if his emotional growth was stunted, his feelings of violence would dominate his sexual feelings.

The impotent man, the homosexual man, the Don Juan, all have repressed violence within that keeps them from being sexually secure. They cannot feel fulfilled and comfortable within themselves; on the contrary, there is discontent, envy and often unending turmoil. The impotent man cannot have a satisfactory sexual relationship with a woman, nor can most homosexuals, while the Don Juan runs from woman to woman because he is afraid ever to trust any one woman and thinks he must prove to himself and to others that he is a "man," substituting quantity for quality, not being able to realize that a real or secure man takes pride in and enjoys a trusting relationship with one woman with whom he can build a strongly interwoven fabric of a warm, mature, human relationship.

A sexually inadequate male may seek power as a substitute for his poor sexual performance. Instead of phallic power in itself, he seeks a symbol of it—money power, political power, the firing power of a gun. This holds true for the men who do not use their aggressive energies wisely, who lack control of their sexual aggression and indulge in "swinish gluttony" as Milton called it, seeking quick acts with many women. They are driven by a greed for more and more power as a substitute for the lack of a deeply satisfying, harmonious orgasm of both partners—their inner hunger producing frustration, depression, hatred or virulent violence.

I think of a man who had a near-nervous breakdown which was attributed to overwork after he became the senior partner of an industrial company. "It was restlessness, not overwork," he said, "because I did not find the happiness I had hoped for." His male security was still threatened by unconscious homosexual strivings. He, like many men, simply could not be satisfied by the material things he possessed. This man could not relate warmly and trustingly to his wife, or for that matter to any other human being. His friendliness was a facade, a cover, the way women "put on their face." He, like so many men, was driven to seek power in organizations, clubs or politics; such men believe that by controlling the destiny of a multitude of men they will symbolically demonstrate their omnipotence, that is their substitution for gratifying sexual power.

Of Herman Goering, Hitler's number-two man—after Rudolf Hess, his deputy, flew to England—fat, vain, almost weighted down by his medals, it was said that "his sexual inadequacy and effeminate nature were hidden under the cloak of virility." In an article "Herman Goering's Pseudo-Froehlich Syndrome," Dr. Robert B. Greenblatt, Professor of Endocrinology, Medical College of Georgia, in Augusta, Georgia, wrote in *Medical Aspects of Human Sexuality* (August 1972), quoting Brendan Behan in "Borstal Boy":

> Hitler has only got one ball
> Goering has two but very small,
> Himmler has something similar
> But poor old Goebbels has no balls at all.

There is a great difference in degree, but not in principle, between a childish Reichsmarschall, a driving tycoon and a poor villager out on a hunt.

The difference depends on intellect, on the intensity of drive, on the scope of goals, and a basic set of values. But what matters most is the self-image a man has about his maleness, the power of his penis and, in case of doubt, a need to display his masculinity symbolically by overpowering or defeating other men. An intellectually brilliant but at times neurotically crippled actor, Franchot Tone, told me that he could not help but react the way he did when, at one time, he physically attacked a stronger actor-boxer in defense of an actress, only to be mauled by his muscular competitor. He just had to prove his masculinity; he was like many others who would get into uneven battles because of a neurotic need to be respected and basically loved by a desirable or beautiful woman, or all women. Even a man of the stature and intellect of a Kissinger, long before he had gotten married, stated with considerable self-irony that he believed that it was more his position and prominence than himself that attracted some of the most glamorous women in the country to his company (including one of my patients, who enjoyed not only his brilliance but the exciting romanticism of dining with a man who was in the glaring limelight of world prominence, guarded by Secret Service men).

Examples of the fusion of sex and power are legion. I think of an air force general, pleasant as a guest, thoughtful and entertaining as a host, who wrote from the battlefield about the glories of dueling in the sky, a murderous game of merciless Russian roulette that demanded complete control of every thought, every muscle of eye and nerve. To kill or be killed was the order of the day, the highest gamble imaginable.

Sexually, this man needed to bolster his masculinity by having the courage to risk his own life or by inflicting violent death on another.

"He really likes to be with the boys," said his wife with muted despair, bravely moving from base to base, keeping the home together. This general did not know what commitment to a family life was, nor about a sense of deep, concerned responsibility. He was married to the air force. His area of interest was the study of war strategies and his dream was of battles in the sky.

It may be of interest to remember the statement of one of

the astronauts, forty-three-year-old Air Force Lieutenant Colonel William R. Pogue, who, after his eighty-four-day Skylab mission said his flight had *humbled* him, that he no longer could operate like a machine but must work as *a human being* "within the limitation I possess." He said that he was going to change also his attitude toward *life* and *his family*.

I think of a military leader, brilliant, vain and ruthlessly ambitious. His drive was to set the world aflame by using his power and superior intellect in the belief he was serving his country; he was actually pushing it into disaster to satisfy his own irrational power-hungry ego. He was stopped by the sanity of his commander-in-chief. Sexually, according to his personal physician, in severe conflict, his military genius had a chance to unfold with all its ruthless arrogance during the war and he could function superbly in an air of excitation, whereas in a state of peace he felt of no use and was fading away.

To these men and others like them, war as a "man's glory" is the unconscious acting out of childhood sexuality and aggression. For the leaders, war is the ultimate in power, a return to an unhindered mastery over life and death. And for soldiers and people with conscious or unconscious violence, war is regression to the hero worship of childhood excitement and a signal for the letting down of sexual bars in the supposed interest of self-preservation. Both the homosexuality in the armed forces, when no women are available, and the rampant promiscuity and rape in an invading army where men hold the exalted position of conquerors, give them a chance to release the violence-sex within themselves. Men who seek a military career, especially in the navy and air force, only too often are running away from the responsibilities of a home and the role of a husband and father. They remain "free"— that is, uninvolved—their status as men enhanced by a uniform and medals, symbols of manliness and bravery, and the respected position of being the defenders of national honor and strength.

While this is an analytical appraisal, realistically speaking it must be stressed that in the uncertain world in which we live, these men are needed and do deserve the people's gratitude, for they are in the first line of defense against possible opposing forces of aggression. And in battle they are being joined by other men with little or no sexual hang-ups who just do their duty and who, because of their valor, shield us. On their vigorous, spirited duty-bound devotion has depended and does depend our feeling of physical security.

That the penis is "power" in the unconscious is shown by the fact that some primitive tribes, when fighting an enemy, would cut off a conquered man's penis and eat it, believing thus they would take within themselves his power. This is a direct expression of the symbolism of all war.

There is the universal childhood fantasy that sex is a violent act, according to Freud. This is a fantasy that we give up as we experience tenderness in love. A man or woman who is unable to be tender in love unconsciously thinks of sex as a violent act. For one thing, a child may interpret the menstrual bleeding of the mother as the result of the father's violence, equating the act of sex with assault or intent to murder. In its primitive, unconscious form, sex may persist as the image of a single act of murder. Mass death in mass murder—that is, war—has the element of an ultimate orgasm, the very end. This fantasy relates to the primal scene which, Freud said, could cause a child who witnessed it to interpret his parents' sexuality as cruel and violent. For centuries children slept in the same room as their parents and today many are still forced to do so and their sexual fantasies are easily aroused. A child may not know what is happening as he witnesses or listens to his parents in the act of intercourse—the labored breathing, a little cry or groan, the moaning, the noise of violent movement—all are mystical and frightening, and the impression they leave on a child's mind is indelible. Parents may not believe a baby is aware of what goes on as they engage in sexual intimacy right under his nose, but a baby, in the absence of reasoning power, is most sensitive to noise, movements and sights. He may not understand what happened until later in life, but he may well retain the impression of something violent, mysterious and disturbing occurring to his mother as, in his imagination, she thrashes around on the bed trying to ward off an attack by a "ruthless" father.

Not long ago in New York, a thirty-one-year-old man fired a gun into the apartment above him, then rushed out into the hall and murdered a neighbor who was newly married. He did it, he said, "because I heard heads rolling around in the apartment above." He said "heads," but he undoubtedly meant bodies. The noise above may well have awakened memories of the primal scene between his parents and their "rolling around." It was not accidental that the killer shot a "newly married man," the one most likely to be engaging most often in sexual activity. Possibly the murderer felt about sex as the Bible put it: "I was shapen in iniquity; and in sin did my mother conceive me."

Many people use the same words about sex as they do about violence or war—wicked, evil, dirty, obscene, destructive, unthinkable. The sexual instinct, if it is to lose its confusing and destructive effect, must be dealt with in childhood. Those who as children do not learn understanding and control have trouble later in accepting sexual conventions or healthy attitudes. Weird and wild fantasies still dominate the confusing, compulsive and often uncontrollable world of childhood sexuality. These fantasies may lead either to open, expressed violence or unconsciously repressed violence turned against oneself. The result in a country with a puritanical heritage is a legion of people who cannot enjoy the pleasures of sex that come with a healthy attitude toward one of the most basic human functions.

We can learn much about ourselves by studying the rituals and ceremonials that primitive man used as a defense against his fears and wishes. These may show us what lies in our own unconscious. In the act of becoming civilized we have acquired a veneer of conformity to civilization, but our heart still beats to the jungle rhythms. Deep within, we may not be very much different from our ancestors who lived in caves and hunted in forests and fought off enemy tribes with sticks and stones. Instinctually speaking, man has not changed through the ages, except that his brain has made him invent more deadly weapons and more terrifying and sophisticated defenses. Neither intellect nor the development of conscience are instinctual.

Whatever early primitive man could not understand, he attributed to magical causes and supernatural forces. He did not understand much about the world around him, and practically nothing about himself and his psychic needs, but he was extremely sensitive to all the sensations of his own physical being. And the most intense pleasure in life came from the act of sex.

Thus primitive man considered the phallus an object of greatest awe and respect. He worshipped it and paid tribute to it in many ways. His first works of art bespoke his preoccupation with the phallus. He fashioned stone and clay in its image. Artifacts of phallic shape have been discovered in Stone Age deposits. Very early rock engravings show men with pronounced phalluses standing by themselves or engaging in some erotic activity. One ancient engraving depicts the sun attached to the phallus of a masked figure holding a spear. Primitive man equated the sun's power with that of a penis. And he equated the penis with the spear, the weapon with which he killed so he might survive.

In one primitive society, if a man thought he was being bewitched by an evil spirit, he would seize his penis and say,

"Let the evil be averted." He believed his penis was filled with such strength that the evil spirit would be destroyed. If, before battle, a warrior lost his nerve, attributing this also to the spell of an evil spirit, he would cast off the spell by crawling between the legs of the chief of battle whose penis would shed its power upon him so he could go into battle strengthened. Primitive men held phallic dances in which images of the phallus were carried high in ceremonial processions appealing to the gods to increase their potency.

But that was in antiquity. A Judeo-Christian morality has done much to confuse basic concepts of sexuality and male security. Today a man may be a hero on the battlefield but a coward in the bedroom, as one patient of mine put it. He was deeply depressed and despondent after his wife left him for another man. He confessed the urge to kill her after she criticized him for being less than a man in bed. "Maybe I am a coward and just not good sexually, as she says," he commented and went on to say, "I don't understand. Maybe I was made impotent by a domineering mother as a boy and have lived in awe of women ever since. But I was no coward during the war."

He described a bloody battle scene during World War II when he was ordered to lead a platoon of men up a strategic hill and take it from the Germans. He ordered his men to assemble and started them up the hill; they ran into the deadly fire of the well-defended Germans, but they managed to keep climbing. He kept encouraging his men to keep going, to storm ahead. His decimated platoon finally took the hill.

"It was a terrifying experience," he said, "but I did not think for one moment of giving up."

Though war is irrational fighting, the assault, the storming ahead, is, in the light of the reality of survival, understandable. The objective is clear. The fear of death is there, yet the only way to live is to kill the enemy. It is savage, atavistic, unworthy of civilized behavior, yet it can be understood.

But the fear of sexual intimacy with a woman, such as this man had, a fear that can lead to impotence and violence, is less easily understood.

What was even less understandable to this man was the change in his wife, for which he blamed himself. She was Viennese and he had met her when he served with the American Army of Occupation. She was soft and lovely and he could give her gifts like coffee and cigarettes. Eventually they had sex. She was the aggressor, seductive and skillful. As a war bride, she came to the United States—as she had wanted. But once she became a citizen, her attitude toward him changed. She withdrew sexually, became cold, critical and contemptuous. He became impotent. But he defended her, even defended the affair she was having with another man, saying, "It's all my fault." He would leave my office encouraged, only to return more beaten and depressed a week later by the bombardment of her sadistic barrages.

As he became more enslaved, paralyzed by feelings of worthlessness, he sensed a growing desire to kill her. He thought, "After all, I have killed innocent people in the war. They did not even hurt me. Why shouldn't I kill her, and then kill myself?" Sometimes he trembled as he spoke, not because of fear of such a dreadful deed, nor of the consequences, but because of the inner rage he fought hard to control. If a man's love for a woman also holds deep hatred, homicidal feelings may arise, because in fantasy the sexual act is as we stated fused with violence. Incidentally, this man, as I learned from his lawyer, died later in an automobile accident.

In a man-woman relationship a seemingly careless remark may reveal a concealed drive for one partner to dominate the other. An advertising man in his late forties spoke about the difficulties he was having with an attractive woman ten years younger than he was who thought that a full year of courtship was long enough for the man to make up his mind to marry her. "We have a marvelous relationship," said the man. "We have a lot of fun together, she is always charming and witty and says that she has never before loved a man as much as myself. . . . But there are some problems and lately some sexual difficulties which have never existed before. She has a terrible temper. Once she even came at me with a poker. She can fly into a rage with such speed and force that any rational conversation is impossible. Either I have to sit through it pretending to be deaf or I have to leave."

He interrupted himself to ask a direct question, one he had wanted to ask for a long time. "Is there a limit in sexual functioning?"

What did he mean—a diminishing function due to age or the like?

"No," he said, "let me explain. My lady friend and I were having cocktails; it was one of the more peaceful times, all was delightful, when she suddenly said, 'Do you know that a man has ten thousand shots to fire—and that's it?' She was talking about sexual intercourse with an ejaculation. 'No,' I answered, 'I did not know that.' But it disturbed me," said the patient. "I pushed it away as we chatted about it, though I wondered where she had gotten her information. But that night I had just dozed off, when I woke with a cold sweat— and I began to count. I remembered my first sexual experience. I was seduced. I was a little over sixteen. Sex was frightening, exciting and rare then. As I was nearing twenty, I had a steady girl friend and later on many. I started counting. A year has 365 days, but I didn't have intercourse every day; still, there would be nights with two or more sexual acts, so I could have had probably four hundred "shots" a year and be possibly close to the ten thousand in twenty-five years—ever since I find myself trying to remember and counting. And withdrawing from women because of the terror that it could be my very last time. . . ." He paused and looked at me. "My friends say it is nonsense. Doctor, is it nonsense?"

"It is," I replied, and explained the sadistic nature of the woman's remark—as well as my patient's masochism, the anxiety and guilt that made him so very receptive to a castrating remark.

One deep-seated unconscious fear of the impotent man is that he may do violence to a woman through his penis, hurting or injuring her, or that she will do violence to his penis, perhaps biting it off. The fear of castration is rooted in the fantasy that once his penis enters the woman she may somehow cut it off, or just snap it off; it will disappear into her mystical, powerful cavity and he will lose it to her and become like his mother or a little girl, minus a penis, nothing there.

As part of the mysticism that surrounds sex, children have the fantasy that both boys and girls originally had a penis, but that little girls have somehow lost theirs, or it was taken from them because they were "bad" (usually because of masturbating or incestuous fantasies). Little girls show a vivid preoccupation with the "gadget" boys possess. I once observed my five-year-old niece trying desperately to pull her small vaginal lips into a long shape to become a penis. The absence of a penis is traumatic to a girl and causes in her a sense of inferiority, or a feeling she has not been "made right." Later in life many a woman is still obsessed by an unconscious desire for a penis for which she substitutes the desire for power and shows a constant need to prove she is "as good as a man."

We then see what is called the "phallic" or "masculine" woman, who acts like a man and is in constant and keen competiton with men. Among the Women's Liberation movement there are maladjusted, power-hungry women who use angry protest or take great pains to conceal their contempt—even deep hatred—of men, often caused by an absent or uninvolved father or an unloving, ungiving mother. Many of these women, though they deny this vehemently, are driven by an often desperate, unconscious wish for a penis. Those who have gone through psychoanalytic discoveries know the truth of this and know too how much deprivation it has brought them and what a destructive motive it has been in their lives. There is a difference between a woman's fulfilling herself in all ways out of choice and a woman who is driven by anger and competition with men to "seize" anything a man has—meaning, symbolically, his penis.

Penis size is frequently a concern to women as well as to men. A man is likely to be worried that his penis is too small, as was, for instance, F. Scott Fitzgerald, according to William F. Lewis, former Fulbright Fellow and teacher at the University of California, in the article "Masculine Inferiority Feelings of F. Scott Fitzgerald," (published in *Medical Aspects of Human Sexuality* April 1973). Declaring that Fitzgerald "was plagued by self-doubts throughout his short, turbulent life," Lewis refers to Ernest Hemingway's statement in his book *A Moveable Feast* that Fitzgerald once said of his wife, "Zelda said that the way I was built I could never make any woman happy and that was what upset her originally. She said it was a question of measurements. I have never felt the same since she said that and I have to know truly." After they made a trip to the men's room together, Hemingway assured Fitzgerald that his manhood was perfectly normal and Zelda was only trying "to put him out of commission," says Lewis, adding, "Yet, despite Hemingway's counsel and a trip to the Louvre to look at comparative male statues, Scott remained dubious."

One study showed that there is little difference in size, once the penis is erect. A man looking down at his penis critically perceives it to be smaller, though it may not be so at all. In another study, presented in an article "Concern with

Penis Size," in the October 1973 issue of *Medical Aspects of Human Sexuality*, Dr. William Peltz, professor of clinical psychiatry, University of Pennsylvania School of Medicine, declares

> The concept is false that a man with a longer or thicker penis is any more effective in intercourse because of penis size than is a man with a smaller penis. In actuality penile size is a minor factor in sexual stimulation of the female partner, so that sexual adequacy on the part of the man is not related to penis size. As has been said, quality rather than quantity is what counts.
>
> So far as *length* of penis is concerned, in terms of satisfaction to the woman, it should be explained that the erotic area of the vagina is around the opening and just inside of it. There is very little sensation farther up inside the vagina. Hence, as long as a penis is capable of making entry, its length is not important in terms of giving satisfaction to the female partner. A relatively short penis can stimulate the erotic area just as well as a longer one can.

(As a woman patient of mine remarked of her husband, "I love his adorable little penis.")

Dr. Peltz points out that when there is worry about a penis being too large, either in length or circumference, such concern is ordinarily experienced by the woman, rather than by the man, and may be based upon her fear of bodily penetration or upon anxieties which arose in childhood, when she may have compared the small size of her own body and genitals with the size of her father's penis. She may be concerned as to whether penetration will be possible or painful. Since the vagina is distensible, there is no basis in reality for worry on either score. Says Dr. Peltz, "It may be helpful to remind her that if a baby can get out, a penis can get in."

The connection between sex and violence has been noted by many psychiatrists who have studied the association between a proneness to violence and sexual inadequacy. Most studies verify earlier statements that doubts in regard to masculinity or fear of homosexual impulses can cause an acting out of aggression or produce an excessive demand for power which means control of others.

Why does a man need to control others? For one thing, he is reenacting his earlier life when he was controlled *by* others—his father and mother. He is doing unto others what was done unto him. He is now also unconsciously getting even with his controlling parents, showing them he is far more in control than they ever were. There is rebellion in the need of a man to control others, as there may be rigidity. There is also fear of what will happen if he ever loses control, fear that he will open his inner Pandora's box of evils.

Only the weak apply over-control. The strong cooperate, share, exchange ideas, work with other men or women. They do not have to manipulate, but advise, offer friendship, help. Their basic philosophy is one of adjustment and constructiveness, not resistance and/or destructiveness.

In a civilized society our sexual instinct needs to be controlled throughout life. Primitive man, many authorities believe, was not able to exercise control of his sexual impulse but indulged it whenever he felt like it, even with members of his own family. As man became civilized, he learned to control his sexual instinct—sometimes too rigidly, to a point of overinhibition.

From our earliest days on, we have to learn to control functions of our body. As babies we may not bite our mother's breast when she feeds us, no matter how angry we feel. And we may not go to the bathroom when and where we will, but must wait for a proper time and place. As to our impulse to have genital sex, we may not have sexual intercourse whenever we want it or with everyone who strikes our fancy or, as the kids put it, with "whoever turns us on."

In a child for whom violence on the part of a parent becomes associated with a sexual desire, or with control of excretory functions, there is apt to be a great need for control of bodily feelings. We saw this in the case of Lee Harvey Oswald, whose controls eventually broke under the weight of repression.

If a boy feels that to masturbate is terribly wicked, for instance, which means his penis is evil, and also feels that his sensuous feelings for his mother are evil, he may become so tormented as an adult that he prefers to live without the temptation of his sexual feelings and may actually mutilate himself, as some have been known to do during a psychotic episode. This is the most severe punishment imaginable, the castration of the self because of incestuous wishes that are so strong they cannot be borne because they are felt as evil. The sufferer prefers to remove all temptation because of his unbearable guilt.

That all of us, even psychiatrists, may have fears about sex was emphasized recently by Dr. Harold I. Lief, director of the Center for the Study of Sex Education in Medicine at the University of Pennsylvania. He declared that the average physician has a far from adequate knowledge about sexuality "and that goes for psychiatrists too," adding, "Although psychiatrists are trained as interviewers and therefore edge out their colleagues in becoming good sex therapists, they also have their share of sexual hangups and prejudices, which tend to weaken their roles as educators and sex therapists." He spoke at a symposium of Human Sexuality Today held at the Carrier Clinic in Belle Mead, New Jersey. More than 600 physicians and their wives attended the symposium which provided current information about sexuality, as well as a gamut of attitudes and opinions, and encouraged the physicians to examine their personal attitudes about sex. The symposium's theme of general sexuality was pinpointed by the slogan: "Yesterday's perversion is today's deviation . . . is tomorrow's variation."

The sexually mature man, confident of his own masculinity, will have no excessive need for power. He is able to control his own bodily desires in order to meet the demands of civilization without feeling repressed or frustrated and he is able to express his sexual desires appropriately and with pleasure and joy. He does not need to take out on other men either an inner violence or feelings of frustration or envy or a driving need to control.

Whenever someone attempts to control someone else, to impose his will on someone else, whether an individual or a nation, he is demonstrating a state of regression into earlier primitive, selfish and most certainly immature behavior. Sex may be used as a means of control, of power, between a man and a woman. Some wives control their husbands by the use of sex, giving of their bodies not because of mutual love but as a means of getting something they want.

When this happens, both will suffer, for it means there is no love in the union, little sharing and no building of friendship. When sex is used as an instrument of power, not of love, there can be no real gratification and, in regard to the relationship itself, no respect, either of the self or of the other person. While sex is an incentive to power, it takes power to control the indiscriminateness of sex.

X

Power Trips in Everyday Life

$\mathbf{A}$ RUSSIAN anarchist, Mikhail
A. Bakunin, an opponent of Karl Marx, once described a
revolutionary as a doomed man because "he has no personal
interests, no affairs, sentiments, attachments, property, not
even a name of his own. Everything in him is absorbed by one
exclusive interest, one thought, one passion—the revolution."

If, in this statement, made a century ago by a political
idealist in a backward Russia, we replace the word "revolution" with the phrase "a man's drive for power," we see the
modern politician. If we eliminate the word "property," leave
in all the others and add "money," we have the successful
businessman.

If we further add "position" and "social prominence," we
see the ideal male in the image of an ambitious woman who,
through marriage rather than her own merits, seeks to

achieve a position of eminence, sometimes even at the price of sacrificing love for power.

There are women who have given themselves a good head start by marrying men who possess position and wealth, having accepted the wisdom of the proverb, *"Bella gerant alii! tu, felix Austria, nube."* (Let the others wage war! You, happy Austria, marry.) (And through marriage, a man, Austria's Emperor Charles V, King Charles of Spain, did inherit an empire on which "the sun never set.")

From time to time the newspapers and magazines publish the success stories of women who, through the men they married, have made a Cinderella dream come true—some because of their beauty, others because of their wit, or their strategic planning, and still others by their artful use of sexuality.

An example of a woman's extraordinary skill in reaching a position of splendor is that of Wallis Simpson, the woman for whom a king of England gave up his throne. The American divorcee's story is of greater interest to us than is that of the rigidly conditioned but severely inhibited king whose passivity and awe of women had reduced him practically to a state of utter dependency.

The future Duchess of Windsor did not use a step-by-step career to attain power. She attained it by one bold step through marriage. A friend of the former king assured me that the king was deeply in love with Mrs. Simpson and that Mrs. Simpson said that the whole thing was "thrust upon" her, indicating that she did not have aggressive ambitions, and had even thought of ending the relationship with the king. But others have described her to me as a very ambitious lady who was not shy about getting what she wanted. And, the fact remains that she *did* stay in the relationship, that she did marry the former king, and that the Nazis considered her ambitious enough to serve as a valuable contact with Edward while he was still king. Hitler hoped to get her cooperation in a plan to make a peace treaty with England, promising that Edward would ascend to the British throne with Mrs. Simpson as his queen.

Soon after the birth of the Rome-Berlin Axis (with Mussolini in the bag), Hitler began to explore a settlement with England on his own terms, according to William Shirer in his book *The Rise and Fall of the Third Reich*. This was disclosed in captured papers of the German Foreign Office. Mrs. Simpson, as a friend of the king before their marriage, was to play a part in helping the crafty German ambassador Ribbentrop to bring the United Kingdom into Hitler's camp.

At one point the Nazis even plotted to kidnap the Duke and Duchess of Windsor in order to induce the former king to work with Hitler for a peace settlement with Great Britain. (Fifty million Swiss francs were deposited in a bank in Switzerland, and the Fuehrer was willing to go higher, so the duke and duchess could lead the life of a king and a queen, even though captured.)

The duke had told the German Foreign Minister von Ribbentrop that he was against Churchill and against the war, and, according to the German foreign minister, the duke had said that if he had remained on the throne war would have been avoided. He had characterized himself as a firm supporter of a peaceful arrangement with Germany. He also believed that continued severe bombing would make England ready for peace.

After the fall of France in June 1940, the duke, who had been a member of the British military mission with the French Army High Command, made his way to Spain with the duchess to escape capture by the Germans. But then the Germans, with the cooperation of Franco's Spain, tried to detain the Windsors in Spain. Churchill ordered the duke to proceed to his post as governor of the Bahamas at once and prepared a letter that threatened him with court-martial should he fail to do so.

According to the captured German papers, the German ambassador in Madrid in a "most urgent, top secret" telegram to Ribbentrop disclosed he had two long conversations with the duke (at one of which the duchess was present) in which the duke expressed himelf as politically more and more distant from the king and the British government, and, the German ambassador said, "The duke and duchess had less fear of the king, who was quite foolish, than of the shrewd queen, who was intriguing skillfully against the duke and particularly against the duchess."

It was then the Nazis plotted to kidnap the duke and duchess, but before they were able to, the Windsors sailed for the Bahamas. The date was August 1, 1940, about sixteen months before the United States got into the war. The Windsors sat out the war in the Bahamas under the watchful eyes of the United States and the British Secret Service.

The disturbing rumors about the duke's suspected treacherous behavior were cut off by a formal statement from the British Foreign Office, declaring that the duke had never wavered in his loyalty to Great Britain during the war; in his own mind, he probably never did. He did not grasp the villainous mentality of Hitler and his regime, just as the Germans did not grasp the English mentality. The duke liked Germany, he liked to speak German, he was against the war and against Churchill. He was a gentle, trusting gentleman. But his wife's world was one of different values. Though she always carried herself with great dignity, she could not remain indifferent to the lure of wearing the crown of England. A grim Churchill, determined to win the war, had cut short an intriguing chapter of love and a commoner's chance to reign as queen of England if the German plan had succeeded.

Another woman, more modest in her end goal and life style, if not in her intensity of ambition, was Elsa Maxwell, a journalist and social columnist. The famous parties she gave

were known as more than just social events, for they served to
help the many she favored become acquainted with "the right
people."

Miss Maxwell was not a glamorous lady, she was short and
fat, but she was nobody's fool. When I was called to see her in
my earlier years of practice, she had been ill and was discouraged because she was not getting any better in spite of intensive
care by her family physician.

Miss Maxwell and I struck a rapport at once, and I was
fortunate in being correct in my diagnosis, as well as in the
prognosis that she would be back at work in a short time.

She liked to talk sensibly and answered questions readily
about herself and her life. "My father," she said, "told me
when I was a young girl that he was sorry not to have given
me beauty." (She knew she was ugly.) " 'I cannot leave you
money nor any great name, nor any position' he said, 'but I
have given you a good brain. Now go on and use it.' And I did.
I have the position I want and I have enough power to get
by."

Our friendship did not last long. My secretary did not understand Miss Maxwell's wish to be treated as a gentlewomanly
personality, not as a patient. One did not send a bill to
Elsa Maxwell. She would make up what she owed in other
ways, like sending a doctor or workman "clients," people of
wealth and influence who, in turn, would send their friends.
My secretary had sent a bill, an unforgivable offense.

The two most powerful women in America, according to
Gail Sheehy writing in a recent issue of New York, are
Dorothy Schiff, owner of the New York Post and Katharine
Graham, publisher of The Washington Post. Mrs. Schiff emer-
ges as a woman whose life was one of struggle to survive in a
field dominated by men. My own impression of Mrs. Dorothy
Schiff is that of a gracious lady with an alert superior intellect,
an attractive, elegant woman whose position of power has not

diminished any of her femininity.

Is the drive for power in women the same as in men? Historically, except for a Cleopatra or a Lucretia Borgia, a Catherine the Great, and a score of other great ladies, women have not been allowed to exert power; they have been treated as inferior creatures, as slaves. The fight for equality is not the same as the fight for power. The fight for equal pay, equal opportunity, the vote, the right to hold public office, all of which women have been waging, is not necessarily a fight for power but for the right to be thought entitled to the same privileges as a man, to be treated truly as a human being.

But, again I say there is a difference in those women who have waged the war for equal rights and those who are envious of and competitive with men.

The drive for power on a personal level differs vastly in form and intensity from aggressive behavior in business or social situations, and nowhere is the psychodynamic interplay as sharp or far-reaching as in the closest and most intimate of all human relationships—marriage. Marriage can take on aspects of an underground tug-of-war, as first one, then the other, pushes his domination (power) on his partner, leaving the latter the choices of resisting or giving in "for the sake of peace," in the latter case presenting the semblance of submission though inwardly smoldering with rebellion. There is a toll either physical or mental on the one who submits and in time, there is often a blowup of the relationship.

Harry B. found his personal life clashing deeply with his rigid set of values. He was a silver-haired, sixty-two-year-old chairman of the board of a large manufacturing corporation in the Northeast with home offices in New York City. He was a notable member of the conservative Eastern establishment and known to be a foxy, scheming businessman, always ready to weigh the opportunities to expand his corporation or to consider a merger as long as he would remain in control. He would never have come to see me or any other therapist, had it not been for a crisis that threatened to disrupt his personal life and possibly cast an unpleasant shadow on his image as the puritanical pillar of society.

Mrs. B. had at one time consulted me because of the reactive depression she suffered after her oldest son was killed in war.

It was a weekend. My wife and I had just arrived at our country home and were longing to relax when Mr. B. called from Palm Beach in a near state of panic. He demanded I come at once; his wife, he said, had locked herself in her room and threatened to swallow a full bottle of sleeping pills if anyone dared to open the door by force.

"She won't see anyone, she won't listen, she won't even talk to the family doctor. I am scared—I told her I would call you."

Even if I wanted to go, how was I to get a plane reservation from the country on a Friday night? "All right," I said, "try to get me a reservation on the first plane in the morning." He called back. Despite all his influence he was not able to get a direct flight to West Palm Beach. "I'll have a limousine waiting for you at Miami." I had to ruin my wife's weekend. We went back home that night.

I saw Mrs. B. the next morning at their home. She had opened the door for me, but had returned to bed and was holding a pillow over her head to stifle her sobbing. She burst out in tears and anger. "That beast," she said, "Mr. Right— Chairman of the Board, member of the President's Business Council, trustee of this and that—"

"What happened?" I finally asked.

Haltingly Mrs. B. began to talk. "My daughter Mary came to visit for a few days. We respect privacy in this house; certainly nobody would ever dare to touch Harry's things, his papers, but Mary was searching for a family picture. She looked in the drawer of his dresser and right on top was an open letter and the picture of a young woman. It was a love letter. Finally she read it. I came into the room as Mary tried to hide the letter from me. I read it too. The young woman looked around Mary's age and her face had a striking similarity to Mary's. So, my noble husband had a mistress."

I tried to pacify her: "We don't really know the full story, but whatever the story, is it worth throwing away a human life for—your life?"

She became angry again. "If he had not lied—God knows, for how long—business trips, excuses. . . . We had talked about what we would do when he retires in a few years. . . . What prospects do I have now—for what people call the autumn years? How can I live with a man who is a cheat? I'll divorce him. I can't take that humiliation—thirty years out of the window."

She talked for two hours, unburdening herself, sobbing from time to time and becoming very bitter when she said: "It was my money he started his business with. I helped him get where he is now and I was with him all the way. He used my family's connections, our social position—and now this." Her tension eased, she was tired.

"I'll see you in an hour or so. What do you want me to tell him?"

"Anything you want . . ."

Mr. B. waited for me in the library. "It sure is a nasty thing," he said. "I don't know how to handle that one. Can I talk to her?"

"Give her some time to rest," I replied. We sat quietly for a while before I asked him: "Mr. B., I have an office and there is a desk with drawers. These drawers are always locked. Nobody else has a key. All that is very confidential, except what is in a bank vault, I put in there. Now, you must have something like that in your office also, don't you?"

He seemed stunned. "You mean to say, I wanted my wife to find this letter? Incredible."

"I don't find it so incredible. If you did not want anyone to see the letter why would you leave it right on top of things in an open drawer?"

"Can't one forget—make a mistake?" he asked.

"Of course," I replied, "but sometimes what we find working in depth is the power of guilt."

"What do you suggest?"

"There are a lot of things that need to be talked out. We need a little time."

Mr. B. drove me to the Everglades Club where he had reserved a penthouse suite for me. He waited for me while I unpacked.

Mr. B. and I began to talk more seriously after we returned to his home. "What I need to know is what you want," I said. "We could try to patch things up—maybe it could be done, I don't know—I am not very much for that. Your wife is a lovely, sensitive woman. She is deeply hurt. She lost her only son and now you. What I need to know is are you in love with that younger woman? I need to know your true feelings. I'll help you to get out of this marriage. I don't believe people should live in unhappiness. But you must be absolutely honest with me."

He was chewing on a dead cigar. He did not like the position he was in. It was evident that he was used to being in control of things, to being boss. His conflict was obvious. Finally, he said: "She just adores me—I think she really loves me—and as to myself? Well, she has brought a great deal of joy into my life. I am dealing with a lot of cynics. This girl is pure. It's not just sex."

"Do you want to marry her?" I asked. "You must tell me what plans you have. You are a serious businessman who, I assume, does not leave things pending?"

"All I know is that having her has made my toughest battles worthwhile. It won't be easy to give her up." He paused. "But marriage is out of the question—I can't do that to Ruth—it would be ridiculous—like I lost my head. Can you picture me, doctor, appearing at a White House dinner with a young chick on my arm? It would be hard for both of us. Margaret is her name, she has done a great deal for me—she has made me feel young and vigorous. Because of her, I have an incentive to prove myself all over again—it's that power thing I have, have had ever since I was a kid."

"What about your wife?" I asked.

"Ruth is a great lady—and in some way I love her, but it's different. She won't accept a compromise. This is not France."

Mrs. B. was adamant. She wanted a divorce. She felt rejected and deeply hurt. "He is dirty," she said. "He is a dirty old man, acting majestic, and now he wants to sleep with his own daughter."

At a moment of deep emotional upheaval, reason is of no avail. Here was a woman, in her mid-fifties, who was ready to throw away her 30 years of marriage. What was she to do living alone? Did she know the misery of loneliness?

And the man? How seriously in love was he? Was it just male pride, infatuation or a great need to fill a void in his life?

It was clear that he was deeply involved with a warm, giving, human being. "In my industry it is either win or perish," he said. "I had no choice but to move on." He realized that family, friendship, social intercourse had been ornaments used to garnish the role he played in business and the position he held. Except for golf, he had cultivated few interests until the young woman entered his life. She made him think of other values, not just the satisfaction in sex. She brought out tenderness he had never dared to show. He had had his own very selfish life and given little of himself.

To my surprise, he accepted my suggestion, upon his return to New York, to come to my office and talk more.

I saw husband and wife individually and from time to time together. Mrs. B. realized that she had accepted all the luxuries he had provided for her but had drifted away. They had to find a new, maturer modus vivendi.

As expected, there was a relapse. The man began to see his former mistress again. A final split-up of the marriage seemed inevitable. This time, Mr. B. admitted to feeling trapped. He experienced intense anxiety, rage, anger and fear that all he had built could go under. The corporation could not afford a scandal—or so he said.

The decision was a momentous one to him, because it affected all his values, beliefs—the final meaning of what his life was all about. It was not easy for this proud man, a ruler in his business kingdom, to discuss his affairs with another man. He felt his inner life was his business and only his.

He told me one captain of industry had resolved a conflict—not a similar one but nevertheless intricate—by putting a bullet through his head. He had thought about it, how easy it would be. But he could never do that. He had not built his empire, overcome a multitude of crises and defeats, climbed up a stony road just to back out. Some young, smooth, eager, hungry wolf would get it. As a farm boy in the valley, he had looked up a thousand times at the big mansion on top of the mountain, and promised himself that was where he wanted to be one day. No, he just couldn't quit now. His enemies, the scandal sheets would poke fun, headline his decision: "Industrialist dumps wife to marry young secretary."

We talked about values, life, happiness, sex. Of course, he could resign due to ill health. That would be a political cop-out, but it's legitimate. He could say: "I am going to devote myself to a cause bigger than myself and not just give money. But I would be a hypocrite. I believe in survival of the fittest; everything else is rubbish."

Mr. B. thought of reconciliation, of compromise, a new life, spending more time with his wife. Then he wondered about seeking an ambassadorship to give her status. It probably could be arranged, but then sitting in Khartoum or Oslo—cocktail parties, dinners—that wasn't for him. Politics is not made by ambassadors anymore.

Mr. B. liked to solve problems by fight, not flight. He enjoyed daily battles with men equally shrewd, games that involved all a man had in guts, in cool judgment and in vision. He couldn't envision a life of happiness with a lovely girl, walking hand in hand through the woods or along a beach. "It's too late for me to adjust to a new life—it's unfair to the girl who could have a home and children. All I know about life is battle. I want to go on and when the time comes I want to die just when my heart contracts to beat, not when it is at rest."

The marriage was mended by work, patience, understanding and consideration for the needs of the other. Mrs. B. had to understand the man who was her husband. His life was action; his pulse was a beat of power.

The healthy choice in the complicated dynamic interplay of two people who wish to smooth out the rough edges of their relationship is to "fight,"—that is, to open up a line of communication, of dialogue, not to repress feelings of hostility but to state what in the behavior of the other is offensive, disturbing or painful. This is a most sensitive undertaking, requiring courage and gentleness, firmness and friendship, but most importantly the care to avoid any semblance of criticism or attack. This can be done by emphasizing one's own feelings and needs, with an undertone of consideration of the needs of the other. The choice of timing and of words are of utmost importance for, in times of anger, reality can become distorted. In the words of Horace, anger is momentary madness.

One morning a charming, well-to-do, upper-middle-class lady turned to her husband without any display of anger or discontent, and said, as he was about to leave for his Wall Street law office, "Honey, I don't want you to come home tonight. I don't want to live with you any longer."

It was not her style to quarrel, nor to go on with a life that bored her, which this one now did, for she had completed her conquest of this man, her third husband. Her subtle domination had not brought her the joy she expected.

This was a woman who could not build a relationship or communicate with a husband because she could not give of herself. In her inner feelings she was still a little girl who wanted to be praised and taken care of or amused. She had never grown up, never explored her own capacities, never exchanged thoughts or values with anyone or tried to find a formula in the marital relationship that would allow both her husband and herself freedom of expression and yet leave room to build the basis of a meaningful life together.

The drive for power can remain a voracious hunger, a never-satiated passion that may destroy a marriage by producing a warped, dictatorial rule of one person over the other. Or worse, by inviting a sadomasochistic relationship with all its destructive effects on the marriage and on children. It is especially pathetic when a person who is superior in humanity and intellect submits to a crude but efficient bureaucrat or crafty businessman because of the former's passivity and fear to act in his own behalf.

The examples of disbalanced relationships in everyday life are legion. There is the husband who, in order to show off his power, embarrasses his wife in front of their guests by making cynical or cutting remarks about her, cleverly couched in the form of a witty joke. Or the sexually frustrated, sadistic pincher of ladies' behinds who is often as indiscriminate as a truck driver who whistles when he sees a pretty girl. Or the discontented wife who insinuates what a superior sexpot she is and how inadequate her husband is in bed.

The insecurity that often exists in the man-woman relationship reminds me sometimes of how, as young men, we tried to reduce the power of a woman by quoting the "scientific" analysis of a chemist who said that after all, "the most beautiful girl in the world is only a lump of charcoal plus some buckets of H_2O and a few ashes." The attempt of our sour-grapes project was a poor cover-up of our own insecurity.

The interplay of power and control on the one hand and fear and submission on the other is evident wherever people are thrown together, not only in marriage but in business, in social or professional situations, in civil service, the military—wherever people depend on each other.

Business offices ought to be functional places with clearly defined areas of work and mutual objectives. Yet too often a business office is a place of intrigue, where unhappiness grows out of the need of one man in power to win control over others. Similar to the sibling rivalry in a home, the drive for power may cause one man to plot against another or to ferment unrest or a teapot revolution in order to unseat another, sometimes even his own boss (the symbol of the domineering father or mother of childhood). Office politics represents one of the greatest scenes of activity in which the drive for power shows itself in clear form.

Women jockey for places of power in business offices, sometimes resorting to a verbal attack on those in higher places, sometimes using sex, to get ahead. Because it has been difficult for women to get ahead, some who have risen quickly have done so by being unscrupulous and uncaring about the careers of others.

The woman who runs the office, the office manager, may unconsciously represent a mother figure as those under her compete for her favor.

Or there is the woman who offers no competition, but whose very sweetness is a form of power—unknown even to her.

Cathy, as everybody calls her, is a very thin, blonde, elegant woman of average height, much younger looking than her 50 years, the prototype of a social figure in a fashion magazine. Cathy is soft-spoken and still has the British accent acquired during school years spent in an English convent. Her parents were divorced when she was very young, her French mother led an active social life and did not want the responsibility of bringing up a child. Cathy's father brought her to England.

After graduating, Cathy returned to the United States, where her troubles really began. Nobody wanted Cathy. Her stepmother refused to let her live with her father whom she adored. She was pushed around from a sister to a brother to an aunt, always in fear of offending someone and being sent away. She was not even allowed to spend her vacations with any member of her family; she had to go with a teacher who was paid for taking her along on a trip. Her teen-age years were so painfully traumatic that she remembers little about them and insists that she bears no grudge against anyone. She adopted a friendly, outgoing and gregarious attitude.

The most remarkable feature about Cathy was that not only did she retain her sanity but in spite of her personal problems, she was able to learn, to improve herself, and to conquer many difficulties by a sheer will to succeed.

Cathy grew into a beautiful young woman, studied drama in college and decided to become an actress—in order to impress her father, who, however, was too busy to pay much attention. With no father around to help her develop trust in men, and with her mother living in Europe, Cathy was not able to identify with true femininity. As she stated in a psychological testing: "I am born a woman—the conflict is—if I could behave as a woman and let the man protect me and provide—if you could behave as God meant you to—behave as a woman—you'd see the happiness of the birds—the cup of happiness."

But Cathy never knew real happiness. She was self-effacing, obliging and deceptively submissive. She picked out actors who were good-looking but weak and irresponsible, because this type of male would be no threat to her. Once involved with a man, she clung desperately to him for reassurance and protection, but since the men she chose were emasculated and passive they were out more to receive than to give and left Cathy feeling inwardly confused, empty and unloved.

Cathy possessed a superior intellect which was diminished by her insecurity and her multitude of problems. She felt it was safer not to stand out; yet when it came to an important decision, she could cut through her layers of massive anxiety and eventually make a realistically sensible one.

Even after her father had died, Cathy was still driven by an inner ambition to make a mark her father would have been proud of. She often thought she should have been a boy and have done some extraordinary work. Only through an outstanding accomplishment could Cathy hope to find the acceptance her family had denied her.

Cathy had a rich fantasy life and a keen imagination. Though her friends were good-natured about Cathy's work in arranging theatrical benefits—they called these affairs Cathy's ego trips—it was she who actually ended up becoming a leader and accomplishing whatever the objective was. She put in enormous work, suffered unbearable anxiety and begged for help, knowing only too well that she had to take care of every detail herself. She knew talent and knew whom she wanted for her benefits; she would go into the office of Sol Hurok, the impresario, sit there and wait and wait until she saw him—and she could negotiate a contract to the point that all a lawyer had to do was to legalize it.

Many of the ladies on her benefit committee referred to her work as though it were a hobby. But it was no minor thing to her. She told me that her goal was "to help to bring about peace through art."

In her seemingly helpless fashion, she attended a city council meeting of her resort town as the single representative of her group; the other committee members did not attend because they were sure that nothing could be accomplished. Cathy spoke and presented a plan she had worked at for years; the council voted to set aside two acres of valuable land within the resort area—tax-free, provided a cultural center was built within two years. And Cathy, the gentle, cultured lady with a subtly concealed drive for power, is now at work to get the funds for building the center.

The deeper the degree of insight a man gains about himself, the more he is likely to come into conflict with his previous set of values and those of society. Objectively seen, many of the values held by adults, values which affect greatly their life-style and their decisions, are still those of their childhood and therefore not in their society's best interests.

Within a family, just as within a nation, some may control others under the guise of "caring." We hear as rationalization, "I tell you what to do and what not to do because I love you, I want to do what's best for you." Children grow up to feel they need someone to control them in order to feel loved, that therefore someone who does not try to control them does not love them. This is one reason it is so easy to get vast masses of people to accept control. Emotionally, in their unconscious, they feel control means the leader "cares" about them. The need to be loved or cared for is so great that people uncritically accept sweet words without examining whether the leader has even the capacity to care for another human being. Anyone who wishes to control or dominate others wants to keep them dependent, does not want them to mature emotionally.

One young man who came for help had great difficulty in talking of his feelings about his mother, who had obviously controlled him all his life. He would show up late for his appointments until he realized his conflict and its depth. His mother was violently opposed to the idea of psychiatric help and threatened to disown any of her children who went into treatment. He dared to come to my office, feeling his mother's values were sick ones, but he was also slowed down (literally) by an unconscious feeling of guilt, because he was doing something of which his mother disapproved. He feared discovery and the loss of a substantial inheritance. He eventually broke off his treatments.

Another young patient, in a similar setting, gained the courage to tell his mother he was getting help. As she realized how determined he was and also how much he had benefited from the help, she lost her fear of being threatened in her relationship to her son and said no more about disinheriting him. Perhaps she is an example of the old saying that the world truly belongs to the brave in spirit if they will only realize it. Not the foolhardy, but the brave.

The closer the circle of people with whom we are involved, the greater the chance of conflict. The ambivalence of feelings is strongest in a family setting or among siblings. If we always possessed clear understanding and objective judgment, we would be able to resolve most conflicts without violence. Or if a relationship had become too destructive we would know when to end it; we would take to flight, that is, we would muster the strength necessary to extricate ourselves from a painful and futile war of attrition—and it does often require enormous strength. Many who have not been able to work out a relationship by fight (adjustment) take to flight and ultimately manage to build a new, healthier and happier relationship. This goes not only for marriage and for friendships but also for partnerships, as well as relationships in all walks of life, wherever people's relationship to one another encourages the process of transference.

One woman decided to go through a day and see in what

ways, open and subtle, other people tried to control her. It was a rainy day and she was recovering from a cold and the first few telephone calls in the morning were from friends who warned her, "Don't go out in this weather! Stay home, or you'll come down with another cold." The warnings were issued in worried, stern tones, the voice, she thought, of her mother in childhood. She wondered why these friends did not give her the right to decide for herself, as a thinking adult, whether she wanted to go out or not.

At lunch, this woman, who was a writer, met an editor who had gone over a manuscript she was writing and made a number of corrections and suggestions. This was another kind of control, but it was a necessity, and she welcomed the criticism for it enhanced her work. She had noticed, however, that some editors made corrections and suggestions in a warm, friendly way, as though wanting to improve the manuscript, whereas others spoke in a pretentious, commanding, hostile, anxious manner, as though fighting her.

At home in the afternoon there were more phone calls from friends and, listening, she was aware of how many times people said "Don't!" or told her what plays to see or not to see, where to go on vacation and where not to go, and implied she would be a fool not to follow their advice.

In the evening she played bridge with two women and a man and became aware of how many times during the evening the other three spoke to her, or to each other, in a way that denoted a wish to control what the other person did. She came under fire for the style of her hair and was practically ordered by one of the women to go to a certain hairdresser; she was called "stupid" because she was traveling from New York City to Los Angeles first class instead of economy, spending money "lavishly," and the dress she was wearing was criticized as too "frilly."

If we listened to ourselves carefully in everyday life or if we watched and listened to others, we might be astounded at the number of times we try to control the life of someone else. True, the control is aimed at so-called "little things," but the motivation is still a drive for power on a small scale which in principle is not different from power battles on a big scale. Maturity, like democratic thinking politically, is based on respect of the integrity of the other person, and on allowing the other, friend or not, to make his own decision.

We should all wish to control our own lives. But to want to control the lives of others means displaying power we do not have and indicates that we do not have our own life under control. We are still obeying voices from the past, the voices of our parents in childhood telling us we were either "good" or "bad." If someone in current life deviates from what we have been taught is "good," he becomes "bad" and threatening, perhaps doing something we wished to do but did not dare. It is rigidity and certainly immaturity to insist that someone do as we do, and not to accept differences in behavior and tastes.

In direct contrast to the one who always orders others around is the person who gains power in a negative way by masochistically obeying every order. Through the ostensible laying down of power, he enchains others, using their need to control as a way of binding them to him. Masochism is a snare, a way of exerting subtle control, of saying "I obey your every command and in return you owe me your allegiance and love—forever."

In the struggle to gain understanding of ourselves and others, we may become confused by what is called facade behavior. We all learn while young to develop a mask to conceal deeper feelings and we may find ourselves enchanted by an attractive and charming facade only to become deeply disappointed by attitudes and a behavior that belies that image. Often there is bewilderment when people find they have not married the person they thought they had; they either blame themselves and their own inadequacy or attack the other for having changed into a nasty "egotist."

A talented fashion photographer married one of the year's prize models. She was a beautiful young woman who had an earnest desire to build a home and family, but found that her husband presented such an exalted figure of nobility that he never could come down to earth. Underneath the facade of power he projected lay a little boy who was afraid to fail or be rejected. It was his vanity that had made him choose a beautiful girl of whom other men would be jealous. It was his pride that made him hold on to a failing marriage. But it was the sanity of the girl that enabled her to end the sham. She had come to me as a patient, to be sure that the failure was not her fault and also to work out not merely her sense of failure and guilt but the insecurity and self-doubt that made her marry such a man in the first place.

To appear civilized—to become a kinder, more concerned human being—demands of most people that they come to terms with their inner nagging drive for power. The more a person knows about himself, the more he matures, the less there is a need for a cover-up facade behavior. The more a person attempts to be honest with himself, difficult as it is, the easier he will find it eventually to live in a world of reality rather than in a make-believe world that will leave him empty and forever discontent.

A man's ego may be strong and determined and appear appealing as long as he deals with outer (extrinsic) values but he may be unaware of how self-defeating he becomes when he is moved by his inner (intrinsic) values. A bookkeeper or schoolteacher, a lawyer or doctor, may perform excellently on the job where he appears competent, but taken out of such a situation, especially when placed in a more intimate, personal one that involves deeper feelings, he may be insecure, frightened and ineffective.

When a person under extreme stress or personal conflict feels his facade crumbling, he may be in danger of breaking down.

Values are socioeconomic, religious, political, racial or philosophical, and all may be the source of conflict. They may contain conscious or unconscious prejudices which in turn cause tension and alienation. In our culture we experience the disintegrating effect of religious prejudice and of racism and a strong ethnocentricism (the polarization of WASP arrogance versus the countermove "black is beautiful"). We have economic conflict between rich and poor, sexual discrimination between male and female, the generation gap between young and old (which, as I said before, I feel is not a generation gap, but a communication gap). And in all these situations, we find a clashing of inner power drives though the specific issue serves as the *casus belli*. The reason for conflict is as wide as the span of the rainbow and as deep as the sensitivity of feelings. Ideals and imagination play a part, as do values of heritage.

Values can be and actually are purely cultural. The American dream, for instance, is American and may have little or no value in another culture. A friend of mine, a professor of philosophy mentioned earlier, who had been teaching the meaning of values for decades, gave his university students this example: A woman in Mexico was selling oranges. A customer, after asking the price, said, "I'd like to buy all your oranges." The woman replied, "I can sell you some, but not all." The man asked, "Why not all? Don't you want to sell your oranges?" The woman said, "Yes, but if I sell you all my oranges now, what will I do the rest of the day?"

There are, as Freud remarked, other values than "power, success and riches." Indeed, in all fields of human endeavor there exist innate drives toward goals other than power or material gain. The fame sought by actors and writers, for instance. Creative people want recognition, the less talented are content with gaining attention. The world honors men such as Michelangelo, Rembrandt, and Picasso in the arts,

Kepler, Newton and Einstein in the sciences, Hippocrates, Galen, Lister, Pasteur, Koch and Freud in medicine, and Gandhi, Schweitzer and Martin Luther King, because of their significant contribution to the progress of mankind. But they all possessed an enormous drive to power which they converted, controlled and sublimated, and by sheer will and self-discipline turned it to the expression their inner calling demanded and their imagination had aroused in them.

In our everyday value system we speak of the good guy and the bad guy, of those who help and those who kill, those who build and those who destroy. There are people who deep within are angry and believe in the inevitability of war, and there are others, including this author, who are convinced of the ultimate victory of peace.

As I have said, some who appear to be the "good guy" may cover up their "bad guy" impulses, one of the things that complicates our already difficult everyday life. I think of a man whose facade of affability effectively covered his sadistic impulses. His friendliness and smoothness of talk convinced the vice-president of an advertising company to hire him. The man, a jack of all trades and master of none, was a good salesman and did so well that the vice-president made him an executive. Then after a few years the vice-president rose to the position of president. His protegé became increasingly jealous and megalomaniacal, believing he had more ability than the new president did and that it was he who deserved the position of president. He became obstructive and began to malign his boss by carefully planting nasty little rumors about him. Preoccupied with his delusions of power and grandeur, he planned a master stroke. Against all rules, he went to see the chairman of the board, motivated he said, by a need to save the company from disaster and wishing therefore to point out the destructive decisions the new president had made; he hinted that the president should be fired and he be given the position.

Eventually he was fired. Then he raged about the unfairness and the injustice to him who had wanted only to save the company, and he embarked on a campaign of slanderous attacks on the president by mail. Soon running out of money, he became an informer, enlarging on half-truths or imagining incidents involving political or other prominent personalities and selling these news items to gossip columnists. He managed a few times to get into the limelight himself but not knowing the difference between reality and fantasy, he became so entangled in intrigue that as a way out he attempted suicide which landed him in a state mental hospital. His was a power trip that broke. (This was the same man who, as I mentioned in the opening chapter of this book, furnished the fallacious information to Drew Pearson.)

A moment of power may come to everyone—even to someone low on the totem pole. During the gasoline shortage, on a very cold winter day, February 5, 1974, there appeared in *The New York Times* under the "Quotation of the Day" the following: "If he's that stupid, he waits in line an hour and doesn't know the rules, I let him get to the pump—and then I break his heart." This was said by a service-station attendant in Elizabeth, New Jersey; gasoline rationing had gone into effect the day before, and only cars with even-numbered license plates were permitted gasoline on even-numbered days and those with uneven numbers on uneven days.

This gasoline attendant was acting out his power and sadism, rationalizing that he was taking a firm stand and enforcing the law; he overlooked the fact that an unfortunate man might have waited an hour or more and then been refused gas because he was not aware of the new rulings.

The deeper the understanding of the psyche of man, the more the wonderment about the infinite variety of man's talents but also his reasons for failure, his genius, but also the causes for his self-defeat. Whoever has the good fortune to work with the minds of people becomes enriched by what he learns and, at the same time, humbled by realizing what he does not know. Sometimes one feels the courage of the scientist who goes on to labor towards greater knowledge and truth in spite of the monumental mountain he must overcome. This had been similar to some feelings I have had when I started writing this book and saw the work, the high, grim-looking mountain ahead of me. Many things have puzzled me about the minds of people, yet there is great gratification in the discovery of one small piece of fact at a time in the often so confusing jigsaw puzzle that is the mind of a patient.

In the power struggle of one man to extricate himself from the Lower East Side poverty in which he grew up was evident a deep ambivalence, a fear of death as well as a fear of life. This man, well-built, affable, attractive, was in his mid-thirties. He was a wealthy international financier who had gained such a reputation for originality that a national magazine wanted to write an article about his rise to success. But my patient refused to give an interview because he had anxieties about revealing personal data.

What had prompted him to come to me was an acute and unbearable state of anxiety, at times actual cold fear. His partner and closest friend, only a few years older than he, had died from a heart attack without any warning. This shook him deeply. In addition, his wife had just confessed she had had an extramarital affair though she had broken off the relationship. He felt whipped, unmanly, wondering where he had failed her. He was aimless, depressed, discouraged, and thought he could die at any minute, as his friend had.

"I have one of the most beautiful offices downtown," he said to me, "but I try to go there as seldom as possible. I conduct most of my business from my Connecticut home because I feel so frustrated each time I travel to New York. I hate commuting on a train full of brokers and bankers, and I hate the traffic after you get there. But then I find I'm frustrated at home as well. Nothing seems to relax me. I'm always exhausted."

Several years before he had seen a psychiatrist because of a depression. He said, "But after six weeks I gave up. I had no rapport with him. He was cold. I couldn't communicate. So I managed somehow with the help of my family doctor to get through the depression. I still don't know what brought it on. I accepted my doctor's explanation that it was overwork, though I doubted it. I did not work hard though I worried a lot. Now I feel the same way, but worse. I don't even want to get out of bed in the morning."

Of all the problems he cited during the initial interview, two seemed to stand out. One was his fear of death, the other, the question as to whether he should get a divorce.

He seemed relieved as he left my office. We had discussed the possibility of his coming for two sessions a week, each of us saying we would think it over before deciding. He had to find out whether he felt any rapport with me. I had to decide if I could work with him.

When he returned within a week, saying he wanted to continue, he added one more problem to his others: "I don't know whether I should go into politics. I've been thinking about it, and I'm in conflict about it."

"Why?" I asked. This seemed to contradict his feelings of utter futility.

"Because I find politics challenging and interesting," he replied. "It probably would absorb me. But, from all I have read about the President and you, it seems like going to an analyst would be the kiss of death for a politician. I'd be dead if anyone ever found out I was going to an analyst."

I reassured him, "Your visits would be kept confidential." But I was thinking, he is only building a little exit door for quitting; his overall picture of depression has not changed.

We then talked about his wife. I asked, "Do you love her?"

"I guess so," he said.

"What do you mean 'guess'? Do you or don't you love her?"

He hesitated, "Well, I have a tremendous emotional feeling for her. I like her. She's a marvelous mother."

That wasn't an answer to my question. I asked again, "What about love?"

"Well—doesn't that feeling cool a little in every marriage after a few years?" He defended his uncertainty.

"Are you aware of any hostility toward her?"

"Not really. I think at times I dominate her too much. I want things done my way. It's generally the better way anyhow."

"Don't you think hostility underlies the need to dominate?" I asked.

He shrugged his shoulders as though he had not thought about this and did not care to.

"Can you express warmth? Are you affectionate?"

He thought a minute, then said, "It's crazy, but since I've learned about my wife's unfaithfulness, I feel much more affectionate toward her. I'm angry and hurt, but I don't hate her. That's what's contributing to the dilemma as to whether I should get a divorce and start fresh with someone else."

In one breath he stated that he liked his wife, felt even more affection for her than before the affair, and in the next, talked of divorcing her. It was evident he did not know what love was. He confused need with love, as a child does.

I asked to see his wife if she was willing to come to the office.

She did, and proved a very attractive, charming and outgoing young woman of thirty-two with an open manner, engaging smile and delightful sense of humor. She said she loved her husband, but felt he lacked the affection and sensitivity she craved, that he took her for granted, and that sex with him had become unsatisfying. She had been a virgin when she married and had started to wonder if other men were like her husband. She had begun to feel increasingly bored and frustrated with her life.

She met the other man, who was divorced, at a party, and they made clandestine dates. She found sex with him exciting and fulfilling, though she disliked him as a person. After a few months of secret meetings her guilt became so overwhelming that she broke off the relationship. It was then she confessed it to her husband. He was angry but more hurt than angry, which, she said, made her feel even more guilty. But ever since, he had been paying more attention to her even though he could not get over his resentment. She said, "I suppose it's the rejection, the hurt of his male ego."

She told me what he had failed to tell me, that he wanted both of them to take part in group sex, an activity she felt to be obscene and degrading, as indeed it is. In psychoanalytic terms, it represents a regression to infancy, an acting out of the roles of voyeur and participant at the same time—the wish of a child who imagines or actually sees his parents in sexual intercourse—for all children would like to be part of this intimacy between parents, even though they are frightened by it.

Since her affair, she said, sex between her husband and herself had improved and so had the marriage. She said frankly she felt happier, more content. When they were first married her husband did not have much money and she had helped out by taking a job. She had admired his rise to success as well as enjoying it.

She told me she was delighted to have been able to talk things over with me and expressed the hope I would treat her as well as her husband. Since he was the patient first, I said I would have to discuss this with him.

He agreed at first, and she enjoyed the meetings enormously. In her enthusiasm she told him this, whereupon he became angry and demanded she stop coming to see me. He, however, continued, though with fluctuating interest.

As the weeks passed, he began to feel more relaxed, though he continued to see his cardiologist once every two weeks, for his anxiety about his heart was still acute. One of his chief complaints was his feeling of exhaustion; he was so tired he flopped into bed as soon as he returned home from his office. When I suggested he play a game of tennis instead, he said aggrievedly, "You want to kill me." But reluctantly he tried tennis, and was surprised to find his tiredness disappeared.

The memories of his youth were of a life of emptiness, deprivation and indifference. He described his father as a very angry man who told him every day that he, the son, was a "nothing" and would never amount to anything, so that he could not expect anything from life. He hated his father but liked his mother, felt sorry for her because she lived in constant fear of his father's anger.

One day when he was sixteen he saw his father strike his mother. Though he was frightened, he interfered, restrained his father from hitting his mother again. Unable after that to regain his composure, he decided to leave home. He said, "I then lived alone until I got married."

"What did you live on?" I asked.

He hesitated, then said, "I gambled. I was always very good in mathematics. My teacher thought I was a mathematical genius. I figured out a scheme to beat the horses."

"And did you succeed?"

"Always," he said.

"Enough to live on?"

He was embarrassed, then said, "In my student years I averaged between $16,000 and $18,000 a year."

Even today that would be considered an enormous sum of money.

"After I got out of college, I figured I might as well go on gambling, and the place to go was banking, he said. "High finance has its drawbacks. It keeps you tense and terribly anxious. The anxiety at times is unbearable but I can't see myself as a college president. I can run things but I need action."

After many sessions, he realized how basically depressed he had been most of his life and how deeply angry. Nobody believed what an angry man he was, except the few who had seen him explode, but that was rare. He also realized that his states of exhaustion came not only from his anxiety, as he had thought, but from an inner violence that demanded all his control.

He felt better, and he came in one morning in a cold, distant mood. He was somewhat restless.

"You want to quit?" I asked.

Surprised and visibly upset, he said "My wife called you."

"No," I said. "It's evident. It's your restlessness—but that's surface—you block fear of what's there in depth, what's causing your anxiety, your anger, your underlying depression. Because it's too frightening."

He overcame his resistance and kept coming for help and eventually was able to face his straightjacket existence, his fantasies of attaining a position of great power in order to feel free, while at the same time nursing a strong unconscious death wish. He had been appalled by any conscious thought of self-destructiveness. He saw himself omnipotent and immortal but at the same time weak, fearful and overly sensitive. He dreamed of being free, unmarried, living on a faraway island, but he knew he could not live a day alone or without the security his wife gave him and the comforts his money could buy. He still had not overcome fully the feelings of being in a trap. He remembered the elation after he made his first half-million and the breakdown he almost had after he made his first million. He was angry at fate, disappointed that money had not brought him happiness. It proved a deception. He felt betrayed. It was as if life had broken a promise. He had no choice but to go on and make his second million while he was searching to do something different. He needed more power to overcome his father's prediction that he would be a "nothing."

He felt dead deep within. He was conscious only of two feelings, one rage, the other, excitement when he gambled or when, in a meeting with bankers, he outlined a great international financing project. He was sharp, alert, inwardly trembling, but felt alive. He experienced anxiety but he came to life. This is the reason perhaps why people often feel compulsive about gambling: it wipes away for the moment feelings that have been in deep-freeze, the deadness caused by an absence of genuine feelings, love, human concern. Excitement is equated with coming alive. There is a sense of magical power when you win and of masochistic pleasure when you lose.

This man gambled only for big stakes, more excitement, more exhaustion. As time went on, however, he was able to take deeper and increasingly less fearful looks at himself. He could accept not merely rationally but on a feeling level his childhood anger at his father, with whom he had felt helpless, the sense of abandonment when he moved out of the house, and the guilt at deserting his mother, leaving her to the fury of his father. One day he would set her free with money. It was painful to realize what he now knew, that he had never been able to feel genuine affection or love for his wife or friends, though he had worked very hard to show love to those around him. But he did love his oldest son, the way he wished his father had treated him.

Now that he could relax more within himself, he found his anxiety on the job was far less. He could feel proud of the mathematical ability which had helped him become so successful in a world of business, rather than feeling embarrassed by it. Most important, he realized that he had been using his power drive on his wife, not wanting her to be free to seek her own fulfillment. She had to be there for him. She loved him, the generous side of him, and she respected the fairness and accuracy of most of his judgments in everyday life, including political events. He understood why his wife had had an affair, that in large part he had brought this on himself, which removed the anger. He developed trust in her almost at the same rate as his self-esteem as a man grew. And then, one day, he said "I think I begin to understand the meaning of happiness."

I present this case to demonstrate the power game played by many who set business above family and money above a search for self-fulfillment.

What matters is not the scale but the principle, not the socioeconomic setting but the raw or balanced display of power. And this measuring of power, this testing of one's strength as a way of dealing with one another is the same in small boys having fistfights and big boys competing on Wall Street, and in women competing at a tea party. One drive for power is pitted against another. Even every blade of grass wants the sun, and every tree wants to grow as tall as its species permits, and as space and soil allows it—though in these cases it may be just survival.

The other day a niece of mine came to see me. Slim, poised, beautiful at age nineteen, she said she was confused. The breaking away from the security of a home, even though she was an A student at Carnegie-Mellon University, had created anxiety. Suddenly she was an adult and, looking at the mystical, threatening enormity of all that was life frightened her. She feared her grades would go down. In the course of her discussion, she described some of the other girls and the games they played to gain attention. "It seems," she said, "they are on their own little power trips." And it seems that the kids' ego trips of yesterday are now being replaced by awareness of a new reality, encompassed in their term, "power trip."

If we all are involved in that power struggle and if we all cannot win—depending on what winning means in one's set of values—and if many do not want to win or feel they do not deserve to win—again depending on one's goals—we have to learn to translate into creative channels the enormous energies generated by the dynamic force which basically still is man's will to live. Survival in modern society means clarity of purpose and determination of priorities or what, in an earlier book, I called the reevaluation of values. To give life meaning requires the development of the art of balancing needs and humaneness, drives and objectives—the wisdom to attain a balance of power.

XI

When the Drive for Power Breaks

"**M**EN ARE strong only so long as they represent a strong idea. They become weak when they oppose it."

This statement by Freud coincides with our concept of a man's persistent drive toward the objective set of values his imagination has produced. It is the ultimate in what meaningfully exalts the creative mind of a man and mobilizes his will, with all its resources, to push toward the formulation and attainment of a goal. It requires visionary power to know how far to set one's goal and it takes wisdom to estimate the obstacles in the outside world as well as the limitations within the self. All goes well when a man knows how to use his ever-present drive, how to channel or rechannel it. This knowledge builds a man's strength, self-esteem and his store of accomplishments. It also increases the chance for his conscious awareness of happiness.

But when a man's drive for power breaks, when a sense of inferiority and a lack of self-worth distort or cripple his belief in himself and the value of his imagination so that he cannot build a goal, when fear paralyzes his creative energies, he becomes weak. For as Freud stated, he then opposes his ideas or denies them. Many a man's creative plans have been buried deep and covered by a blanket of forgetfulness, because he cannot take failure. The child in a man may build goals that are too high for his wings and too powerful for his strength. He may then decide to live out his life narrowed down by fear and corroded by a sense of insecurity and failure, caught by a growing self-contempt and an inability to free himself from childish dependency—to cut the Gordian knot.

Such conflict appeared in a young man who traveled two and a half hours to my office in the hope of bringing order to his confused state of mind. A sharp intellect had gained him a position in the advertising office of one of the country's great industries. And yet he felt weak, passive and stymied. He recognized that his passivity was somewhat like that of his weak father. He had more intellect and a better education than his father but a similar fearfulness. His position in the industry was safe but the scope of his work was limited. He was thinking ahead to where he would be in ten or twenty years. What was he to do? Did he have the strength to change, the courage to seek work he truly liked, to give up security for a possible chase of the rainbow?

Another man in the same office, twenty years his senior, to whom he told his plight, sympathized with him, saying, "How well I understand. I was a coward. I should have left here when I was your age. Now it's too late; I have a wife and four children. I'm a vegetable. I hate myself. How can anyone respect me if I don't respect myself?"

"We all can't be chiefs," said my patient, wanting to comfort the older man. "There must be Indians too, in order for a company to run."

He told me, "I felt like an Indian when I was growing up, ordered around by my father, who was constantly losing jobs, had little money and was always afraid of tomorrow. There never was money, only fear, and such fears grow deep within one."

One cannot push a patient before he is ready to change. This young man was only too painfully becoming aware of the example his father had set and the imprint it had left on his mind.

"How do you learn to overcome fear?" he pleaded. "How do you build confidence? How does anyone become strong? Are some born strong, others weak?"

It does little good to quote worn-out phrases, such as the Chinese adage that a journey of a thousand miles begins with one small step. Or the German proverb that an accomplished master does not just fall from heaven. Or Vergil's words: "It gains strength, as it goes." A patient has to feel the change from within. The process is not one of "building up" courage or artificial self-esteem; it is not as simple as the mere power of positive thinking. Energy is produced every day, physically and psychically, and it is often the overcontrol, be it from fear, guilt, or anticipatory anxiety that eats up energy or inhibits its use. No car can move as long as you keep your foot on the brake—that is the negative power of inhibition.

Eventually the young man made a decision. He sought and obtained work he liked, the editorship of a national magazine in New York City. He used his heretofore repressed drive for power in the development of his talent and his creativity, and his self-esteem grew.

But many do not dare take their foot off their psychic brake and thus don't move on. They clutch desperately to the little security they have, as did the older man in my patient's office. Many more do not even recognize their conflicts; all they know is that they have a vague feeling of discontent or tension, or sometimes of sickening inadequacy.

"The greater the feeling of inferiority that has been experienced," said Alfred Adler, "the more powerful is the urge to conquest and the more violent the emotional agitation." The repression of this emotional agitation, or power drive, creates a clash of two forces, one that wants to move on aggressively creatively and the other that is inhibitory (fear of failure or inadequacy). The effect of blocking one's aggression, the conflict between acting or not acting, is a tug of war that produces procrastination and at times unbearable tension.

But the tension can also be chronic if no decision is made and no action ever taken. Such a state produces a need to seek relief. This relief may be provided by a regression into fantasy living or to the lower creative level of raw sex. Or it may take various forms of escape—such as overeating, oversleeping, alcoholism, drug addiction.

The United States has seen its citizens go through some of these regressive phases. One occurred around World War I when alcoholism became so widespread that it led to the debacle of Prohibition—the compulsive, missionary, over-zealous crusade that opened the door to a thirteen-year era of speakeasies and organized crime. A second has occurred in relation to the Vietnam war, with drugs replacing alcohol. It is a well-known psychological fact that regression may occur when guilt or anxiety becomes too great. But there have been other elements, such as anger in young people who were forced to kill or feared being killed, or who felt outright hate at the immoral deeds or corruption of authorities in power. Intense repression of the wishes to act out aggressively may result in feelings of depression and destruction of the self.

The conflict in Southeast Asia had led to a reaction—hate begets hate—as youth tried to protest what they thought was an immoral war, and were beaten, clubbed or shot, and, in despair, sought oblivion via drugs. The years of marijuana, the "fix," goofballs, the uppers and downers, heroin and LSD, have been accompanied by a rise in crime as organized crime moved in to supply what was needed to ease first the inner pain and then the tension produced by dependency on the drugs.

The soldiers in Vietnam, many of whom felt guilty at killing other men against whom they bore no hatred, and many bored and frustrated, have been easy targets for the "connection," the dope peddler, both in Vietnam and on their return home.

A desperate population, comprised in large part of bewildered parents, turned to the government for help. The parents of young soldiers blamed the military for taking away their sons, exploiting them for an unglorious military venture, then sending them home emotionally sick, broken, addicted.

I have listened to the tales of young people, including many in college, tales full of anguish and fear, and rage, tales of young people who wanted help. The larger number, like hunted animals, were on the run, not believing anyone cared or would understand them. They were also on the run hoping not to have to fight in Vietnam. Many took to drugs, wanting to escape awareness of what might lie ahead—death on the battlefield, and, at home, an unfeeling, pompous establishment speaking of commitments. They grew beards and long hair and wore jeans, and rebelled at everything they were told was "nice" behavior.

Rescue operations by psychiatrists sprang up, such as Synanon, Odyssey House, Dr. Casriel's AREBA (Accelerated Reeducation of Emotions, Behavior and Attitudes) and many others. As one young woman said after a first visit to AREBA, "It's like a home"—a home she never had. What she meant was the communal spirit, the openness and the readiness of each one in trying to help the other with feelings akin to love. Doctors know that humans who are emotionally healthy will not easily fall victim either to alcoholism or drug addiction, and they know also that to fight these addictions, the victim needs help in understanding what in his psychological makeup has made him seek out the specific addiction.

Besides the many efforts by local health centers and city and state drug clinics, President Nixon created in 1971 a federal law enforcement agency within the Justice Department to deal with the problem. He also set up an office to deal with prevention within the White House. He sent one of his staff assistants, Jeffrey Donfeld, to see me in New York, to ask whether I would be interested in participating in a consulting capacity in the new "Special Action Office on Drug Abuse Prevention," which I assumed would be an unpaid job.

I had to think about it, for I was not sure what my role would be. Then I learned that my boss would not be some White House staff member but the President himself. I went to Washington to discuss the addiction problem with the director of this new office, Dr. Jerome Jaffe, to find out specifically what my job would be. We met in September 1971 (with Mr. Donfeld representing the President). Immediately Dr. Jaffe asked me how I would go about the prevention of drug abuse. I replied that I had hoped to learn from him what I could do. He again asked me to present some of my ideas. I said that what was needed was a program to explore, and possibly cure, areas of conflict and confusion in the minds of adolescents, with the intent and hope of making them resistant to the need for, or the lure of, dangerous drugs.

Without preparation, I had had no chance to prepare a plan—I outlined such a program and put it into the form of a memorandum which, on September 23, 1971, I sent to the President (*See* Appendix), since the office was run under his jurisdiction.

The aim was to prevent adolescents who are confused or in conflict from falling victim to the lure of dangerous drugs.

The plan was to form a body of already trained guidance counselors and supplement their number with young volunteer teachers trained by psychiatrists or psychologists in the techniques of group therapy (I later added the role-playing technique). There would be special classes, attended by *all* children, and the children would *learn to become their own therapists*—under the guidance of trained counselors or special teachers. Verbalizing their problems (fears, hates, unworthiness, domination, depression, and the like) would not only be therapeutic but make the children aware of conflict situations in others and then in themselves. It would stimulate an interest in helping others and accepting help in return.

Children in trouble, I pointed out—children who later could become a threat and/or a burden to society—can be reached best by their peers, that such a group generally generates more rapport and interest in active participation than can parents or teachers.

There was a need to work with parent-teacher associations and to enlighten the public about the meaning of the plan and to reassure them that their *children were not to be brainwashed* but to be taught to avoid drug addiction and how to live peacefully and creatively within a group.

I pointed out that not only could children learn to accept a larger group in a kind of peaceful coexistence, but that for parents, resistance to a large project might be no greater than resistance to a small or local plan. And I stressed that *all* children should participate in the program—the rich and the poor, the black and the white—because the effectiveness of the project would depend on a cooperative spirit, on a feeling of relating to one another in an air of freedom and equality.

As I saw it, what would make my plan original would be: the involvement of the total child population of the country —this would require in addition to trained personnel to call on volunteer teachers who have interest and enthusiasm and who would be trained in courses and symposia at hospital centers in each state to be repeated every three months—and the role the federal government would play in executing the program.

I stated that the problem of drug abuse and juvenile delinquency could be conquered only if all the existing state and city projects were coordinated: one approach, one method. The plan, if properly executed, could free our society from a dangerous sickness that is costing our country far more in loss of property, damage, productivity—and lives—than a fraction of the money needed to cure the disease.

I admitted that it is not the government's job to undo the failures of parental homes and inadequate education, but that *we the people pay the price for this failure:* our lives are threatened, our streets unsafe, our survival as a healthy nation in jeopardy.

And I wrote the President that I would be at his disposal anytime he wished to discuss this problem with me.

Later I modified my plan by suggesting the use of role-playing (to discover fear, hostility, intense shyness) as the focus of a class in school, beginning with kindergarten. Since there exists in the United States not even a fraction of the trained psychologists needed, I suggested the training of volunteer teachers in symposia held in the capitals of each state which would qualify them to lead classes of about ten pupils. Similar to the principle of group therapy, the children themselves would be the therapists while the teacher guided the role-playing. Dr. Jaffe estimated the cost to be about three billion dollars, a sum that I said scared me, whereupon he remarked, "That is not much for a project of this magnitude."

Dr. Jaffe however was so intensely involved with lowering the percentage of drug-addicted veterans by the use of methadone (which has since been reported as killing more users than heroin), that everything else seemed to have less urgency for him. And perhaps he was not assertive enough when he presented plans to the higher-ups, possibly to the chief advisor on internal affairs, Mr. John Ehrlichman. Since I did not hear more about this project, I assume it was shelved. The press never learned about it, and thus there were no repercussions to this plan of mine as there had been to the first one. That first (1971) plan was kept alive by inquiries from research centers, and by press references to "the Hutschnecker memo."

In another *New York Times* editorial, headlined "The Lessons of Eagleton," which appeared one week before the 1972 presidential election, I summed up my thoughts on the prevention of drug addiction and crime by stating:

> An all-embracing and truly preventive plan ought to begin with programs that encourage children from six to sixteen to learn to understand one another. This plan, based on the new technique of role playing goes far beyond the prevention of drug addiction or delinquency for which the plan was originally designed.
>
> This would do more than to wipe out delinquency and tendencies to violent crime and drug addiction. It would in the long run help the development of healthy citizens and mature judgment but it would also *build* a vast *pool of healthy stable competitive leaders,* capable of using their creativity toward the growth of a nation as well as a brotherhood of man.
>
> It might cost this nation an estimated three billion dollars, far less than the amount that would be saved from loss through violence and destruction and very little when compared with the budget of $79.5 billion we spend for arms in 1974 (and an estimated $85.8 billion for 1975), especially if we realize the values we would be buying for ourselves, our country, for our future generation and for our world.

At the present time we are still far from any decision to implement a drug or crime prevention program by the federal government.

There is, among many human problems, a sociological one

that is very serious. It is poverty. Poverty places people, masses, in a state of misery and helplessness and inhumanity that perpetuates itself because the drive for power is broken, replaced by feelings of despondency and futility and a vain hope of deliverance by a religious miracle or a political revolutionary.

I have come to consider poverty more a mental than a social illness. It is endemic in India, South America and many backward countries in Africa and Asia. The ruling classes there do not want a change, but we in the United States can bring about a change if we want to spend the money and apply our will. The children of the poor should be trained in school by teachers of the highest quality and high pay, who teach the values a depressed and negatively oriented home cannot provide and which the sickness of poverty will prevent being taught.

Masses of people, especially in the slums and black ghettos, who have little chance to help themselves, suffer because they have by conditioning become beaten down, hopeless, apathetic, with little initiative and minimal family cohesiveness, factors as the Milton Eisenhower Report points out that breed crime. Their natural drive to power has been squelched or sometimes activated by violent, radical groups that demand taking by force what the white majority has accumulated—either by work and saving or by exploitation.

We live in an age of violence and open rebellion. Complacency and indifference have for too long caused the greater part of the population to close its eyes and become blind to misery; it acts like the old steel baron who, while he was dining, called in his servant to remove a beggar because, he said, "It breaks my heart to see him hungry."

"If there is genius among these poor people, he will make it," is one callous way to rationalize poverty. The reality is that the majority of the poor show mass regression into the helpless status of a child who turns to society demanding, "You must take care of me." With the inability to assume responsibility goes a loss of self-esteem that has helped to create an enormous dehumanized welfare system composed of people with a twisted sense of pride. For able-bodied people, not to work is parasitic and destructive to them and society. People must be helped to stand on their own feet and be prepared for work. Again, one has to begin with the child, where there is a receptive brain and an imaginative mind. Those who do not want to work, except for the sick, the aged or the crippled, should receive psychological help to remove the mental blocks, for poverty can be and often is a sympton of mental illness.

The philosophy, "I will get myself fired and live on unemployment," is morally and sociologically that of a sick state of mind and symbolic of a corrupt system. The able-bodied who refuse to work should not live off the sweat of those who will work. When this happens, something has gone wrong with the human spirit, a healthy power drive has been broken early, on an individual or collective level, and that is why I believe such people need help to have their self-worth restored. Psychiatry knows preventive and therapeutic measures that can be taken if lawmakers with understanding will introduce the necessary bills and provide the funds.

The squashing of an ego can take place in a mansion as well as in a tenement, sometimes with similar disastrous results. The wife of one of this country's leading industrialists came to me for help. After the initial greeting, she immediately apologized for the lack of care and time she was able to give her son because of the social and other obligations that went with her husband's position.

In a society that is as highly industrialized as ours, and as competitive, the inability to function is, with the exception of the handicapped, the ill and those with brain damage, generally due to the psychological factor of inhibition.

Pavlov created behavior in dogs that resembled that of persons who live in fear and who have no incentive or ambition. They exist in a state that is like the somnambulistic phase in hypnotism: a limp, ambitionless twilight zone. Beyond this, Pavlov produced paradoxical behavior; that is, by crossing signals he induced animals to show an exactly opposite reaction. For instance, by the exposure to prolonged stress and a mix-up of signals, a dog would walk away when food was presented and, when food was taken away, return to look for it. We find this in persons we call oppositional, those who automatically must do the opposite of what is demanded. This is an indication of a serious mental condition.

Our contemporary society cannot be punished for some of the sins of our ancestors. Personally, I accept the system of free enterprise as one that is basically healthy because it produces an enormous incentive to the growth and development of the total personality. Or rather, it should, if a man wants to be a beachcomber, let him be a beachcomber, but he must not live at the expense of those who work. People who love parasitic existence are sick people. There are neurotic reasons why a person shows indifference to, or disinterest in, using his productive potentials.

We must learn not to detest failure or to give up on those who fail because their drive for power has been broken. But we must not accept slum populations or masses of poor as an inevitable social condition or a regrettable drag that we allow, and even support, because of guilt or fear.

If we, the productive part of the population, want to live with dignity, we must try to bring dignity where it has not had a chance to develop. There are any number of agencies with programs that aim to help, though many seem discouragingly inefficient. Sometimes there is a lack of enthusiasm, of genuine human interest, but most of the time it is just that help comes too late to those in need.

The key to alleviating slum conditions is education, as all

studies have concluded. Thus what we can do, rather than giving endless handouts such as welfare, is to start a massive program of reeducation, not only in schools that teach the three "R's" but schools that try to prevent damage to the young human psyche. Such a task, long overdue, is so great that it could only be achieved on a governmental scale and it is for that reason that I presented the two earlier outlined plans to the President, though there may be, as I stated, better ones. But proceed we must, in spite of those who, because of their perverted sense of values, will give priority for government spending not to what should be on top but to the bottom of the list.

Russia knows the value of work to a man. When I went to the Soviet Union in 1959 as a member of the United States Committee of the World Medical Association (now open only to member countries, not individuals), the group leader asked me to be spokesman for the two psychiatrists and respond to the greetings of Professor Timofev, Vice-Director of the Bechterev Mental Hospital in Leningrad and also the chief psychiatrist of the Soviet Army. After he gave the history of his hospital and its work, we were led on an inspection tour and were very impressed by the patients' being trained in a variety of occupations. According to Pavlovian principles, the tasks of the patients are selected according to how ill the patients are: the sicker the patient, the simpler the task. As a patient improved, more complicated tasks were given him, symbolic of the process of recovery. The workrooms at the hospital looked much like a small factory; the patients were producing pajamas, underwear, belts, shoes, hammocks, TV antennas, among other items. There were toolmaking, metal and wood shops. All the manufactured goods were useful products, and the emphasis was on helping the patients return to the normal life. Schizophrenics worked side by side with epileptics and neurologically sick people. Significantly, the patients were paid full salaries and given pension rights. This, it was believed, would restore a patient's self-respect, his sense of reality and usefulness. We heard a description of how a deeply depressed man who refused to move was induced to make a useful object. A trainer would come to his side every day, demonstrating a simple movement, until one day the patient carried it out himself. Then the trainer showed him a second, and a third movement until the man learned how to make a fountain pen, an enormous achievement. We were given a pen as a gift, with the name of the hospital on it.

The point made here is that the patient's self-esteem and sense of worth was restored by seeing products he made bearing the label of the hospital and also by the pay he received, pay that equaled that of workers in factories (I think, with a deduction for the hospital). Later on the patient would return home and the family would be paid for his room and board—to free the bed—and the patient would return to the hospital daily for work.

During the question and answer period in Professor Timofev's spacious office, I asked:

Q.: Do you use psychotherapy?
A.: We talk to patients when necessary.
Q.: For how long?
A.: That depends.
Q.: Do you talk for an hour?
A.: Not that long.
Q.: For ten minutes?
A.: Longer than that if necessary.

The information I tried to elicit from the professor was his attitude towards psychotherapy. I could have asked directly whether Russian psychiatry had been using psychoanalysis, which I finally did. The answer was "No—we are not sure that Freud was correct." But they do have their own type of psychotherapy.

Professor Timofev was a polished, worldly man and very polite.

"What about homosexuality?" I inquired.

"We have none—it's a crime in the Soviet Union and is punished."

"How about drugs?"

"We don't have that problem, except for some cases in Central Asia." This was in 1959. I don't know about the problem now.

He then asked me, "What about alcoholism in the United States?"

"That is a problem," I replied.

It seems the number of alcoholics is higher in the Soviet Union than in the United States, where the latest figure places it at nine million.

After the conference we were treated to a lunch of a large bowl of fresh caviar, cold sturgeon and other delicacies, and vodka.

It was a warm and cordial good-bye, and we reciprocated by giving farewell parties for the heads of the various departments and their assistants in Kiev, Leningrad, and a most successful one in Moscow. Generally, the longer they lasted, the more fraternal the spirit. (The Scotch we had brought was a favorite drink.) The Russians made every possible effort to demonstrate their friendship. I once asked a Russian, not a physician, through my interpreter, "Why are you all so very friendly?" and he said, "During the war you were the only ones who helped us—we shall never forget that." It was evident that the Russians had an enormous respect for Americans and tried to recapture the cordial relationship they had at the time when they were our allies.

They tried to minimize the cold war by playing the role of perfect hosts. My interpreter, considered their best (she had accompanied Mrs. Eleanor Roosevelt and various American congressmen), turned to me after we left the hospital and said, in a very emotional tone, "When you don your white coats [like those the Russian doctors were wearing] you are not Americans or Russians or Germans—you are doctors," to stress the mutuality of purpose and goal and possibly the hope for a world of peaceful coexistence and friendly cooperation.

During that same trip, one other American psychiatrist and I visited the Pavlov Institute in Koltushy, at that time a rare privilege, for it is a temple of science that has the status of a national shrine.

The Pavlov Institute consists of a theoretical division in Leningrad and an experimental institute with about twenty laboratories in Koltushy, eighteen miles north of Leningrad.

The theoretical basis of Russian psychiatry, as well as the treatment for mental, nervous and many physical disorders such as essential hypertension, is based on Pavlov's work at Koltushy, a small village of scientists. During the war the Germans occupied Koltushy and killed all animals, among them many generations of conditioned dogs used for the study of genetics. Now new generations of conditioned dogs are being bred in order to resume the study of behavior and genetics.

I read a paper at the New York Academy of Science on "Medicine and Psychiatry in the U.S.S.R.," which appeared in the *Transaction of Academy*. (Ser. II, Vol. 22, No. 8, June 1960) and in *Psychosomatics* Vol. 1, No. 5, September-October 1960. In it I said:

> The discovery of the unconscious and its profound effects on the mental and physical functioning of man is perhaps the greatest contribution psychology has made to medicine in the first half of this century. Indeed, the majority of researchers in the United States and other countries of the Western World consider the vast quantity of mental life, which at one time had been conscious and then became repressed or which never has reached

consciousness, to have a more powerful effect on the psychodynamic functioning than the conscious mind. . . . [Soviet medicine] "rejects the concept of the unconscious as it does Freudianism or any related school of psychoanalytic thought.

(Though recently there have been reports of some doctors being more receptive to the studies on the unconscious.)

I concluded however that the cordial reception our Soviet colleagues extended to us and their full cooperation in allowing us to examine facilities which had been closed for so many years were hopeful signs of a closer and more fruitful exchange of concepts toward the mutual goal of all physicians, a peaceful, healthier and saner society of man.

That makes it all the harder to accept the fact that the Soviet Union has been revealed by such outstanding men as Solzhenitsyn and Sakharov to use mental hospitals to suppress political dissenters: such people have been imprisoned as "antisocial" and "not in touch with Socialist reality." When, for example, a former Soviet army general tried to defend a group of Crimean Tatars charged with anti-Soviet activity, he was arrested, ruled insane, and sent to a mental hospital. That was in 1969; he was still there as of May 1974, according to *The New York Times*. What a terrible travesty of Pavlov's dreams of the ideal man, and his hope that "exact science about human nature . . . will deliver man from his present gloom and purge him from his contemporary shame in the sphere of inter-human relationships."

Returning to the problem of self-defeating behavior in people, be it alcoholism, drug addiction, ineffectiveness in work or inability to hold a job, there are in it elements of fear or of a weak, beaten-down ego that has enslaved natural, healthy self-assertion. The drive for power has been broken with little chance of repair.

If, after World War II, we, the victorious nations, had destroyed the industrial capacity of Germany and Japan, and had broken the will to rebuild their countries, and if we had kept them in an enslaved and economically impoverished state, we, the victors, would have created welfarelike conditions with two alternatives: the drive for power could have been kept down by force to a poverty level and a behavior pattern established, similar to that of Pavlov's fourth group, the weak inhibitory type. Or, and this would have been more likely, the simmering rebellion would one day, like a smoldering fire, burst into flames of open, violent warfare in an effort to regain independence.

The psychodynamic forces in the individual do not differ in principle with those of a group. If there has existed an assertive power drive that has broken under stress, the individual has a chance to recover. He can regroup inwardly, change objectives and pick up the battle with life with clearer coordination and greater effectiveness. The weak, inhibitory individual cannot by his own efforts build an effective ego unless, like the man in the Bechterev Hospital who was taught step-by-step how to make a fountain pen, he is helped to build or cultivate an undeveloped or crippled ego or a natural drive for power. He may never become a conqueror but then the world does not need masses of conquerors.

If we, members of a healthy society, learn how to restore effective functioning in the many who have been chained by an unkind fate or by debilitating mental functioning, we will move towards a less violent, less neurotic and more mature society. Again, let us remember, nothing is stable, all exists in a flow. Man's genius, if given a chance, (and the money), can make as great a contribution to the field of human interaction as to the feats in the field of technology.

XII

Power and Peace

POWER AND peace seem to be in contradiction with each other, for we tend to relate power to aggression and aggression to the very opposite of peace—war. But men who have worked with intensity, who have been preoccupied with a task of profound interest or creativity, whatever the scope, have experienced the feeling of being fully at peace with themselves.

To feel at peace comes from a state of complete absorption, from channeling all aggressive or creative energy into physical or mental activity toward a desired objective. The successful mastering of innate resistance leads to mixed feelings of exhilaration and tranquility. Peace may be found in the resolving of inner conflict or at the height of concentrated activity or in rest after work in a state of contentment.

Power is needed to accomplish a task of creation, whether that creation is the building of a house or the completion of a garden or the writing of a scientific paper. As we have said, to produce something that did not exist before, that in the end has meaning or is pleasurable, and that is the product of one's imagination—all of this is creative. I remember, nearly three decades ago, watching a frail old man strike mighty blows at a mass of copper to give it the supersized human form his creative mind had envisioned. In brief, creative power is the uninhibited energy that is poured into one's work, whatever the field, be it writing, painting, an experiment, putting one brick on top of another or planning a special Thanksgiving dinner. Creative energy flows as a river in one direction and with as much intensity as a person is capable of. Those who have the ability or the courage to let go with a sense of abandonment, in work or love, know that the greater the abandonment, the greater the feeling of peace. This is what I mean when I use the term peace in this connotation: it is harmony, inner balance, not absence of toil or fight. As an inner experience, it is of a different, warmer, more active quality, than viewing a beautiful sunset by the sea.

Peace or war, at the height of an all-out effort, have a related fury of excitement, but the one builds and the other destroys, the one produces and the other devours. Peace requires cultivation and is truly creative, rewarding and harmonious, while war, though also requiring creative thought and sweat and toil and preparation, is brutal and cruel. Peace is a conquest of love over hate, war, of hate over love.

Those whose power to love and, consequently, to create has been broken or never developed will choose war in order to experience an intoxicating sense of power or excitement, similar to that of the man who felt truly alive as he gambled, all other feelings numbed.

I have slowly come to believe that we do not have both a creative and a destructive energy but only one energy, one drive, that can be poured into either creative or destructive pursuits; that one man uses power and fury for constructive creation the way another man uses it at the height of a battle. Vincent van Gogh wrote in a letter to his brother Theo: "I can very well do without God both in my life and in my painting, but I cannot, suffering as I am, do without something which is greater than I, which is my life—the power to create." The power to create is the true meaning of peace and may explain why so few people are peaceful or why mankind has not kept the peace but taken the easier way to release restless, un-coordinated energies—by war, the way two boys fight.

Since many men are uncertain about their own basic values (and their manliness or femininity), they are also uncertain about the "call" of the creative urge that may be the expression of their inner self. They may choose goals that are selfish and greedy or use power not as a means to a happier life but as an end itself—a despotism to control all or to gather up, to possess, all.

Most people do not possess the demon within of a van Gogh, or the drive of a Henry Ford, or the sense of mission, as my friend Harrison Salisbury described the courageous stand of Solzhenitsyn, but each can in his own way try to learn that the use of power, that is, the use of creative energy for meaningful goals, will deliver him from the lure and subsequent anguish inherent in violent behavior.

A few years ago, a French diplomat (whose father had the distinction of being prime minister a dozen times after World War II) drove me to his home in Versailles for dinner. His English-born wife was suffering from peculiar painful headaches that no one seemed able to cure. She told me that she loved to paint, and I asked to see her studio. Once in it, I was fascinated by the forceful strokes and colors in her paintings. She was standing behind me and I turned and said to her, "Do you know how much violence there is in you?"

She did not seem surprised. She replied, "I know, but now my doctor says I must not paint, it's too exciting. My blood pressure is high."

I paused, then said, "I hate to contradict a colleague but you must paint more, more and more or—" I wanted to say "You die," but modified it to "You will have more trouble." And then I added, in a mutter, "Where is your violence to go?"

"I agree," she said. "If I stop painting I know I will die."

The next day both she and her husband came to visit me at my hotel. She brought me a present, a watercolor of Venice in flaming colors. I looked at it, then I said, "It's all blood." I meant the colors looked like blood. She nodded with an understanding smile.

While it is true, as Ernest Jones put it, that "the control man has secured over nature has by far outrun his control over himself," we can learn to conquer the need for violence (war) and begin to grow up and learn to enjoy the fruits of peace, that is psychic peace. It is, as we said, a matter of absorption and devotion: whether we give of ourselves fully in the work we do or try to get away with the least amount of giving. One person may clean the streets with the pride of a man who wants to do a good job, whereas another may brush along aimlessly, his only interest getting through the day. The first man may never feel the need to fight, the second may need a fight to release some of his slumbering, unspent energies. We can, as many people do, find sports and hobbies to absorb our aggression.

As we have seen, discontented men in power, men with an insatiable hunger for glory, may be driven to gain control, to dominate others. They may arouse others who are equally discontent, who cannot let go fully or enjoy or give of themselves and cannot therefore experience the full excitement that comes from creation—from doing something that has meaning, and from being able to love. All of them may mumble that war is terrible and must be banned, and yet they will react to the contagion of mass excitement, of which the most primitive and therefore violent is the contagion of war.

Our present political and military concept of peace still seems to follow the fourth century Latin adage: "*Si vis pacem, para bellum.*" (If you want peace, prepare for war.) Consequently, we have built at enormous costs organizations such as NATO and SEATO, military power alliances meant to act as a deterrent to the outbreak of war. We say that security demands these protective measures because of an active Communist imperialism that preaches world revolution.

Rightly or wrongly, the Communist bloc feels equally threatened and has built its own Warsaw Pact and a powerful arsenal of offensive and defensive weapons. And so the world exists in a state of a near-alert—a silent confrontation with a potential of "overkill" that devours stupendous sums of money taken from hard-working people and used for the perfection of sophisticated weapons for mass killing, not for wiping out poverty and illiteracy or for progress in becoming truly civilized.

The irrationality of this course of action seems finally to have become apparent to even the suspicious minds of many of the apostles of destruction and hate. As a result there has emerged, in Washington and the Kremlin, the workable and infinitely more rational policy of *détente*. Secretary of State Henry Kissinger went to the real heart of the matter when he said, in early 1974: "The accumulation of nuclear arms has to be constrained if mankind is not to destroy itself."

It is unfortunate that the parents of détente have been fear of death and destruction and recognition of one's power limitation rather than love and a genuine desire for peace, or we would have disarmament. But we must be grateful for small steps toward peace. A treaty to limit the arms race, even in a most modest form, may secure an absence of war, though that is still far from a positive, creative concept of peace. We must break with the age-old conditioning of power politics that have led in this century to two world wars and scores of bitter, smaller wars. Albert Einstein, with his lucid and penetrating sharpness of thought, said, "The unleashed power of the atom has changed everything except our thinking." We have no choice but to adopt a new thinking if we do not wish to drift toward a catastrophe beyond comparison. We require a substantially *new manner of thinking* if mankind is to survive.

The tragedy, as psychology has taught us, is that many people do not cherish life, and many makers of international policy, though educated and polished, are nevertheless nihilists at heart, playing a game of Russian roulette where the stakes are masses of lives other than their own, often sacrificed for their narcissistic glory.

Psychopolitics would be a beginning, the infant of a different kind of thinking. It is built on the thoughts and work of many who have gone before. Its concepts are pragmatic, educational and above all, *preventive,* using every method the field of psychology and related fields, including axiology, has produced to decipher the working of the minds of people and, more importantly, to test and to secure the sanity of our political leaders.

Where was the visionary judgment of leadership, our own or that of others, in 1914, or 1939, or, in our country, before Korea, or Vietnam, or the day the Gulf of Tonkin Resolution was speeded through Congress? When certain congressmen asked me, during the Ford hearing, what we discussed when he came to see me, my eyes glanced down the rows of the congressmen, thinking, where were you during the Tonkin debate?, as I replied, "We discussed the wisdom of staying out of involvement in Southeast Asia." It has too often become a grim reality, as Haile Selassie, Emperor of Ethiopia, put it, that "throughout history it has been the inaction of those who could have acted, the indifference of those who should have known better, the silence of the voice of justice when it mattered most, that has made it possible for evil to triumph."

The problem is not the long line of statesmen who mask

their greed for power under the guise of liberators, missionaries and St. Georges; the problem is that psychopathological men have ruled history and we have no guarantee that psychopathology in our leaders will not reach the height of obsessive-compulsive-destructive behavior and send the world up in flames—turning it literally to ashes.

Psychopolitics aims at reforms. We must seek methods to stop mentally unstable leaders from continuing to drag nations along the bloody road they thus far have traveled. We need new thinking, as Einstein said, though new thinking by some may be a problem, as evidenced by the statements of a historian as distinguished as Arthur Schlesinger. In a keynote address before the Eighth Biennial Divisional Meeting of the New York State District of the American Psychiatric Association on March 15, 1974, in New York, titled "A Historian Looks at Psychopolitics," he took great pains to attack me personally and my plan to combat crime. He also said, "No amount of psychiatric exorcism would have done away with the intractable problems that confronted Lincoln," an attack on my statement in a *New York Times* Op-Ed page article referring to Lincoln's mental illness. If a scholar of the stature of Schlesinger believes that our constitution is sufficient to protect us from unstable leaders, then he is merely a learned dogmatist who records history but contributes little to the prevention of war. But that he devoted his address to psychopolitics at least indicates the impact my concept had made on him.

The right kind of new thinking will lead to action that prevents destructive aggression, that stems from the mobilization of man's creative forces for peace. It is rather naive to console oneself with the belief that the Department of Defense is a Department of Peace. It still is what it was named for years, a Department of War. The time has come for a real Department of Peace and this was the thought I wanted to present to President Nixon when I originally went to the White House.

This was the meaning of my suggestion of an "Agency for the Exploration of the Psychodynamics of Peace," a painful compromise but a necessary one to win a first step against reactionary thinking, the opposition of Congress, and foremost, incredible as it sounds, the President's all powerful, Machiavellian former White House chief of staff.

President Nixon's preparations for reelection, and Watergate, made any pursuit of my plan impossible. But ideas born of deep conviction never really die; they are only shelved. To stimulate the interest of other people, to unburden my heart, and to let the White House know that my struggle had not ended, I published a summary of my thoughts, based on the second paragraph of the Constitution of UNESCO, that reads: "Since wars begin in the minds of men, it is in the minds of men that the defenses of peace must be constructed."

I wrote down six points while in the plane on my way to Washington to have lunch with President Nixon when he was Vice-President, in the mid-fifties. (The slip of paper stayed in my briefcase for a few years, then proved to be embarrassing at the Soviet border in Kiev when a luggage inspector found it. He was suspicious and called as interpreter a supervisor, a stern-faced woman in her thirties. She read the paper slowly—spent twenty minutes on it—then she permitted us to go through.)

The points were described in "The Road to Peace," an editorial I wrote in *The New York Times* on March 30, 1971 (later printed in the Congressional Record of July 19, 1971), the full text of which is in the Appendix.

In it I stressed six points: first, and foremost, that "Peace is more than the absence of war—just as health is more than the absence of illness." I wrote of changing the concept of peace from a passive one to a new dynamic way of life, and of my dream of the creation of a Department of Peace to balance the existing Department of Defense. I suggested that a Secretary of Peace be present at all policy-making decisions.

The last paragraph of the editorial was chosen to silence critics during the height of the Cold War. It read:

> If we accept the premise that the defense of peace must be constructed in the minds of men "then the problem is for people to get together and leap governments—if necessary to evade governments—to work out not one method but thousands of methods by which people can gradually learn a little bit more of each other."
>
> It was Dwight D. Eisenhower who made this statement in 1956 when he spoke of how "to help build a road to peace."

The defense of peace is in the hands of the people, or it should be. An agency for the exploration of the psychodynamics of peace could, I would think, be established by a presidential order. But if it did need the support of the legal representatives of the people in both houses of Congress, who, I wonder, would vote against it? If enacted, it would involve the government and the people in a dialogue toward what would be perhaps the most gigantic program of education ever attempted—*education for peace*. As John Dewey said, "Since a democratic society repudiates the principle of external authority, it must find a substitute in voluntary disposition and interest; these can be created only by education."

People must be taught the meaning of peace and how to liberate the energies bound up in boredom, discontent, self-destructiveness and hate. People must learn how to elect peaceful leaders who are aggressive yet strong, who are emotionally secure enough to be peaceful. As Freud said, *"What this world needs are men of passion who can control that passion."* And we as people must become mature and responsible enough to participate in the process of choosing candidates. Just to vote and then complacently lean back in front of TV is a dangerous act of negligence, as we are beginning to learn.

Several years ago the president of a psychological society suggested the development of a pill for political leaders that would make them peaceful. This is an absolutely absurd, naive idea, even if said half in earnestness. But even if this man were serious, the question arises as to who would administer the pill and why a leader would take it. Furthermore, if a leader has attained his position because of his aggressive way of handling problems, why would he want to give it up or why should he be psychologically treated? We do not advocate a diminishing of aggression, only a prevention of the acting out of overaggression that has its roots in hidden violence.

Knowledge is power, we learned in school, but the controlled know-how of action is superpower. It is not what we hear, learn or read that, from a point of progress, matters. What matters is the absorption of a thought as though it were our own, and then its application to action or inaction. "What thou inherited from thy fathers, acquire it to make it thine," said Goethe.

If we want peace we have to understand its full meaning, learn the enjoyment that comes from a transformation (or sublimation) of raw aggression into what is creative, and then fight for peace—overcoming within ourselves resistance and self-destructiveness, and overcoming from without the threats and opposition to anything that deviates from the conventional and familiar. That is why I say that peace is dynamic, not passive, and entails the full and free use of power inherent in man. Again, peace in everyday life does not mean to avoid a battle, but to ask ourselves the meaning of the battle, what values we are fighting for. Peace also means tolerance and humaneness in coexisting with fellow men who may think differently from us.

Again and again, I say, instead of Power for War, let us

have Power for Peace.

Let us build trust among ourselves and all other nations, as trust is a first bond of friendship, or for that matter of love. Fifteen years ago when I was one of fifteen physicians who visited Russia on the inspection tour I mentioned in the previous chapter, I walked through the Snegirev Maternity Hospital in Leningrad. On my right walked the director, Professor Dodor (I never knew her first name), and on my left, a young, attractive woman, the best interpreter in the Soviet Union, who had attached herself to me because of her great interest in psychiatry.

We came to a huge ward filled with beautiful, pink-cheeked babies. Suddenly, as we stood in the middle of it, Professor Dodor, a rather plump woman in her fifties, with a jovial, friendly manner, stopped, looked at me, then, with a wave of her ample hand that took in the babies on the ward, announced "All these babies must die."

I was stunned. I asked, "Why?" thinking, they must have some dreadful disease although they looked healthy.

"Because you Americans are going to make war on us," she said.

I paused, then replied, "My dear professor, I am not here in any official capacity representing the United States. But I assure you of one thing. We Americans shall never make war on you if you don't make war on us." Her whole face lit up, as if the Messiah had spoken. And when she appeared at a farewell party we gave for the heads of the hospitals we had visited, arriving with some of her assistants in tow, she joyously ran to me and kissed me on both cheeks and turning to the rest of her group, pointed at me and announced, "He said, 'There will be no war.' "

Several days later, bored with a general medical lecture in the largest Moscow hospital, I decided to shop at the large department store called GUM. My special limousine had gone off somewhere so I jumped on a streetcar without the faintest idea of where it was going. I knew GUM was at Red Square. Not knowing Russian, I said to the conductor, "GUM, GUM." Nobody seemed to understand where I wanted to go.

Finally, one very tall Russian passenger said to me, "Ah, GUMA, GUMA," then took my hand, led me off that street-car and onto another, and sat next to me until we stopped near the department store. He got off with me, embraced me, saying "Eisenhower! Khrushchev! Ah!" shaking my hand, delight on his face (Eisenhower was expected in the Soviet Union for a visit). This man had made a detour to make sure I got where I wanted to go. There was joy and excitement on his face at being able to help a lost American, and I saw this same excitement on the faces of many Russians I met, as I greeted them with the three words I had learned that worked like magic, *"Mir i druzhba"*—peace and friendship.

But Eisenhower and Khrushchev never met that year. A few weeks after my trip, one of our spy planes was shot down flying over Russia and the pilot, Francis Gary Powers, taken prisoner. This incident put an end to the proposed summit meeting to discuss a possible end of the cold war.

The Russians are fearful and suspicious. No wonder. Within three decades the Germans invaded Russia, twice, devastating their land, committing atrocities unequalled in history. There was intervention by an International Anti-Soviet Army right after World War I to defeat the new Soviet state, and a long, bloody civil war until 1920 with a loss in those three wars of thirty million people—about the total population of Spain. The people of Russia want peace, just as the people of the United States want peace. But the leaders do not seem able, at this point in history, to trust each other, though they are able to whip up the people into a mutual fear of each other.

We have been equally distrustful, fearing an overthrow of our government by force. It seems to me it would be a very weak government if that were possible.

The American leaders have supported anti-Communist regimes because they say that Communism is a threat to democracy and they want to impose democracy on Communist countries. Democracy cannot be imposed; it has to grow out of the will of the people, just as independence grows out of an individual yearning for it. You cannot "impose" good mental health on anyone nor can you "impose" democracy on a nation. The individual, the nation, changes only as he enters into a good relationship with someone who provides him an example of a better way of living.

Mediocrity ruled and determined our foreign policy for nearly three decades before the emergence of Henry Kissinger. To checkmate Communism, we have supported with men and guns and money corrupt regimes which did not have the support of their own people. And so China fell and Cuba and a half a dozen other little countries. And people became confused about the meaning of democracy. The Communist countries might become more democratic if they saw in our growth and prosperity the advantages of democracy to the nation and the individual.

Similar to insecure individuals, nations seem to be motivated by two factors: the drive to power and the fear of extinction, which has been stated to be the chief cause of the fierce imperialistic arms race of the Soviet Union. But trust and good will between nations would reduce the fear of extinction, and the drive to power could then be used constructively. Unfortunately, as we have seen, most politicians in action are like aggressive adolescents, threatening, boastful, always ready for a good fight. No longer can we allow them to make decisions which might again involve innocent men in worldwide slaughter.

A letter from one agonized father, a man I do not know, appeared in *The New York Times* Op-Ed page on February 19, 1974. The father, Robert C. Ransom, a corporation lawyer in New York, started off by saying he never thought he would visit the bleak coastal plains between Quang Ngai and My Lai where his oldest son, Mike, was killed in Vietnam nearly six years ago. But he went as a lawyer, joining four other Americans in a trip to assess the prospects for peace in Vietnam. He said he had heard much about the abuses of the legal and judicial system there and wanted to see if they were true. He wrote, "I would not have believed it had I not seen for myself what can only be called a total police state."

He had long ago concluded, he said, that his son's life was "wasted by his own government in a war that his fellow countrymen want only to forget," and that he had reluctantly "come to believe he [his son] died for a cause that had brought only discredit and shame to the United States."

He said he went to Vietnam because he hoped he might find some consolation for his loss, some evidence that his son's sacrifice had somehow served the Vietnamese people. "I wanted to find the honor promised by our government when we signed the Paris agreement in January 1973," he wrote. "Sadly, it must be said that none is to be found. The very use of the word when applied to the conduct of the government of Nguyen Van Thieu is a mockery. . . . Nor is there any peace in Vietnam. . . . Responsible sources said at the time that there had been at least 119,849 casualties since the 'cease-fire.' "

He described President Thieu's palace as "a fortress," and said that on every block in Saigon he encountered policemen and paramilitary forces equipped with United States M-16 rifles and sidearms. He spoke to many persons who had suffered torture and the brutality of prison life. He said, "The palpable presence of terror was everywhere—in the sure knowledge of these people that any apparent opposition to the government or the indication of a desire for peace, would be met with reprisals against members of their families, even young children, in the form of seizure and subjection to the inhuman incarceration so prevalent."

One of his group attended a Saigon military court where defendants were tried without benefit of counsel, given five-minute hearings, and in every case convicted of "political" crimes.

He said that 80 percent of the costs of the Thieu government were borne by American taxpayers and there was little evidence that American money was being used for anything but support of the Thieu military regime, instead of going for food and housing for the devastated villagers of Vietnam. He reported, "With horror, I observed a family of six, near starvation, eating a meal of chopped banana stalks just to fill their stomachs." He saw no sign of "sophisticated American medical assistance," and noted that even the food supplies paid for by the United States did not reach the intended beneficiaries "because of the ever-present graft and corruption at all levels of the civilian and military bureaucracy."

He concluded:

The fact is that the American presence now, as before, remains a disaster, not only as a result of the wartime devastation, defoliation and displacement of people, but as a continuing financial presence that maintains a government of military officers that clings to power no matter what the cost to peace, freedom and democratic principles.

I wish every member of Congress, before they vote more funds for President Thieu, could share my experience. The Paris peace agreement was supposed to guarantee the right of self-determination to the Vietnamese people through democratic liberties and elections. It was supposed to provide the honor in my son's death.

It is doing neither.

Three days later there appeared a front-page story in *The New York Times* written by John W. Finney in Washington, reporting that the defoliation damage caused by the American use of chemical herbicides in the Vietnam war was expected to take at least a century to heal. The study was made by the National Academy of Sciences, a group of leading scientists that often serves as arbiter for the government in matters of scientific controversy, and was authorized by Congress in 1970 to determine the impact of the extensive use of herbicides in the war by the military. Their report stated that herbicides caused "serious and extensive damage" to the inland tropical forests along the South Vietnamese coasts. In addition, there were indications that the herbicides used for the destruction of crops caused deaths among children in the hills of western South Vietnam.

In addition to the ecological damage, the study concluded, the use of the herbicides had an adverse psychological effect, turning Vietnamese opinion against the United States.

Senator J. William Fulbright had been fighting for greater understanding of the relationship between American foreign policy and the behavior of our leaders. In May 1966, as chairman of the Foreign Relations Committee of the United States Senate, he called in a psychiatrist, Dr. Jerome Frank, of the Johns Hopkins University psychiatry department, to explain how hostilities that emanated from misunderstandings could cause wars. In an article, "Psychological Aspects of International Violence," which appeared in the book *Dynamics of Violence,* edited by Dr. Jan Fawcett, Dr. Frank stated:

Just as domestic tranquility in the United States depends on restoring a sense of community to all Americans, so world peace requires the creation of a sense of community to all the world's people, transcending their national allegiances. In the past, there was no prospect of achieving this goal, but now for the first time tremendous advances in electronic communications and mass transportation may be bringing it within reach. We have not, for example, even begun to use the potentialities of international communication satellites to increased international understanding.

With potential enemies, these means offer new opportunities for constant communication without the distorting effects of intermediaries, such as the hot line, and for direct surveillance by satellites. Both of these methods should yield more accurate information as to the opponents' intentions and capabilities. In itself, this would impose restraints on preparations for hostilities by both sides, and would also help to reduce any distortions of the enemy image.

He claimed that "public opinion is an important inhibitor of violence within communities," and that "one can discern the beginnings of a world opinion whose increased power can . . . be seen."

He further said that social psychologists have shown that the most powerful antidote to enmity between groups is cooperation toward a goal that both groups want but neither can achieve alone, and that "at first glance survival would seem to be such a goal, because all people desire it and its achievement requires international cooperation."

He warned that in addition to building attitudes of cooperation, some of these activities should provide outlets for man's aggressive competitiveness, "which must be rechanneled if it is not to be released periodically in war." He said the conquests of outer space and of the undersea world meet this need because they demand the fullest exercise of courage, determination and "all the other manly virtues."

In June 1969, Senator Fulbright called on another psychiatrist, this time the famed Dr. Karl Menninger, to present to the Committee on Foreign Relations some of the "general insights of psychiatry" as it applied to the outstanding issues of foreign policy, "so that we will be better able to understand the political behavior not only of other nations but especially our own."

Dr. Menninger said that "to many of us the war in Vietnam seems a prime example of self-destructiveness, one more likely to spread Communist and other evils than to control them. Youths are being sacrificed; money, materials, the country, our own national image, and in many places our goodwill are being destroyed in a continuing, pointless, and—as it seems to many of us—futile military bonfire." He spoke of the universality of aggression and vindictiveness, predaceousness, greed and envy and said that since life depends upon averting the consequences of self-destructiveness, as well as of external dangers, "it must depend also upon the control of aggressiveness, that this is what civilization is all about."

The philosophy of psychiatrists, he said, puts a high value "on mutuality and understanding, on helpfulness, on cooperation, and on conservation, rather than upon destructiveness for any purpose." Declaring that "civilization is, and always has been, a struggle," he said,

> Civilization is a never-ending series of conflicts but it should be conflict to prevent conflict, not to enhance it. . . . Life is too precious to waste or to be wasted. . . . Our world, for all the scars we have inflicted upon it, is still too wonderful, too magnificent, too holy, may I say, to be destroyed by our sloth, our pettiness, our hates, our heedlessness, or our failure to use our intelligence.

Listen to the words of a West Point graduate, Cornelius McNeil Cooper, Jr., in his successful appeal for an honorable discharge as a conscientious objector:

> I believe that if I kill my brother, I kill myself a little, if not completely. Thus I cannot participate in war in any form and retain my humanity, and cannot face the possiblity of life without my personal humanity.

In the meanwhile, the long American military involvement in Southeast Asia has ended and the Nixon administration has brought about a cease fire in the Middle East. While both are gratifying accomplishments they constitute, at best, an absence of war and not a true, lasting peace as outlined in this chapter. Indeed, a great deal more of good will and understanding and friendship must be mobilized if we the people want to help the world spin on its axis, not ever again for the purpose of war and death, but for peace and for life.

XIII

Power: The American Dream

Every human being with a healthy will to live has a natural drive for power, a drive that goes beyond his need for mere survival. It is an urge to unfold as much of his inert potentials as his courage will allow and a wish to gain recognition that aims to give back to the world what he has received from it, possibly more. There is also a constant struggle to balance the flight and power of his imagination with the demands of the culture, the moral code, and the socioeconomic structure of his society.

The drive for power can be neurotic, unrealistic and so turbulent that it strives for a ruthless, godlike omnipotence. Born out of man's weakness, it can serve to elevate him—though only for a moment—to a position above all others. It is for this that some people kill.

The drive for power rules the life of nations as it does that of individuals. Both nations and individuals set their own stan-

284

dards. India for generations has existed mentally in a state of passivity and is physically almost in a state of near-starvation. The United States, on the other end of a wide scale, calls for the greatest possible production and the highest possible accomplishment. It demands a full use of the aggressive drive for power. It lives up to the image of a conquering pioneer spirit that has opened up a vast land and is making use of its resources. And with this spirit has come an unequaled standard of living. With it also has come the term "The American Dream."

Our American culture sets a high priority on achievement. The need to excel is a conditioned process deeply ingrained in childhood. The philosophy of "making good" is evident as a driving force in a country that has coined the phrase "the sky's the limit."

When Richard Nixon gave his acceptance speech in Miami in 1968 after he had won the nomination of the Republican Party for the Presidency, he made a brief reference to his poor boyhood days and then, in an emotional undertone, added, "I have always believed in the American Dream."

Four years later, elected to the Presidency for a second time, in an atmosphere described by the press as a coronation, he again mentioned the American Dream as the idealized final goal of a man's utmost accomplishments in life. As he stood in the glare of the television cameras, a lone figure in the immense hall, his face projecting an unusual softness, he seemed to be enjoying the moment that spelled fulfillment of a lifelong dream. And as the world watched this scene, Nixon at that very moment did indeed symbolize all that ultimate power and glory represents in a world of reality.

Few have ever risen as high as Richard Nixon, though many have climbed the ladder of success as high as they could. Only a few could set a new goal for themselves after there were no higher peaks to climb. Following an ultimate in success, the emotionally unprepared fall. They want the good

life without knowing what it really is. For any peaceful enjoyment of one's autumn years, there must be a balance of
extrinsic and intrinsic values. A man, if he does not want to
fade away, must go on creating values that equal his degree of
maturity. Goals and objectives change, as does a man's pace.
But there is a need to shift gears or there will be inner turmoil, emptiness or death in the rocking chair.

Hollywood portrays success stories that glorify the overcoming of defeat, the eventual winning. Little attention is
paid to those who fail, those who may end up in a doctor's
office or a mental hospital. The lure of reaching a distant star,
the whip used to drive oneself there, remain powerful incen-
tives in a culture in which millions follow the set formula of
working hard for long hours, bravely overcoming all the obstacles along a stony road, to be eventually rewarded by sharing in the good life of the land.

Success is equated with happiness standardized by the
norm of a dream house, economic security and a respected
position in the community. To have done the best according
to one's ability and to have reached the set finishing line is the
concept of the American Dream.

But the stark light of success throws deep shadows. The
man who has reached his summit, who is still geared for
action, is now confronted with a need to shift gears, to adjust
to a reality that offers no higher peaks to conquer. This, in a
high-powered individual, may lead eventually to self-
destruction, as with Alexander the Great after his conquest of
the world. President Truman said of Alexander's death: "And
then the people around him made him think he was immortal
and he found that thirty-three quarts of wine was too much for
any man, and it killed him at Babylon."

Less dramatically, many never even come close to touching
their star. Some, after a glowing start, break down along the
way despite what once seemed a smooth road to success.
Some give up after a few feeble attempts, as stated earlier,

when their drive for power breaks. Still others seemingly without ambition, never start, not seeing a chance to become famous, important, wealthy—or even noticed. These failures, as we saw, are the poor in a land that is rich. Whatever their wealth, they are poor in the sense that they feel unworthy; they have no meaningful goals, nothing important to say, no sense of the excitement that makes it worthwhile to get up in the morning. They dissipate their innate creative energies or they labor under an overcast aura of futility. When triggered by some minor setback or failure, they react in a conditioned way by turning a great part of their aggressive drives against themselves and become ill-humored and depressed. Those who cannot pull themselves out of the pit of their depression remain unproductive, perhaps even acting out suicidal tendencies. The dissatisfied, the hopeless, the helpless, make up, I would guess, at least one-fifth of our nation.

One man who faithfully followed the ideal of the American Dream and in his rise to prominence succeeded both in a spectacular unfolding of his talents and in the careful, sensible use of his aggression nevertheless just barely avoided self-defeat.

This man, Mr. M., was in his late forties, of superior intellect, tall, slim, confident, self-controlled, and a poised, polished speaker. He would never have entered a psychotherapist's office had it not been at the urging of his wife. He was making a major concession to what he thought was her emotional and romantic nature, for he failed to grasp the deeper reasons for her anxiety about their marriage. From his point of view there was nothing wrong. He thought of himself as an ideal husband. He neither drank nor smoked. He came home for dinner on time. He had a respected position with a handsome income. He had recently bought a large house in a fashionable suburban community, which fit into his concept of an enviable life.

At first he had shrugged his shoulders over his wife's discontent. But it made him feel angry and insecure, causing him to retreat into the sanctuary of his library, as he retreated when as a boy into the loneliness and safety of his room in the attic. He rationalized his wife's complaints as premenopausal mood swings.

But his wife knew better. She saw her marriage in jeopardy though she did not know how to get this problem across to him. Having gained considerable insight about herself in an analyst's office years before, when in her early twenties, she was prompted one day to confront her husband with the plea that he see someone.

"Someone" meant me. (She had read a serialization of *The Will to Live* and decided I would be the right man for him.) "I had carefully chosen you," she told me when I met her. Her husband, wanting no trouble at home, yielded to what he considered a nonsensical demand, but nevertheless a veiled ultimatum by his wife. He made an appointment to see me, and arrived punctually and seemingly complaisant.

Mr. M. displayed the sophistication of his diplomatic training. He was controlled, answering questions readily but disclosing very little about himself. He did not visibly betray discomfort in a setting in which someone else was asking the questions and very personal ones at that. He arranged his appointment for 7:45 A. M., so there would be no interference in his workday routine and so nobody would know he was seeing a doctor twice a week, to him a suspicious routine. The fact that someone might find out he was visiting my office troubled him. He needed the reassurance of professional confidentiality.

On his fourth visit I asked a question that seemed to hit him like a shot. I said, "Why do you come? You really don't want to be here—is it because of your wife?"

For a moment he lost his composure. He did not answer at first. Then he said candidly, "No—I come to please my wife."

"Why then this waste of time and money just to please one's wife?" I asked. "Why not quit and tell her honestly how you feel, that you see no real need for this type of exploration, of having your brain picked apart. Especially since you are a man who has learned early in life how to handle his own affairs."

It was a difficult session. "I admit I do have some anxiety," he said, as though thinking over what I had said. "But who doesn't have anxiety at times—and especially these days. Or occasionally, there is a bad day in the office. Of course, no job is perfect, but I always seem to manage. I think I know how to handle people."

He left my office in a deeply pensive mood, as if sensing there was trouble ahead. Before he left, I asked if he would object to my seeing his wife. He said, "Not at all."

She came willingly. She was almost as tall and slim as he, very attractive and conservatively dressed. She answered my questions with ease and with a warm little smile. But it wasn't long before her voice broke and she began to press a tissue against her eyes.

"Please forgive me," she said.

She scolded herself for her weakness, for not handling herself better. And yet it was evident she wanted to talk. All at once, everything that had been pent up for so long started to come out. She felt she was losing her grip, that she had become "irritable, quarrelsome, really nasty," she said, and "I think I am heading for a breakdown."

The idea of sending her husband for therapy was a last, desperate hope for saving her marriage. The thought of leaving him was unbearable and yet she could not continue a relationship that left her so lonely, depressed and unfulfilled. The marriage had become a bond in name only. His real marriage was to his career. His one and only objective in life was to move on. It was not so much money he was after, it was power. Obviously he could not stop in the middle of his work. She understood that. But she felt outside, alienated.

She admitted she loved her husband and admired his brilliance. "He is a genius," she said with pride. "Everybody recognizes that," she added. But this actually made things worse. She was living with a man who was like a boarder, a polite, immaculate and responsible boarder.

He had his little quirks. In everyday life he was a little tight with money, but he was overly generous with Christmas and birthday presents. He was obstinate in some ways and submissive in others. It was all so very confusing. She had tried to find a key to the confusion. The knowledge that her husband had grown up without affection was an intellectual reality, but where did that leave her? It did not meet her needs, nor those of the children. His lack of affection for the children hurt her.

She said, "I don't want to burden him with my problems. He has so many, as it is—but I just can't carry the load of daily living alone. The children need a father who cares. I am tired of making excuses for his 'benign neglect.' "

She added, "I've thought of how life would be without him—the loneliness, what I would do with my time. A woman alone is a big bore; nobody wants her anyplace."

She spoke calmly for the most part, becoming agitated only when the conversation touched on her husband's personality. She described him as being cold-blooded—an icicle, like his mother. He used withdrawal as a means of punishment. An argument would end abruptly; he would disappear, work in his library, come to bed late to avoid talking to her or having sex. There were increasingly longer intervals between sex episodes.

"Why did you marry this man?" I asked. "You must have known what he was like."

"I knew," she said. "Before I married him, I went to see a psychoanalyst. I was afraid of becoming an old maid. I had a thing about it, and living with Mother was no bed of roses. To complicate matters, I had set high standards for myself—too high. But my prospective husband seemed to fulfill them. He was very attractive and his mind overwhelmed me. My analyst pointed out that I would always be well taken care of but warned me that, when it came to personal warmth and affection, I should not expect too much. But I was one of those girls who believe that love cures all. I was going to shower him with love, and every problem would be solved. And so I decided to marry him. It was a challenge to my love to melt his iciness. And I thought I had learned enough to be able to cope with anything that might arise."

She left my office feeling better because she had been able to express some of her thoughts and feelings.

When her husband came for his session the following week, he was uneasy. He told me he had never really listened to his wife's complaints, had treated them as he had his mother's. Both women made constant demands. So he had closed his ears until the curtain fell on the lecture, so to speak. It was a matter of time and control. He had learned early in life to let the drops of discontent of others roll off his back. He now questioned how wise it had been to tell his wife about himself, his early anxieties, his unhappiness. She could use the information as a weapon. I encouraged the patient to discuss personal problems not to reveal what he had talked about in my office. He admitted how much his new awareness of his detachment from criticism and complaints shocked him.

He had never thought about his uninvolvement, his inhibited and embarrassed displays of affection. He felt nobody really understood him but had consoled himself with the fact that everyone respected him and that deep within he was noble, a martyr, working as hard as he could to make it possible for his family to live in elegance and comfort. This achievement had salved his hurt ego.

But what was the truth? Was this man basically as kind and noble as he believed he was? Or was he fulfilling his own self-centered and compulsive need for power?

Once the word was spoken, he admitted he wanted power. This was his secret ambition. To gain power was the mainspring of his thinking, scheming, planning and driving himself. One day he would show the world his gallant St. George qualities as he slew all the dragons. He would be hailed as one of the country's great business leaders.

But the evil was the accumulation of his own violent, denied feelings, the rage at growing up with a mother and father he thought critical of him and uncaring and selfish. The drops of discontent had not rolled off his back.

He needed power to protect himself from the father who ridiculed him because he did so poorly in sports, sneered at him for avoiding fistfights with the other boys. Power would compel his mother to pay attention to him, make her and the world watch him, listen to him. And then perhaps everybody would love him.

These were his top-secret thoughts, his childhood dreams of one day being all powerful not for anyone else's ears, only for himself, during his off-and-on escapes into a vivid world of fantasy. His daring in letting out more and more of his innermost feelings in my office surprised him, and frightened him as well.

It took some time before he could lose some of his defensiveness and start to develop a sense of trust and a gentle dependency on me. He was learning the meaning of the term "transference," in which the patient bestows on the doctor all his feelings, both of love and hate.

He started to see his father more the way he was, powerfully built, a show-off when it came to displaying physical strength. He had always been afraid of his father, resenting the ridicule of his weakness. His father's bullying was meant to impress his mother, who, however, remained unimpressed. She seemed to sense her husband's own weakness underneath the need to bully. But he, as a boy, was terrified of his father most of the time. His pale face and frail body were a source of his father's contempt, and he felt weak and ashamed. His mother was no help, for she too often mocked his lack of masculinity. To escape these daily little cruelties, which, in the life of a child, add up to one great cruelty, he took refuge in his attic room and dreamed up plans for showing everyone how mighty he was, how sparkling his intellect and how sharp his wit and then he would put his parents to shame. Beautiful women would love him and seek him out, and then his mother would feel sorry that she had misjudged him and finally—finally, she would love him too.

Mr. M. was very harsh with himself. He was overcritical, as often is the case with mentally very alert patients for a period of time. But he was changing. Many things he had accepted on face value now appeared in a different light: his elaborate home, his social position, his attractive wife, his good-looking blond children, his status in the country club. It had all been real and enjoyable but symptomatic of the mold into which he had been pressed, or had pressed himself. He had thought it was proper, a model of the typical, happy American family. Now, all looked a sham.

Occasionally, very occasionally, we slid into philosophy and we spoke of what a man is, what a man has, and how a man may stand in the esteem of others, ideas expressed by Schopenhauer, the German philosopher.

His creative mind had had no difficulty charting a course of action that would enrich his worldly goods and earn him the esteem of the outside world. But the first phrase, "what a man is," had been for him from time to time a source of troublesome introspection. His busy life, the extra work he brought home on weekends, did not leave much time for self-examination or rumination. Nevertheless, this question would suddenly come to mind, triggered by seemingly unrelated incidents, and cause him a mild discomfort and frustration. He would ask himself what kind of man he was, and what it was that made a man a man, and what the meaning was of the more sophisticated term, "male identity."

He had always hated bullies, sensing that their bullying was a cover-up for inner weakness, as it had been in his father, rather than an expression of strength. He now understood how to handle bullies without responding in kind. He compared his actions with that of other men and asked himself: How does a strong man act? What is strength? Is it a covering up of weakness, or is it a special kind of quality? Is one born with strength or does one develop it, and if so, how? How does a man combine gentleness with masculinity? And, more puzzling, how is a man aggressive with women without being rough and demanding—and without frightening them? Confused about his own emotional needs, how could he be aware of the emotional needs of someone else—that is, a woman?

A new vista opened up when he became aware of the enormous rage, anger and hostility that seethed in his unconscious, and realized how much effort it had taken all his life to repress these unacceptable feelings. It was disturbing and confusing to him and yet the awareness gave him a theretofore unknown sense of freedom and inner security, which made him more considerate and thoughtful. He resisted the pretense of empathy. What he felt, he dared to express. He reported to me with satisfaction how much his new understanding of people helped him in dealing with his boss, the chairman of the board and also in handling those who worked for him. He was the president, the youngest ever, of a rapidly expanding corporation, noted in the world of business and high finance; he was respected by some, envied by others, an easy target for criticism, just as he had been as a boy. In the past he had had to attribute his success to something outside himself and so had never fully enjoyed his success for fear his "luck" would leave him. But now he felt a greater sense of security in making decisions, trusting his own judgment, and building a stronger optimism about himself.

In spite of these inner gains he still experienced periods of depression. It was not easy for him to accept the realization of how uninvolved he had been at home, how little time he had given his wife and children. Even more devastating was the painful discovery that his drive for power, which took up most of his energy, had crippled his capacity to feel genuine affection for his family—left him as unfulfilled as his wife and children. His inability to give fully to his wife sexually had been a symptom of his withdrawal, of his punishing his fantasied mother on another level. His sexual freedom depended on his mood, on how relaxed he was or how inhibited, which was determined by how well he could apply his energies to the acquisition of power. He still thought in terms of substitution: power for love.

Having gained this awareness, he was troubled about what to do. Should he reduce his aggressive drive in business and spend more time at home? This was not possible, nor was it advisable. He was used to racing his psychic motor like a high-powered car, even when in neutral. He now had to realize it was not a matter of giving up his aggressive drive and spending hours at home, but of his depth of feelings about and interest in his wife and children during the hours he was with them. There was a need to balance his values, to look at his career not as an end in itself but as means to an end, namely to achieving a comfortable family life and enjoying his success at work by sharing it with his family.

The sessions became enjoyable and gratifying. He was making enormous progress. He felt happier as a man; sex had become more fulfilling and more frequent. His wife was thrilled. And yet, though she was pleased by her husband's progress, she began to show ambivalent feelings about the changes in him, for they forced her to make adjustments too. Her own drive for power started to emerge as she felt more secure, hence more competitive. Freed somewhat from her debilitating depressive state, she strived for more control in the community and took part in many of its activities.

A crisis arose when he was called to take a top post in Washington. This seemed the fulfillment of all his ambitions. He would become famous; his parents, his home town, the nation, the world would have to take notice. His head swam with excitement. The challenge was almost irresistible—it was the fulfillment of his very own American Dream.

It was a painful decision to reach—to weigh, to reason, to remain calm and objective though his heart beat fast at the thought of what was at stake—and he often felt exhausted at the excitement. He had to consider where the new post would lead and where his loyalties were—to his company, to his family, the children, the school they did not want to leave, the friends they did not want to forsake, or to the country and its administration, one he had to accept and fully believe in if he took the new post.

A vague, faraway question came into focus. The question of life and its meaning. What would truly bring him fulfillment? Joy? There had to be enjoyment in the very exercise of a job, not some future reward. There had to be recognition of values of his childhood—the lure of the American flag or the large government limousine he would ride. He had to decide what was reality in his life and what was illusion.

He had only a few days to make a decision. He knew it was a momentous one. Would he regret missing out on a rare chance if he did not accept the post? And, if he took it, would this further restrict his chance for happiness with his wife and children?

He recapitulated points of our earlier discussions, that an excessive drive for power is born out of weakness, that it moves on wings of aggression to overcome inferiority, that it sustains the will to live as long as it serves as a means to an end but that when it becomes an end in itself, it turns into a raw, corrodingly destructive force.

The essence of his struggle seemed to be a choice of power versus love, outer success versus inner happiness. It was not a case of aggression versus nonaggression but of what values he considered important.

He made his decision. He told me later, "I went to Washington and declined the post. I gave my reasons openly but firmly, in a man-to-man way."

It may have hurt him a little to decline, but it did his ego good to be able to decide in favor of giving up a glamorous, high-pressured job so he could feel more peaceful within himself.

If we could only have peace in the world as easily as this man found peace—by balancing his need for power against what he really wanted to build for his children. Here was a man who at long last was able to use his drive for power in a constructive way, a way that brought happiness to his wife and children and most of all to himself. For years he had used the power drive to rush headlong into supposed success only to find unfulfillment in his life. Now he no longer needed the world's approval. He had his own, the only approval that counts.

This happened at Christmas, and, to my surprise, I received a gift and a letter from his wife. I quote part of her last sentence: "I want you to know that what happened in our home, our marriage and with our children *is* a miracle and a dream come true."

And the lesson? There is nothing wrong with the American Dream if we build our future in a world of reality and don't turn it into a dream of glory and power—don't see ourselves walking over our land in New England or sitting on the porch of a home in Florida, or California, once we have reached our home stretch of success.

Life is not static. It makes its own demands. Creative energies must be spent if we don't want them to become stagnant and destructive. We may slow down our pace or change our goals but as humans we cannot escape the question: Is reading our paper or spending our days on the golf course or fishing all that is left for the driving man's mind in a quest of self-fulfillment?

We can do all these things, but we can never retreat from being involved with life. Sex never ceases to make its demands, which need to be considered, as do the substitutes, the sublimations. The question is: Have I done my work in the best way I know how? Have I been able, after an experience of humiliation, to regain my self-esteem? And have I really lived with values that are mine, and not those of Mr. and Mrs. Jones?

This is important, for when death comes, it must come in an hour of quiet, of peace, and not in the painful struggle of a man who has not balanced his books or his drives for power.

As a rule, a man dies the way he has lived, with violence or modesty, discontent or harmony. To spend an hour with oneself thinking about what to do when the peaceful hour of the sunset comes is to take life in its fullness, not only the stormy part, the winning part, the show-off part, but the summing-up part, the acceptance part, that closes the circle of the American Dream.

XIV

The Balance of Power

ONLY A poet would say, "One word of truth outweighs the whole world."

These are the words of Solzhenitsyn in his 1970 Nobel Prize for Literature lecture, a speech he wrote but did not deliver. He referred to the writer who lives in "this cruel, dynamic, explosive world that stands at the edge of its ten dooms," and expressed the hope that

World literature has it within its power in these frightening hours to help humanity know itself truly despite what prejudiced people and parties are attempting to instill, to communicate the condensed experience of one region to another in such a way that we will cease to be split apart and our eyes will no longer be dazzled, so that the units of measurement on our scale of values will correspond to one another, and some people may come to know the true history of others accurately and concisely and with that force of perception and painful sensation they will feel that they have experienced it themselves, and by this token be guarded against subsequently repeating the same errors.

It may well be that the power of the poet's word can touch the hearts of readers more readily than the intellectual presentation of the scientist. And yet, while both present an appeal for truth, one by an inspirational arousal, the other by addressing reasoning power, both aim at bringing people closer together, offering them a deeper understanding of one another, and, by creating a feeling of security, both allow the promotion of peace and friendship on a worldwide scale.

Because I believe that the struggle to attain these goals is the responsibility of every member of the human race, I decided to take to the pen. The presentation of new ideas is, I feel, within the scope of the doctor, for doctor comes from the Latin *docere* which means a teacher, an instructor. One word of encouragement at the right time may evoke a sympathetic response in a reader, may have the power to ignite a spark of hope in a downcast mind, to lead to a way to overcome a mood of despair.

In the field of psychology, it was the written word that communicated to the world Freud's concept of love as well as his concept of self-destruction, his uncovering of the mystery of the unconscious that explained how civilized man, individually or as a group, could at times become a creator of undreamed scope and at others be drawn into disaster, his own or the world's.

And when Solzhenitsyn speaks of "the spirit of Munich" that has existed and continues to exist, and asks what literature can do "in the face of the pitiless assault of open violence," he touches upon the question that is on every decent person's mind and which for years has preoccupied this author's mind and stirred him to present his thesis in this book.

Here we come to the first of several conclusions: Man has open to him a way to forestall his doom, to free himself from the shame and brutality of cruel and inhuman actions by an uncompromising search for—Truth.

This sounds simple, because most people are brought up to speak the truth, but as judges know and all physicians know, not every patient who comes for help is *able* to speak the truth. Everyone knows that not all people are truthful. And there are people who do not know the difference between the truth and a lie. Some will lie even though they gain nothing from the lie. While most people as children are taught a code of ethics, they also learn early in life how to tell a lie to avoid the pain of punishment, or to imitate a parent who lies. As I often say to my patients, "It seems that many forget on Monday what they have learned on Sunday." It has always puzzled me why grown people will lie about a misdeed they have committed, and I find it particularly disturbing in men in position of great political power.

Many political candidates use obvious lies when they make campaign promises they cannot possibly keep, or when they try to turn a slim possibility into an absolute reality. Or when they conceal facts and intentions. Public relations people, a new breed of hocus-pocus conjurers, figure out carefully how far a politician can bend the truth in order to win votes.

All this opens up the question as to what choice for peace or survival we, the people, really have, once we surrender the power of our vote to a man who then has the power to act in our behalf. In a curious way, our leaders can make us unwitting conspirators in a crime about which we know little, because of the secrecy that surrounds men in high office. Leaders without congressional approval have often enough paved the way to the incitement or the actual start of a war without justification, a war that in the end, if we believe in moral judgment, turns us from victors into victims, no matter what its outcome.

It would be easy if the spoken or written word could prevent man from repeating errors, but depth psychology has taught us that man has learned nothing from disaster. If man had been able to learn, would we have had a second world war after the first? Or would people ever have advocated a "preventive war"? We might well ask ourselves, Have we really learned anything in the field of international affairs?

While I share Solzhenitsyn's hope that the writer who discloses the lie under which we live and who helps to discover the truth, will help the world in "its white-hot hour of trial," we must face the fact that man is a conditioned animal and thus is continually subject to two enormous problems: his conscious mind may not be aware that he lies, so that he can do nothing about it, and the complexity of his inner world and the adjustments he has made to the world of reality, may make it difficult for him to cope with his deep, inner feelings, the ones that control his value judgments.

And there is that third problem ot truth in regard to political leaders. By the time we, the people the world over, discover the untruth, the damage has been done, a crime has already been committed.

Man is moved every minute of his life by value judgments which are specific for a specific culture and for the specific set of values of the individual. These judgments determine his plans, ideas and actions. His behavior is actually the sum of his conditioned reflexes, which are greatly affected by his value judgments—his own and those of society. And they are and remain to be strongly affected by his first conditioning and his underlying emotional conflicts.

Civilized man is conditioned to his group, his own little peculiar defenses, his pragmatism—all of which have the power of a conditioned reflex, and it is this automatic response-behavior that so often leads in political life to overaggression and the use of the power drive against the betterment of mankind. The military may not even be aware that it is lying when it pretends that it is acting "in self-defense" of a nation or of a ruling regime.

This leads to the second important conclusion: We must gain awareness of what lies in our unconscious in order to know the truth within our hearts. All the gifted writers of our century have known this—be they Thomas Mann, Eugene O'Neill or Tennessee Williams—and have found their own perceptions borne out by Freud's revelation of the role of the unconscious in ruling our lives.

Because of the power of the unconscious, the writer alone may not succeed in the gigantic task of changing the world. Perhaps he should accept the help of the physician in preventing large scale disaster or mass suicide or mass insanity—war.

It is this wider role of the physician that attracted me to the working of the human mind: not the purely scientific part, nor the purely speculative one, but the combination of the scientific and the artistic-perceptive parts that helped me form my own school of thought and eventually stretch the physician's role into the field of psychopolitics.

I believe that if we can know truth, and develop self-awareness, we can also develop trust, the third concept necessary to forestall doom. For trust, as we have stated, is the basis for any meaningful relationship, be it friendship or mature love. If we trust, we can communicate. We can also afford to behave as civilized human beings without fearing violence from a supposed ally or an imagined enemy.

The hope of one of this century's noblest spirits, Pavlov, that science and only science would deliver man from the shameful conditions that prevailed in the field of international relations, has so far not been realized. Science has not brought us peace or freedom from international tension. His own country, one that revered Pavlov's work, has misused his unfaltering faith in the creation of the ideal man, for nowhere except in Hitler's Germany has the concept of human rights been more inhumanly violated than in Stalin's Soviet Union.

Few have listened to what scientists have had to say; the majority of politicians and the military have been quick to grab the discoveries of scientists for their own, chiefly destructive purposes, but have been slow to improve the lot of man. In the field of interpersonal human relations, the larger number of scientists, though sympathetic to helping the wretched of the earth, has more or less remained neutral and uninvolved as far as actively helping people is concerned. But in spite of its abuse, science, real science, is a search for truth and therefore forms a fourth concept necessary for the prevention of doomsday. Science has dominated and greatly changed life in this century.

I was tempted to write an appeal to the physicians of the world to unite in a *world study of psychopolitics*—that is, to widen their field of saving lives, of fighting premature death, of preventing plagues, to get out of and to go beyond their offices, clinics and laboratories and research centers and work on the prevention of the most shameful disease of man—war. Again I say, psychodynamic psychology could help people detect the false propaganda of the false apostles *before* they elect a political leader. And I repeat that a leader who lives on excitement like a gambler, and who is basically self-destructive, must inevitably lead his nation into disaster of one kind of another.

What is important at this time is that we physicians, who communicate with our patients, begin to communicate with our colleagues the world over, with or without the structure of a new formal organization. Psychology belongs to all, not to one privileged section of medicine, and psychiatry belongs to all physicians, not only those who wish to play the role of high priests. It belongs to all those physicians who feel the responsibility to prevent the destruction of lives beyond the scope of their hospital or office activity.

We need to treat and prevent especially mental illness not

just in those who, according to our laws, are a threat to themselves or to others. The treatment should include leaders who have never broken a law and will never break a law, but who, because of their power drive or because their minds may be ruled by the unconscious concept that there is a "devil," which means an easy replacement by an "enemy," and therefore dangerous. A chief of staff whose bona fide job it is to protect a nation, may, if he is mentally unstable, develop a "*maladie professionelle*" and go haywire, scheming and dreaming of preventive war and "total victory" in his fantasy of killing forever the devil in man. And, as we have seen, the fantasy—an unconscious process—may all too easily, in this irrational world, become reality. It has happened, and many minds are busy scheming how to make it happen again, or we would not have the concept of "overkill": to kill a man or enemy is not enough; we must pump more lead into his body.

When Aristotle spoke of "the insolence" of the demagogue, he could have added "arrogance"—a quality the weak often use as a cover-up after they have gained a position of power but have not emotionally grown up to become compassionate, tolerant human beings.

Life is a maturing process, though not for all. Some learn and some do not. As people, we must demand that the leaders we elect, the leaders who have the power to determine our destiny, possess truthfulness, self awareness, self-control and strength of character. Men who can "trust" will not need the defense of supersecrecy which, in the affairs of state, should have gone out with Metternich, or at least the beginning of this century. Big children play a game with the stamp "top secret," and treat the people like little children—too young to know, too immature to understand. It is arrogant, omnipotent, adolescent thinking to use such terms as "eyes only" classified, or "top secret" for thrilling self-importance—and often to bury acts of misjudgment, fraud and error from the eyes of a trusting public.

As for self-awareness, this goes for both the people and their leaders. Insight will make people aware not only of their own neurotic behavior but that of a leader, of the deeper part of his personality and whether he is basically motivated by love or hate. For this we need not go to a psychoanalyst. As Otto Rank, a pioneer psychoanalyst, once said, "The only therapy is life." I myself learned from life not only self-understanding and therapy for myself, but also how to help others in the complicated process of psychotherapy.

In dealing with how to seek a balance of power, I have left out the two emotions which are man's highest and most exalting ones, happiness and love. This was not an oversight. In everyday life, both terms are used to a point of oversaturation. But both feelings, particularly the experience of happiness, are *consequences* of how well we manage or balance our own particular drive for power.

First, a word about happiness. In an earlier book called *The Will to Happiness* I stated that only after many years of practice did the simple truth of one of my professors come to me, namely that "the enjoyment of life is inborn in all living beings." Happiness, then, is a natural state, not merely the absence of pain, as Freud put it, and we, the people, destroy it for reasons mostly unknown to us. Happiness comes from using our power drives meaningfully, creatively, that is, fully, and towards positive purposes or goals. Happiness then is the accomplishment of a task to our own satisfaction and, before that, the experience of intense involvement with some work: the striving for and making of an accomplishment produce a feeling of happiness.

Happiness and love are often felt at the same time, one as the result of the other, but they are not interchangeable concepts. Love is more than being in love or being loved, though both are indeed exalting experiences. Love is primarily giving and sharing in all aspects of human endeavor. It is concern for the other and it is the full use of Freud's erotic or creative instinct. "Not to love before one gains full knowledge of the thing loved presupposes a delay which is harmful," said Freud, and, "When one finally reaches cognition, he neither loves nor hates properly; one remains beyond love and hatred. One has investigated instead of having loved." If we like ourselves, we can love and if we can love maturely, not only because of what we get out of another person, but because of our inner capacity to love and give, we can love humanity. And if we can love humanity, which is caring and wishing to contribute to its happier existence, we certainly will ban doomsday forever.

Part of the plan I outlined for schoolchildren—role playing in classes to give them a chance to be their own therapists— would help in giving them more self-awareness, which is self-analysis, and in their interaction they would learn therapy. This in turn would teach them how to get along better with other children, how to care for one another, to develop compassion or perhaps even love. This kind of schooling into adulthood would give a deeper understanding of the conviction of Diogenes who said, "It takes a wise man to know a wise man." With self-understanding, we would learn to choose more wisely our friends, our marriage partners, and our political leaders.

The word "wisdom" is a complicated one. It is a mixture of many things: the power to discern the healthy from the sick, the neurotic from the destructive, the good from the evil. It includes the choice of values by which we wish to live, which help us to survive by building security in ourselves so we can be tolerant and live peacefully with our neighbors.

Wisdom comes from experience and knowledge: it is something a farmer may have and a university graduate may never achieve. Wisdom tells us when our drive for power turns into a dangerous overdrive so that we know when to stop. Alexander the Great did not know what to do with his overdrive and killed himself. Napoleon could not stop and had to go on to

Moscow and defeat. Both of them had tremendous power had they known when to shift gears from violent acting out to using the dynamics of aggression for creative purposes, as with atomic power. But they could not, for this would have required an inner wisdom, a wisdom and balance they did not have, and which seldom exists among military leaders, men who must make war and conquer the world. Many political leaders lack inner balance; some have been mentally depressed people. War is a state of supreme excitation and therefore an enormous lure as well as a strong defense against a mental depression, a need which may account for the fact why many political leaders resort so readily to confrontation, rather than to communication. Such a choice may temporarily "cure" the individual himself but at the sacrifice of others, of innocent lives.

Healthy functioning demands a balance of power, in the life of a nation or in an individual. Medical students learn the concept of homeostasis, the maintenance or steady (balanced) states in the organism by coordinated physiologic processes. Walter Cannon, an American physiologist, introduced this term in 1922, teaching that all organ systems are integrated by automatic adjustments which keep within narrow limits both outside and inner disturbances with the aim of establishing balance. And Claude Bernard in the middle of the last century coined the term *milieu intérieur,* the internal environment on which health depends. All internal fluids bathe all tissue elements and secure all life by maintaining inner stability.

The ancient Chinese concept of Yin, the female element that stands for darkness, cold and death, and Yang, the male counterpart that is heat and the source of life, is foreign to our Western thinking and certainly may not be to the liking of Women's Liberation movement but nevertheless illustrates the idea of balance.

Erasmus of Rotterdam, a friend of Thomas More and Henry

VIII, taught of the importance of going the *via media* to avoid the extremes, to seek the balanced life, or, as we might say, to learn to apply the balance of power.

But a state of balance is possible only if we, as people, learn to avoid inner breaks and splits by repairing rifts and states of disbalance. A split within is illness, a split without is war. Men can move against one another or towards one another. This is true for the individual who is in conflict, at war, within himself, or for groups, or nations. What we need to learn is to recognize and to solve our inner conflicts so that we feel secure enough to move *towards* another human being— intimately towards a husband, a wife, a friend, and, in a larger sense towards humanity. When we choose to move away from another person we choose isolation and antilife.

If we choose survival rather than self-destruction we must aim for peace. If we wish peace, we must learn how to manage the enormous powers that are inherent in man in his struggle to become a wholesome human being to live with a sense of security in his society and to know how and by what values to choose his leaders.

A healthy relationship between peoples and their leaders depends on the wisdom in all of us to attain a balance of power within ourselves, in our relationship to others and to the spinning world around us. Only such a state of balance can give us inner peace and that natural, joyful state we call happiness.

But this awareness or supreme feeling of content and pleasure can evolve only if we keep before our mental eye the sober reality that we humans, all of us, have but one world to live on, a world from which there is no escape other than death, and therefore we have no choice but to share it with one another. And this we can do the way the child secures his emotional survival which is by learning to cope with his two most powerful emotions: love and hate.

This first primitive coexistence sets the pattern for what is called our ambivalence—all of our opposing feelings, needs and wishes—which makes it possible for us to function in a world of reality, to control feelings of violence without becoming submissive and to seek self-fulfillment without hurting another. Ambivalence forms the basis for man to become civilized.

But ambivalence as a concept is without value unless we gain the awareness of the hate we bury, the greed we negate, and the passions we deny, so that we can use all our knowledge of self and our perception in the all-out, never-ending battle against the onslaught of massive negative and destructive forces. Only then can our basic and often un- or underdeveloped positive feelings of love, creativity and ability to enjoy our life have a chance to unfold. Only then can we maintain at all times the inner delicate balance of our potentially dynamic drive for power.

Appendix

Drew Pearson, Address to National
Press Club, November 14, 1968

Washington (UPI)—Columnist Drew Pearson, who has been involved in disputes involving several presidents, has raised the question of why Richard M. Nixon, now President-elect, consulted a New York physician several years ago.

Pearson related to an audience at the National Press Club Wednesday that he was told the visit concerned "psychiatric problems" and occurred at some time in the 1958-61 period that Nixon was Vice-President.

The physician is *Dr. Arnold A. Hutschnecker,* currently a psychiatrist with offices at 829 Park Ave. in New York. Dr. Hutschnecker told UPI that when he was treating Nixon two or three times a year from 1951 to 1955 it was "for strictly medical problems."

Hutschnecker emphasized that while he had gradually changed his practice to psychiatry over the past several years, at the time Nixon was consulting him he was practicing internal medicine.

Ronald Ziegler, Nixon's press secretary, questioned at a news briefing about the columnist's remarks, said: "I won't be drawn into a discussion of a Pearson utterance that is totally untrue, as most of his statements and utterances are."

Pearson, who spoke at a National Press Club luncheon, mentioned the Nixon medical matter while responding to a question as to how closely he checks material for his column.

Pearson said that in the process of checking rumors, he telephoned Dr. Hutschnecker about 9:30 A. M. October 31—five days before the election—"and he told me he had treated Nixon when he was Vice-President."

311

Pearson took this to mean he had treated Nixon psychiatrically. The doctor had patients at the time and asked Pearson to call him again at 4 P.M.

"I called the doctor back at four o'clock and he said, it's true that Nixon did consult me, but this was for problems of internal medicine and it was not for psychotherapy," Pearson said. The columnist said he decided to write nothing, although he wondered why Nixon would go to New York to see an internist. He added: "Now subsequently Dr. Hutschnecker has told others and confirmed the fact that in the interim between my call at 9:30 in the morning and 4 P.M. he got a call from the Nixon office and that he had changed his story to me. And he did confirm to others that he had treated or advised Nixon over psychiatric problems. And he had expressed some worry privately that Nixon had problems—or did have a problem—of not standing up under great pressure."

Dr. Hutschnecker, interviewed by telephone, said that he had not said he had treated Nixon for any psychiatric reason.

"If Mr. Pearson made that statement, he fabricated it," he said. "I did not make it."

The doctor said he treated Nixon from about 1951 (the year Nixon was elected to the Senate) through the first couple of years of his Vice-Presidency, which began in 1953.

"I was engaged at that time in internal medicine, so Mr. Nixon came at that time for strictly medical problems," Hutschnecker said. The visits were "at rather rare intervals, maybe two or three times a year." He would not elaborate on the reason, beyond saying "for general consultation."

The doctor said that "we came to an understanding that because of his exposed position he should get someone in Washington"—indicating that this was because as Vice-President, Nixon was more in the public eye and always accompanied by a Secret Service man.

Dr. Hutschnecker, who came to this country from Germany in 1936, described himself as now "engaged in psychotherapy which is psychoanalytically oriented treatment of emotional problems."

He said he has written several books on psychosomatic medicine, which concerns the relationship of psychological elements to bodily ills.

Jack Anderson and Drew Pearson
November 20, 1968 Column

Several of my editors have been complaining that I should have written the account of Mr. Nixon's psychotherapeutic treatments in the column before the election instead of talking about the matter at the National Press Club after the election.

Under the circumstances, I owe them and my readers an explanation. It is true, as some have pointed out, that if this had been published before the election the outcome might have been different. The problem of new confirmation and its timing is exactly what I was trying to illustrate at the luncheon which the Press Club had set up in my honor.

During the question-and-answer period, I was asked the criterion for news in the column.

Then, as a serious illustration of the problem of a columnist, I told of the report that kept cropping up during the campaign that when Nixon was Vice-President he had undergone psychiatric treatments, and that finally I had obtained the name of his doctor, Arnold Hutschnecker of New York, and had called him at about 9 A. M., October 31.

I now find upon checking my calendar that I called him on October 29 and that the time was nearer 10 A. M. I told the doctor I understood he had been giving Mr. Nixon psychiatric treatments and had been concerned as to whether his former patient was the right man to have his finger on the nuclear trigger.

Dr. Hutschnecker confirmed that he had treated Mr. Nixon, said that it was a delicate matter and that he was reluctant to talk about it. He had a patient with him, he said, and asked me to call back at 4 P. M.

* * *

I then asked Jack Anderson to telephone Nixon's communications director, Herbert Klein, and ask for comment. Klein flatly denied Nixon had ever consulted a psychiatrist. At 4 P. M. I telephoned Dr. Hutschnecker a second time. This time he said that he had treated Mr. Nixon for a brief period when he was Vice-President but only for problems involving internal medicine.

In view of Dr. Hutschnecker's statement, I killed the story I had written on Mr. Nixon, although it seemed to me strange that Nixon should go all the way to New York to consult a well-known Park Avenue psychotherapy specialist concerning his internal medical problems when some of the best internists in the U.S. are located at Walter Reed Hospital and Bethesda Naval Hospital, where the Vice-President could have had their services on the cuff. Perhaps I was derelict, but at that time I did not pursue the matter further.

Subsequently, and toward the very end of the campaign, further information came to my attention that Dr. Hutschnecker had told friends he received a telephone call from Nixon's office between my morning call and my 4 P.M. call on October 29 which had led him to change his earlier statement to me.

We also learned from one of Dr. Hutschnecker's friends that he had definitely been concerned about Nixon's reaction under pressure; second, that he had received a call from Mr. Nixon in 1960 requesting him to come to Washington for consultation. According to the dates given me by Hutschnecker, this was long after he claimed to have stopped treating Nixon.

In addition, I was told by Dr. Hutschnecker's receptionist that she had handled a call from Nixon as late as 1961. She informed me that at that time, and for three preceding summers when she had been Dr. Hutschnecker's receptionist, his patients had been given fifty-minute appointments each, which indicated psychotherapeutic treatment.

*   *   *

Some of this information, I admit, was learned during the closing days of the campaign, and I could have published it at the last minute. But, as I explained at the Press Club luncheon, I decided it was unfair to use it so late. It was one of those difficult decisions a newspaperman has to make.

But now that the campaign is over, I continue to be convinced that a President or candidate for President should make all the facts public regarding his health, mental or otherwise, just as Dwight D. Eisenhower did after his heart attack; and that there should be no covering up of the facts or blatant denials such as issued by Ron Ziegler, Nixon's press secretary.

[For denials of Mr. Pearson's above-stated falsehoods and untrue statements, see pp. 7-8]

"The Lessons of Eagleton"*(New York Times,*
Op-Ed, October 30, 1972

The tragic episode of Thomas F. Eagleton last July, of first winning the Democratic Vice-Presidential nomination and then losing it on grounds of three psychiatric hospitalizations, has opened up an intense debate about the question of mental stability of our political leaders. Generated by deep anxiety, the debate continues, at least in medical circles.

This anxiety is only too well justified, for never before in history has one man had as much power as an American President.

Now there is added anxiety about the presidential running mates, who heretofore played a rather secondary role. Twice in less than two decades Vice-Presidents have become Presidents. In each case they have led the country into war. The question for historians to answer is how sound was their judgment and how essential to our natural survival were these wars?

Leaders are driven by their inner aggression and an often gnawing hunger for a plus of power. And since in the words of Erich Fromm, "The lust for power is not rooted in strength but weakness," the need to compensate may become obsessive, compulsive and relentless. Childhood experiences of inferiority and helplessness generate a drive to prove to oneself one's worth, or one's very existence.

Aggression, when it is positive and realistic, is a healthy, forceful, goal-oriented drive. But it must be balanced so that it may serve the individual and help him to make use of his potentials in a constructive self-fulfilling way. Aggression that is unrealistic becomes destructive and may be directed against society or oneself. The long line of mad leaders throughout history had been men who were whipped by their pervasive delusion of grandeur and an inability to control or sublimate their destructive and unconsciously homicidal aggression.

The realization of weakness or inadequacy is not necessarily a detriment. On the contrary, it may generally serve as a stimulus to mature. In fact, it has given many leaders a powerful incentive to overcome handicaps, as was the case with Teddy Roosevelt.

The classic image of the heroic seems to be on the wane, not because man has become more mature but because the risks of a total holocaust have become so much greater.

A new ideal of leadership seems to emerge. It is based on the preponderance of the creative instinct over the destructive drive and of controlled judgment over impulsive pressures. In today's world, a leader's greatness seems to lie less in a dramatic display of might than in a less spectacular policy of patient negotiation and of resisting the urge of acting out inner aggression to back up a political philosophy by military might.

It is a symbol of statesmanship if a leader dares to change the trend of well-established foreign policy in order to build a bridge of understanding with his antagonists and a peace that is based not on fear but on friendly relations. Whatever the scope of action, control of self is the key word. In a politically explosive situation, the exercise of control is a supreme test of a leader's inner strength.

Eisenhower, at the height of the cold war, resisted the relentless pressures around him and actually paid with his health for his promise to keep the peace.

The strength of character of an American President is not only challenged by the constant threats and provocations of a restive world, but by some of his overaggressive and sometimes mentally unstable advisers. There were the mentally disturbed first Secretary of Defense, James Forrestal, and John Foster Dulles, with his constant brinkmanship, and Mr. McNamara, who saw human lives in the light of cold computerized statistics, to name only a few.

In the life of any nation, there may be, of course, unprovoked bona fide attacks, not always on as huge a scale as those hatched by psychopaths such as Hitler or those who ordered the bombing of Pearl Harbor. Leaders of vision may at an early stage even have prevented that disaster.

To make the point, I would like to quote Haile Selassie's wise and valid words: "Throughout history it has been the inaction of those who could have acted, the indifference of those who should have known better, the silence of the voice of justice when it mattered most, that has made it possible for evil to triumph."

Failure to act may be as destructive as is over-reaction. The criterion is an objective evaluation of a crisis. If a threat to survival is not real but exaggerated or even imagined, if a theory that a small war might prevent a big war is considered valid, then the neurotic judgment of a leader can push a nation into a bloody quagmire.

How can we as people distinguish between mentally healthy leaders and men who under an appealing facade hide an inner rage and a mind in disarray? How can we know whom to trust, who will keep his word or who might betray the trust of the people?

Pavlov could by his scientific method of conditioning produce aggressive behavior and leadership and so did the fathers of John F. Kennedy, Frederick the Great and Thomas F. Eagleton. These three fathers were overly ambitious men who carefully or brutally groomed their sons for their future tasks. All three young men performed superbly. All three were ill; Frederick the Great had the mood swings and depressions of a homosexual, John F. Kennedy suffered from Addison's disease and Senator Eagleton had three nervous breakdowns.

Does that mean that neurotic men cannot be great leaders? Is there one man of stature who has not gone through the tortures of the damned and who has not gone to the rim of an abyss before his upturn to a meaningful and creative life began? Does the so-called "normal" man, who has a minimum of trouble because he functions like an automaton, make a better leader?

The answers lie in the personality structure of the man who strives for leadership, and whether his drive to power is motivated by creative or destructive forces, whether he wants to serve the people or whether he needs the people to serve him and his ambition.

As a nation, we need safeguarding principles. Are there really any? Doctors have suggested that Presidential candidates ought to make statements about their health as they do about their financial status.

This writer, while endorsing this thought, does not believe it to be a foolproof guarantee. Also, it could involve a candidate's physician and bring him into conflict with his concern of protecting a patient's confidence. In the Eagleton case, his physicians did refuse, and rightly so, to make any statement as to their patient's health.

Evidently, the fear in the case of Eagleton was that under the pressures of his high office, he could break down and then possibly make unsound or destructive decisions. This was obvious in the controversy that captured the headlines of the press.

Generally speaking, it takes insight and enormous courage for a person to decide to go through a process of self-examination as in psychotherapy, when he must come to grips with the person he really is and his place in a world of reality. Consequently, to consult a psychiatrist is not necessarily a sign of mental instability and may often speak more for than against a political leader.

In our search for security, we need some safeguarding principles to do away with the worry every four years about how well put together a candidate is.

Nearly twenty years ago, I suggested that mental health certificates should be required for political leaders, similar to the Wasserman test demanded by states before marriage. Valid psychological and axiological (value) tests exist today, which would pinpoint psychopathology, so that mentally unstable individuals would be prevented from attaining jobs of political importance. More sensibly, testing should be required at a student level, before a candidate has acquired a position of power.

An all-embracing and truly preventive plan ought to begin with programs that encourage children from 6 to 16 to learn to understand one another. This plan, based on the new technique of role playing, goes far beyond the prevention of drug addiction or delinquency for which the plan was originally designed.

This would do more than to wipe out delinquency and tendencies to violent crime and drug addiction. It would in the long run help the development of healthy citizens and mature judgment but it would also build a vast pool of healthy stable competitive leaders, capable of using their creativity toward the growth of a nation as well as a brotherhood of man.

It might cost this nation an estimated three billion dollars, far less than the amount that would be saved from loss through violence and destruction and very little when compared with the $76 billion we spend for arms, especially if we realize the values we would be buying for ourselves, our country, for our future generation and for our world.

"The Stigma of Seeing a Psychiatrist"
(*The New York Times*, Op-Ed, November 20, 1973)

"If one thing was made perfectly clear in this first slow, polite day of Senate committee hearings on the nomination of Representative Gerald R. Ford to be Vice President, it is that consulting a psychiatrist or psychotherapist is still an unforgivable sin for an American politician." Thus wrote Linda Charlton in The New York Times.

On that first polite day before the Senate Rules Committee, Gerald Ford denied that he had ever been a patient of mine and said with emphasis: "Under no circumstances did I see him (Dr. Hutschnecker) for treatment and under no circumstances have I ever been treated by any psychiatrist."

When questioned by the committee's chairman, Senator Cannon of Nevada, about the purpose of his brief visit to my office on Nov. 21, 1966, Mr. Ford replied that he had dropped in to "say hello" and as to the conversation, "Dr. Hutschnecker gave me a lecture on leadership or about the role of leadership in the American political system."

On Nov. 7, I appeared before the United States Senate committee in Washington as a sworn witness. Asked by the various Senators what my relationship with the Vice President-designate had been, I confirmed Mr. Ford's statement that he had never been a patient of mine and had come to my office only once. As to the personality of the former lobbyist who had charged Mr. Ford had been a patient of mine for about a year, I stated in the closed session the abhorrence I had felt at what seemed to be a deliberate attempt to destroy another man (Mr. Ford) politically.

In a book he wrote, the ex-lobbyist made statements so obviously perfidious that the chairman wondered whether this man lied deliberately or whether he did not know the difference between reality and fantasy. Why was the ex-lobbyist lying?

I gave my answer in the following way: Schopenhauer, the German philosopher, talked about two types of writers, one who writes out of conviction and the other who writes for money. There is a third type of writer, I said, one who writes out of vengeance.

"I did not sue the man," I answered the chairman because I did not want him to gain any benefit from his misdeed through publicity. A megalomaniac has little difficulty saying anything that comes to mind and will suit his purpose. According to the newspaper reports, the committee, after having heard the ex-lobbyist, believed that there were grounds for the Department of Justice to examine the possibility of perjury.

What gave this case, however, special significance is not whether Gerald Ford had seen me professionally—he did not—but the fact that an alleged psychotherapeutic treatment could become a national issue, partially holding up the confirmation of Mr. Ford. I found this point so disturbing that I did not wish it to be pushed into a dark corner and then forgotten.

In 1968, when the late Drew Pearson, a syndicated columnist, made a similar though more devasting allegation, that President Nixon had been a former patient of mine, I was forced also to correct falsities which were of greater gravity. But the element of superstition was similar, as evidenced by the strong advice Mr. Nixon was given that it would be unwise for him as a political leader to continue to visit a physician who was changing his practice from internal medicine to a psychoanalytically oriented psychotherapy.

This point was made again by the crisis of Thomas Eagleton, who first won and then lost the Vice Presidential nomination on grounds of having had three psychiatric hospitalizations. I refuted then the idea that a neurotic man could not be a great leader.

In this last third of our century, when man has demonstrated that he can land on the moon and return safely, when scientific knowledge is available to study human behavior and when emotional reactions in our human intercourse, be they positive or negative, can be interpreted with a fair amount of accuracy, can we continue to treat the psychoanalytic field and its application to political leaders as a dread-inspiring tabu?

To consider a branch of medical knowledge and practice with suspicion or condemnation is not merely an act of cruelty toward people in need, it is almost an act of negligence for a Government not to avail itself of the merits of this discipline.

The Ford and Nixon cases prove that for politicians of their stature it would be a kiss of death, had they sought help for the stress of their burdensome office by an analyst. But doctors who have conquered most of the plagues and thereby dispersed medieval super-stition, now question, as research goes on, whether the time has not come to liberalize our hangover in time and spirit from the era when witches were burned and the "devil" beaten out of unhappy people. Most doctors, and certainly those in the field of psychoanalytically oriented psychology, reject dogmatism and intolerance.

To accomplish a new way of thinking, I move toward a new discipline—that of psychopolitics, a study of the effect the psycho-logical make-up of political leaders is having on the political life and the present events of a nation. Let us imagine, for instance, what torture and misery would have been spared a man like Woodrow Wilson and the world if he could have had competent psychiatric help before slipping into the darkness of his depression.

Or, if the towering figure of Abraham Lincoln could have been helped to understand the nature of the anguish produced by his inner conflicts. It would not have diminished his greatness and perhaps there would not have been any need for the bloody killings of the Civil War.

General Pershing had a psychiatrist on his staff. I cannot help think if an American President had a staff psychiatrist, perhaps a case such as Watergate might not have had a chance to develop.

A President has a personal physician to watch over his physical health. Why could a man of outstanding leadership not have a physician watching over his and his staff's mental health? Why should that be considered unacceptable and be interpreted as sig-nifying mental instability or incompetence? And why must a leader in our time carry the enormous stress of his office without the benefit of physicians, experienced in objective interpretation or problems or of curing possibly debilitative reactions if they occur, as was the case with Wilson and Lincoln?

The help a political leader might seek under stress to secure his emotional stability is not weakness but courage and is as much in our national interest as it is in his. Why condemn any such attempt as an unforgivable sin?

Memorandum on the Problem
of Violent Crime (January 9, 1970)

Dear Mr. President:

In my search to find more effective and inexpensive methods of how to remedy the problem of "Violent Crime", I have met with a professor of philosophy at the National University of Mexico who had developed a new "Axiological Testing" (the measurement of values). According to the Social Security Administration of the Mexican Government, this testing method of personality features has proven to be so effective that this agency, after having used it for several months, is now going to make a psychological census of the whole country, in their words: "like a thorax census to detect tuberculosis."

This surprising and revolutionary undertaking by a Government has a striking resemblance to my own suggestion to have the total young population in this country tested, proving that new needs require new steps of action. The new test, I had it done on myself, has easy applicability, it is swift (10 minutes with the use of computers) and it can be applied to a large number of populations. Its cost is estimated to be 50 cents.

Since I had been assured that a future delinquent "sticks out like a sore thumb" I am now comparing the "axiological" method with those used in the United States in order to determine the most reliable and most economical method, possibly a combination of tests for different age groups, (of course it could be later on used for the older population as well).

The program, as outlined in my preliminary report, is in no way meant to replace the Eisenhower Committee's recommendation but ought to be looked upon as an augmentation of it. The approximate cost of my program will be a fraction of the Eisenhower Committee's estimated 20 billion dollars.

It is my hope, Mr. President, that you may give my project your kind consideration and since Mexico seems to be on the move now, put our country in the forefront of not only curing a cancerous social illness, that of violent crime, but to pave a way of preventing other debilitating problems as well, such as the high rate of drug addiction, of drop-outs, of unwillingness to work and of aimless rebellion.

The world-wide importance of a Government attack on so much misdirected human aggression on a grass-root level is self-evident and could indeed amount to another "giant step for mankind", if I may borrow the beautiful words of our astronauts.

Respectfully and with warm regards,

Memorandum on the Problem of Violent Crime (March 10, 1970)

Dear Mr. President:

Today I write to you as a friend rather than as a concerned citizen writing to his President. Your suggestion on December 1, 1969 to submit to you my opinion on how our crisis of violent crime could be solved, by means other than an increase in law enforcing agencies, has led me to a further study of the problem. The only solution that holds out any promise of success lies, I believe, in the earliest possible detection of future delinquency and which can be done successfully (and will show up emotional disturbances as well) at the age of 6-10.

The Harvard people who developed the Glueck Prevention Test responded with enthusiasm and willingness to cooperate with me although I avoided mentioning our meeting and your personal interest in this subject. Through them I learned that the Prediction Test will be done soon in the Philippine Islands and I reported to you already that the Mexican Government is conducting a census of the whole population by applying the Hartman Value Test. Both Mexico and the Philippine Islands are poor countries and I feel that the United States, the richest country in the world, must not fall behind.

It is for this reason, that I write to you for should there be little likelihood that—because of priorities or other reasons—you could not consider accepting a plan of early detection and treatment of future delinquents at this time, I would like to set up a pilot project myself, on a modest scale of course, to prove the validity and worth of detecting future delinquency and of treating at an early age violent tendencies by channelling these complex aggressive drives into creative pursuits.*

However, before moving toward such a goal, I would like to ask your permission to use the basic material which I have submitted to you and also, I would like, if I may, refer to your personal interest in this problem because you deserve the credit for having directed my attention from the wider aspects of an Agency of the Exploration of Peace toward this related but more detailed social illness.

Respectfully and with warm personal regards,

Memorandum on an Agency for the Study of Human Aggression (May 12, 1971)

Dear Mr. President:

. . . I would like to renew the plea I presented to you on December 1, 1969, to consider the formation of an agency for the study of the dynamics of human aggression and for the prevention of war. . . .

The great chance such an innovation could have at this time, is to reunite our divided country, to restore confidence and to help America to regain prestige and to enhance its leadership in the world. Moreover, such an agency could represent an unusual living monument not only for those young men who have died in battle but would also commemorate the sacrifices the American people have made for sustaining that long war in South East Asia.

History has taught us that military or political solutions—though they have their place—have nevertheless proven not to secure a lasting peace. Scientists on the other hand, when working as a team, have landed man on the moon. Scientists working as a team can teach people how to think and feel peacefully and how to channel, by sublimation, their hostile aggressive forces into creative and constructive pursuits, for their own happiness and for the good of the country and the world.

So far scientists have never worked systematically or on any scale toward peace and though such an endeavor would be a long and

---

* In the meanwhile, however, Dr. Hartman died, disrupting the execution of a project we both planned.

thorny road, it could become *your historic mission* to initiate such a novel experiment. It would electrify the hope of the world, for instead of anxiously waiting for peace, a creative action on your part would have an immensly inspiring and upsurging effect on the morale of people everywhere.

The agency could be a small one. It could begin with a handful of people, devoted to explore and develop the dynamics of peace, thereby avoiding any costly bureaucracy you had talked about. It would boil down to develop programs and workshops in schools and colleges and churches and to demonstrate practically how violence can be conquered and how the enjoyment of work and constructive play can become the best defense of peace. It would work in conjunction with other agencies and with scientists in other countries. Though I would be happy to devote my life to that work, I would gladly accept anyone you would choose to nominate as the head of such a new agency.

Of course, I realize that the innovation of any new idea, similar to the one I outlined, might be attacked as being overly idealistic and not practical. This has been the case throughout history. Yet, Pestalozzi's one room school has grown into universally accepted school systems all over the civilized world. What we need is a beginning and you, Mr. President, have the power to begin.

If you see any merit in my thoughts, please allow me to talk to you more about it.

I am with devotion and warmest personal regards,

Memorandum on Drug Abuse Prevention
September 23, 1971

Dear Mr. President:

The meeting I had with Dr. Jaffe and Mr. Donfeld on Friday, September 10th, to discuss the problem of drug abuse was pleasant and productive. Having been asked by Dr. Jaffe about some ideas, I presented points of my personal interest within the larger framework of your new drug abuse office. One thought of prevention was to explore and possibly cure the areas of conflict and confusion in the minds of adolescents in the hope of making them "immune" to the need for or the lure of dangerous drugs.

A Plan:

The idea I presented to Dr. Jaffe—and I was happy about his sympathetic attitude—was an attack on the problem at its root: the neurotic personality of the adolescent.

The plan is to form a body of already trained guidance counselors, increase their numbers but seek out volunteers among young teachers to be trained in techniques of group therapy. Special classes should be formed within the school program, to be attended by *all* children. Psychodynamic principles of group therapy ought to be applied according to the various age groups of children, *so that they themselves learn to become their own therapists,* of course under the guidance of trained counselors or special teachers. By verbalizing their problem (fear, hate, unworthiness, domination, depression, etc.) and by identifying with the problems of others, adolescents would be inspired to develop a sense of responsibility and enough interest in the problems of others to a point of desiring to help them and in turn to be helped by others.

Children in trouble, the lonely, the angry, the withdrawn and children with character disturbances—who later in life become both a threat and/or a burden to our society—can be reached best by their peers, especially if a cured addict is stressing the miserable and humiliating existence of an addict. The group as a whole or a few individuals of the group generally generates more rapport or greater power of pulling problem children into an active participation than do parents or teachers. As a rule, when a rejected or deprived child feels to be accepted by his group or as soon as he wins group respect, he generally begins to cooperate and to work along with the group.

I found Mr. Donfeld's presence most helpful. He pointed out possible opposition by conservative groups to the plan. Thinking about it, I feel the resistance could be overcome, if the purpose of the new classes is properly explained and if the parents and the public are being reassured that the *children are not being brainwashed* in any way but are being taught how to avoid drug addiction and how to live peacefully and creatively within a group. Instead of forming small cliques of one or two friends and then ignoring the rest, children besides forming close friendships could learn—what is necessary, if we wish a nonviolent society—to accept a larger group in a kind of peaceful coexistence. Also, resistance to a large project may not be greater than resistance to a small or local plan, probably even less as the experience of mass psychology teaches.

Picking up another of Mr. Donfeld's points, there may be no need for psychiatrists or psychologists to make a physical appearance at the school, although many schools have increasingly accepted already the services of school psychologists. The teachers who volunteer would be trained in courses and symposia at hospital centers in each state by experienced psychiatrists who practice group therapy. There should be repetitive courses perhaps every three months.

Considering the cost of such a program, I suggested at the meeting that we should start with the fourteen-year-old children because they seem to be the most endangered ones. But I made the point that all children would have to participate, the rich, the poor, the white and the black, not only because all children at that age have problems but the effectiveness of the project will depend on a cooperative spirit and a feeling of relating to one another in an air of *freedom and equality.*. This approach holds the promise to develop healthier, happier and more productive children and because of this a diminishment of drug addiction but also of delinquency and crime.

It was a pleasant surprise to find Dr. Jaffe receptive to another plan I suggested that would involve all children from six to sixteen. Such an approach, I believe, would not only prevent drug addiction and other self-defeating personality problems but possibly cure the problem of delinquency, which actually is the other side of the same coin. Forces of aggression are active in both, drug addiction and delinquency. Hostility and aggression turned against the self causes depression and pain which adolescents seek to relieve. One of the reliefs is provided by addictive drugs. The acting out of hostile-aggressive impulses leads to acts of violence and destruction. In drug addiction we often find a mixture of both, passivity and violence. Crimes are committed only too often to obtain the money for buying drugs.

I do not claim my idea to be original* because pilot programs are actually being conducted in various parts of the country. What would make the plan original, would be:

to include to the trained personnel enough teachers with interest and enthusiasm—
the involvement of the total child population of the country—
the role the federal government would play in executing the program.

A chance of successfully conquering the problem of drug abuse and juvenile delinquency is possible only if all of the existing *state and city projects are being coordinated into one unified approach and method.* Such a plan would come close to the ideal of prevention. It would free our society from a sickness that has reached dangerous proportions and that is costing the nation far more in loss of property and damage and productivity and a desire in young people to work, to say nothing about lives, than the money it may cost to cure the disease.

While it is not the government's job to undo the failures of parental homes and inadequate education *we the people pay the price for this failure* by finding our very lives threatened, our streets unsafe and our survival as a healthy nation in jeopardy.

Surely it is not easy to teach children love, but with patience and the help of mature teachers, we can teach children tolerance, responsibility, respect for fellow men and for our free society. Also, I believe we would end up with fewer mental hospitals, fewer prisons and a diminishing of the present polarization of our nation. Of course, there are more points to be made in regard to the value of the project, but I am also aware, of course, of the enormous difficulties.

Until I hear from you, Mr. President, I plan to give the scope of

---

* Although when I wrote this plan I thought it was a new idea.

the Special Action Office on Drug Abuse Prevention more thought and I will be at your disposal anytime you may wish to discuss this problem further.

"Suggestion: Psychiatry at High Levels
of Government" (*The New York Times*, Op-Ed, July 4, 1973)

Absolute independence is an illusion: unrestrained self-assertion would lead man on a road back to the jungle.

Independence is a state of relative freedom from domination within boundaries drawn by tradition, the culture and the laws of society.

Inherent in man is his drive to power. The will of the aggressive to subdue the passive causes, if successful, a subjugation of individual or group independence. Unless beaten into complete submission, the subdued resist, for man in order to create needs freedom from fears and controls. Throughout history, he has risen therefore to fight against oppression and tyranny.

In pursuit of such an ideal, a spirited group of men met to turn their dream into reality. On July 4, 1776, in the name of the newly formed United States of America, they presented one of the most stirring documents ever written by man: the Declaration of Independence.

Today, when children in America learn by heart—that all men are created equal—that they are endowed—with certain unalienable rights—that among these are life, liberty and the pursuit of happiness—they also learn that "governments are instituted among men, deriving their just powers from the consent of the governed."

And it is this sentence that provides the key to the startled reaction of the American people when they learned that their cherished guarantees of liberty had been threatened. Men charged with the responsibility of being the guardians of their basic rights had dared to violate a sacred trust. And a method, low on the scale of human values, one we have attributed contemptuously to totalitarian forms of governments only—namely spying on one another—had been used by some of the guardians themselves.

A deeply disturbed nation had been watching—in rapid progression—the unfolding of bizarre deeds and the painful spectacle of a group of men who had held powerful positions only yesterday, giving the image of frightened small men as they confessed their crimes and, worse, seemed to have difficulty in dealing with the first law of morality: Truth.

The evidence is growing that a conscious level of intellect, even in its sharpest form, may not unravel fully the motivation for some of the absurd tales presented.

The understanding lies in the psychoneurotic personality structure of some of the people who displayed a minimal capacity for human understanding and a greater need for omnipotence. An emotional immaturity and an obvious identification with an image of power was evident in some of these men's nearly blind loyalty and hero worship.

In a professional life, such as mine, one learns to refrain from rash judgments of people—and many times I have thought of Spinoza's impassioned words: "I have striven hard neither to laugh at any of man's doings nor to detest nor cry about them but only to understand them."

But understanding does not mean that a disturbing reality, which affects a whole nation, does not hurt. Nor does it mean to excuse crimes committed against the basic rights of the people. Whether shocked or dismayed, we must try to learn the lesson from a human disaster.

Perhaps we, the governed, have been too complacent and ought to strive for greater participation in government, oppose secrecy and paternalism and resist the shifting of power away from the people to those who govern.

There can be no independence without responsibility, nor can there be freedom without the determination to defend it. Now that the American people have become aroused, and display their strong will for justice, integrity and the preservation of their rights, they may gain a greater understanding of the full meaning of independence.

It is more these reasons and not because of sensationalism that the greater majority of the people support so strongly our First Amendment guarantee of a free press, and freedom from search without a warrant.

When we review the last two decades with two undeclared wars, with an unleashing of dormant human aggression and violence and a protesting movement of the young people, and when we further consider all the unmeasurable human suffering, the loss of life, of wealth and of prestige our country has undergone, we may perhaps wish to take a second look at all "the best and the brightest" in the nation who, while serving as advisers, advocated and concocted tough policies or armed intervention, when goodwill negotiations could probably have served all concerned better.

Now that the tragedy of the cold war is coming to an end, those who opposed these ventures find indeed how poor in judgment, in wisdom and vision these advisers have been and to what degree their own voracious ambition or irrational fears of imaginary attacks has caused them to plot holy wars in the name of self-defense.

What method of measure can we apply to evaluate the integrity or honesty of purpose and humaneness of a person who is about to enter a position of power in any branch of Government?

Having been concerned with the mental health of political leaders for over two decades, this writer has been attacked for having suggested that candidates, before being allowed to enter a political race, ought to be cleared by a board of physicians and psychiatrists to make certain they are healthy in mind and body. Or in order to avoid a possible argument of governmental interference, that the evaluation of mental health, like physical health—should take place in childhood so that parents are made aware of problems and have a chance to have their children helped.

Personally I can't shake the belief that had we applied personality evaluation—either psychological or the newer and more precise axiological (a mathematical method of value examination)—our maturer members of Congress might have questioned and possibly fought harder against the tragic ideologies of the cold and the two shooting wars.

The revelations of top secret files have only helped to demonstrate what the psychologist has been aware of: how easily an aggressive human mind can inflame others or be inflamed and how equally easy a casus belli can be manufactured.

Perhaps the time has come for us, the people, who love our country, who respect its laws, who cherish freedom and who are responsible and independent men and women and who believe in the progress of our civilization to apply psychodynamic principles and to explore possibilities other than purely political to secure that our best and brightest leaders are also our mentally and morally healthiest and soundest.

Progress demands that the many people who still consider psychiatry a branch of medicine only for the insane be made aware of their prejudice or ignorance and be helped to accept not only the curative but also preventive principles in this as in all other areas of medicine.

Today, in view of our country's enormous power and its responsibility, this writer believes that both a clinical as well as a psychoanalytically oriented physician should take part in the policy-making of our Federal or local governments. While some of these doctors may not always be infallible or the wisest, they have at least been trained in assessing human behavior objectively and can raise their voice when human ambition and greed or drives for an uninhibited use of power seem to be getting out of control.

Imperfect, perhaps, it would be a beginning. Such an innovation would be a rational step forward in view of our struggle for world peace, freedom and respect for the dignity of the individual and his rights. It would secure our own individual independence, allow healthy interdependence and foster the "pursuit of happiness" in the spirit of 1776.

"The Road to Peace: I" (*The New York Times*, Op-Ed, March 29, 1971)

In 1953 I attended a reception that marked the conclusion of the seventh session of the General Assembly of the United Nations, a session that had been particularly stormy and frustrated. When one of the diplomats asked me to which delegation I belonged, I replied, only half in jest, "To none. I am just a physician, but if you diplomats cannot achieve peace, perhaps we doctors will."

The delegate was surprised, for making peace is considered the province of statesmen and the clergy. Yet is it not true that when they fail, it is the physician who is called upon to heal the victims of their defeats, either on the battlefields, in mental hospitals or in institutions for the crippled and disabled?

So why shouldn't we doctors address ourselves to the prevention of war? In the words of the American Medical Association, we doctors are equipped for the first time in history to "help mold citizens of tomorrow and influence the trend of human destiny."

Actually, our course of action has been clearly stated in the constitution of UNESCO. Its second paragraph reads: "Since wars begin in the minds of men it is in the minds of men that the defense of peace must be constructed." The question then is how to implement this principle since the world is not ruled by mature, empathetic psychotherapists but by politicians, partisans or revolutionaries, not always the best-adjusted people and often driven by an inner unrelenting compulsive will to power.

Reading our daily newspapers we may feel sickened by a war that nibbles away life tissue like a cancer and which governments seem unable to bring to a halt. But the incredible fact is that deep in their unconscious there are people who feel ambivalent about violence and not appalled by it since the acting out of violence or even watching it serves as a release from unbearable tension or boredom (war pictures, violence on TV). It has therefore never ceased to have an appeal to those people who have difficulties coping with their inner restive aggression. However, to more secure peaceful and adjusted citizens, those with compassion, displays of violence, including those we have seen in the streets and campuses of America, are disturbing, horrifying and intolerable.

But open outbursts are only part of our problem, for we must deal with another concealed and more dangerous type of violence that exists in the minds of men in position of power behind polished desks whose rationalized opinions as theoretical experts or advisers help form the decisions which lead to conflict, torture and violence on faraway battlefields. Since punishment does not prevent either crime or a drive to war it is perhaps useless to ask who are the more guilty, the men in the field who are indoctrinated to kill with no remorse—such as the lieutenant who brushed off the accusation of having "wasted" 102 men, women and children as "no big deal"—or the civilized men behind polished desks who by means of projection attribute their own unacceptable and unconscious aggression to others, the enemy.

We then have the vicious circle of two hostile groups or ideologies which feed on one another's fear, hate and distrust (the issue changes in each century). But the drive to war for a righteous cause remains, fanned by men who tend to advocate—as they must because of their basic hostile-aggressive personality structure—ever stronger acts of confrontation, making weaker the chance for negotiations.

It may well be as Ernest Jones (quoting Freud) put it, that "the very emphasis of the commandment 'Thou shalt not kill' makes it certain that we are descended from an endless chain of generations of murderers, whose love for murder was in their blood as it is perhaps in ours." As civilized people we would perhaps have overcome this dreadful heritage and its legalized form, war, if there did not appear from time to time false apostles capable of stirring up the lust for blood as evidenced by Hitler's statement that "the very first essential for success is a perpetually constant and regular employment of violence."

But our theme is prevention. Knowing that man for millennia has been conditioned to war, we physicians in all countries must move to enlighten all people so that they can assert pressure on their governments to apply newer scientific methods of detecting and curing by Pavlovian methods the disposition to violence (the mass-expression of which is war).

The question of how we may approach the problem will be tackled in tomorrow's article.

"The Road to Peace: II" (*The New York Times*, Op-Ed, March 30, 1971)

In the mid-fifties I drew up a six-point program, which, in 1969, I sent to both Presidential candidates, being fully aware of the long and thorny road it would take to make an idea of this kind palatable. In the meanwhile, I have learned that independently a bill about a Department of Peace has been introduced in Congress (Hartke-Halpern).

My points were:

Peace is more than the absence of war—just as health is more than the absence of illness.

Since decisions of peace and war are made by human beings, the psychological make-up and mental functioning of the people in power will in a last analysis be the decisive factor of how innate human aggression will be employed in decisions about peace and war.

In order to attain real and lasting peace, the concept of peace must be changed from a passive, non-aggressive concept to a new dynamic way of life. The energies of repressed human aggression (absence of war and/or violence) must be liberated and channeled into meaningful, creative and productive pursuits.

The ideology and practical application of peace will demand a gigantic program of education and reconditioning of thinking, so enormous that it must become the main business of government.

To study, to develop and to execute a program of the dynamics of peace, a new agency must be established. Techniques of sublimation of human aggression must be developed and perfected. A Department of Peace must balance the existing Department of Defense (formerly War).

The Secretary of Peace must mobilize all human energy toward the benefit of all people and beyond this to all mankind, for happiness cannot flourish long in one part of the world if there is hunger, oppression and violence in another. The Secretary of Peace must be present at all policy-making decisions to safeguard peace by presenting controlled alternatives to the old conditioned violent solutions by the use of physical force, whenever political negotiations appear to fail.

That we have not blown each other into nuclear dust has not come because of governmental love for the human race, but because of sheer fear of dreaded retaliation. Most people, especially the young, want peace because of their healthy will to live.

So far, the Great Powers seem to move painfully slow toward building peace, blaming obstructions on a reluctant enemy. So fear and suspicion perpetuate an irrational arms race at incredible costs.

What can we individual people who abhor violence—war—do? In defense of peace we could begin by urging our lawmakers to help restore the prestige and physical power of the United Nations. The United Nations should be supplied with a strong international police force. But we must have no illusions—the will to peace must come from within.

On national levels we must move toward an agency whose business is peace and nothing but peace. But our concept about peace needs to be changed. Even if the governments should pronounce general cease-fires all over the world, if they deprive war of its glamour and profits, such a plan would not banish war because it would leave unchanged man's inner proneness to violence.

Therefore, doctors must work with their governments and be given the chance to start in childhood applying the techniques of sublimating trends to violence to suitable ways of self-expression in work, of learning to get along with other people and of gratifying leisure activities. People must learn freedom from fear so that they can learn the meaning of love. And people must learn a new reality—that millions for peace would do more for them than billions for defense.

A Department of Peace would not produce a magic cure but it could become the coordinating agency for exploring the dynamics of violence and supervise the manifold ways of conditioning the human mind to react to signals of aggression with new, controlled, assertive and yet peaceful responses. The principles of reconditioning must be coordinated with our system of education. As I have said in "The Will to Happiness": Reconditioning to peace has not failed, it just has not ever been properly applied and certainly never been accurately practiced.

If we accept the premise that the defense of peace must be constructed in the minds of men "then the problem is for people to get together and to leap governments—if necessary to evade governments—to work out not one method but thousands of methods by which people can gradually learn a little bit more of each other."

It was Dwight D. Eisenhower who made this statement in 1956 when he spoke of how "to help build a road to peace."

Bibliography

Adler, Alfred. *The Science of Living.* New York: Greenberg, 1929.

Casriel, Daniel. *So Fair a Horse (The Story of Synanon).* Englewood Cliffs, New Jersey: Prentice-Hall, 1963.

Chapiro, José. *Peace Protests: Erasmus of Rotterdam and Our Struggle for Peace.* Boston: Beacon Press, 1950.

Crissey, Elwell. *Lincoln's Lost Speech.* New York: Hawthorn, 1967.

Einstein, Albert. *Essays in Science.* New York: Philosophical Library, 1954.

Eissler, Ruth S. *Psychoanalytic Study of the Child.* New York: International Universities Press, 1957.

Feifel, Herman. *The Meaning of Death.* New York: McGraw-Hill, 1959.

Freud, Sigmund. *The Basic Writings of Sigmund Freud.* A Brill, ed. New York: Modern Library, 1938.

Freud, Sigmund. *Civilization, War and Death.* John Rickman, ed. London: Hogarth Press, 1953.

Freud, Sigmund and William C. Bullitt. *Thomas Woodrow Wilson.* Boston: Houghton Mifflin Company, 1967.

Freud, Sigmund. *Three Essays on the Theory of Sexuality.* Translated by James Strachey. London: Imago Publishing Company Limited, 1949.

Fromm, Erich. *Escape from Freedom.* New York: Harper & Brothers, 1956.

Fromm, Erich. *The Art of Loving.* New York: Harper & Brothers, 1956.

Group for the Advancement of Psychiatry. *VIP with Psychiatric Impairment.* New York: Charles Scribner's Sons, 1970.

Halberstam, David. *The Best and the Brightest.* New York: Random House, 1971.

Hartman, Robert S. *The Structure of Values*. Carbondale: Southern Illinois University Press, 1967.

Hartman, Robert S. *Value and Valuation*. Knoxville: University of Tennessee Press, 1972.

Hitler, Adolf. *Mein Kampf*. Munich: Franz Eher, 1933.

Horney, Karen. *Self-Analysis*. New York: W.W. Norton, 1942.

Hutschnecker, Arnold A. *The Will to Live*. Englewood Cliffs, New Jersey: Prentice-Hall (Cornerstone), 1951.

Hutschnecker, Arnold A. *Love and Hate in Human Nature*. New York: Thomas Y. Crowell Company, 1955.

Hutschnecker, Arnold A. *The Will to Happiness*. Englewood Cliffs, New Jersey: Prentice-Hall (Cornerstone), 1964.

Jones, Ernest. *The Life and Works of Sigmund Freud*. New York: Basic Books, 1953.

Kant, Immanuel. *Moral and Political Writings*. New York: Modern Library, 1949.

Kessler, Jane W. *Psychopathology of Childhood*. Englewood Cliffs, New Jersey: Prentice-Hall, 1966.

Laswell, Harold. *Psychopathology and Politics*. New York: Viking Press, 1960.

L'Etang, Hugh. *The Pathology of Leadership*. New York: Hawthorne Books, 1970.

Lippmann, Walter. *Early Writings*. New York: Liveright, 1970.

Lorenz, Konrad. *On Aggression*. New York: Harcourt, Brace & World, 1966.

Luthin, Reinhard. *The Real Abraham Lincoln*. Englewood Cliffs, New Jersey: Prentice-Hall, 1960.

Mazlish, Bruce. *In Search of Nixon: A Psychohistorical Inquiry*. Baltimore: Penguin Books, 1973.

Menninger, Karl. *Love Against Hate*. New York: Harcourt, Brace & World, 1942.

Menninger, Karl. *Man Against Himself*. New York: Harcourt, Brace & World, 1938.

Merriam, Charles. *Political Power: Its Composition and Incidence*. New York: McGraw-Hill, 1934.

Miller, Merle. *Plain Speaking: An Oral Biography of Harry S. Truman*. New York: Putnam, 1974.

Munroe, Ruth L. *Schools of Psychoanalytic Thought*. New York: Holt, Rinehart and Winston, 1955.

Nietzsche, Friedrich. *Der Wille zur Macht*. Leipzig: Naumann, 1901.

Nixon, Richard M. *Six Crises*. New York: Doubleday, 1962.

Pavlov, Ivan Petrovich, *Conditioned Reflexes and Psychiatry*. New York: International Publishers, 1941.

Pavlov, Ivan Petrovitch. *Essays in Psychology and Psychiatry*. New York: Citadel Press, 1962.

Salk, Jonas. *The Survival of the Wisest*, Vol. 12. New York: Harper Row, 1973.

Schopenhauer, Arthur. *Parergh und Paralipomena*. Leipzig: Insel Verlag.

Schopenhauer, Arthur. *Die Welt als Wille und Vorstellung*. Leipzig, Insel Verlag.

Shirer, William L. *The Rise and Fall of the Third Reich*. New York: Simon & Schuster, 1959.

U.S. Congress. Senate Committee on Rules and Regulations. *Nomination of Gerald Ford of Michigan to be Vice-President of U.S.* Washington, D.C.: U.S. Government Printing Office, November, 1973.

U.S. Congress. House Judiciary Committee. November 20, 1973.

Wertham, Frederick. *Sign of Cain*. New York: Macmillan, 1966.

Wimm, Ralph, translator. *Psychotherapy in the Soviet Union*. New York: Grove Press, 1962.

ARTICLES

Hutschnecker, Arnold A. "Health and Wholeness," *Ohio State Medical Journal* (1959).

Hutschnecker, Arnold A. "Medicine and Psychiatry in the USSR," *Transaction of the N.Y. Academy of Sciences of Psychosomatics* (Journal of the Academy of Psychosomatic Medicine) (1960).

Hutschnecker, Arnold A. "Health and Personality," *Industrial Medicine and Surgery* (February 1961).

Hutschnecker, Arnold A. "Anticipatory Grief," *Archive Foundation of Thanatology—Symposium with Department of Psychiatry Columbia University* (1973).

"La mort est-elle un suicide, un suicide déguisé," Anon. *Réalité* 190 (Paris: November 1961).

Lewis, William F., Ph.D. "Masculine Inferiority Feelings of F. Scott Fitzgerald," *Human Sexuality* (April 1973).

Moulton, Ruth, M.D. "Penis Envy," *Human Sexuality* (October 1973).

Peltz, William, M.D. "Concern with Penis Size," *Human Sexuality* (October 1973).

Index

341